REFERENCE GUIDES TO RHETORIC AND COMPOSITION

Series Editor, Charles Bazerman

REFERENCE GUIDES TO RHETORIC AND COMPOSITION
Series Editor, Charles Bazerman

The Series provides compact, comprehensive and convenient surveys of what has been learned through research and practice as composition has emerged as an academic discipline over the last half century. Each volume is devoted to a single topic that has been of interest in rhetoric and composition in recent years, to synthesize and make available the sum and parts of what has been learned on that topic. These reference guides are designed to help deepen classroom practice by making available the collective wisdom of the field and will provide the basis for new research. The Series is intended to be of use to teachers at all levels of education, researchers and scholars of writing, graduate students learning about the field, and all who have interest in or responsibility for writing programs and the teaching of writing.

Parlor Press and The WAC Clearinghouse are collaborating so that these books will be widely available through low-cost print editions and free digital distribution. The publishers and the Series editor are teachers and researchers of writing, committed to the principle that knowledge should freely circulate. We see the opportunities that new technologies have for further democratizing knowledge. And we see that to share the power of writing is to share the means for all to articulate their needs, interest, and learning into the great experiment of literacy.

EXISTING BOOKS IN THE SERIES
Invention in Rhetoric and Composition (2004, Lauer)
Reference Guide to Writing across the Curriculum (2005, Bazerman, Little, Bethel, Chavkin, Fouquette, and Garufis)
Revision: History, Theory, and Practice (2006, Horning and Becker)
Writing Program Administration (2007, McLeod)
Community Literacy and the Rhetoric of Local Publics (2008, Long)

Community Literacy and the Rhetoric of Local Publics

Elenore Long

Parlor Press
West Lafayette, Indiana
www.parlorpress.com

The WAC Clearinghouse
http://wac.colostate.edu/

Parlor Press LLC, West Lafayette, Indiana 47906

© 2008 by Parlor Press and The WAC Clearinghouse
All rights reserved.
Printed in the United States of America

S A N: 2 5 4 - 8 8 7 9

Library of Congress Cataloging-in-Publication Data

Long, Elenore.
  Community literacy and the rhetoric of local publics / Elenore Long.
      p. cm. -- (Reference guides to rhetoric and composition)
  Includes bibliographical references and index.
  ISBN 978-1-60235-056-4 (pbk. : alk. paper) -- ISBN 978-1-60235-057-
1 (hardcover : alk. paper) -- ISBN 978-1-60235-058-8 (adobe ebook)
  1. Literacy--Social aspects--United States. 2. Communication in social
action--United States. 3. Rhetoric--Political aspects--United States. I.
Title.
  LC151.L66 2008
  302.2'244--dc22

                              2008009334

Series logo designed by Karl Stolley.
This book is printed on acid-free paper.

Parlor Press, LLC is an independent publisher of scholarly and trade titles
in print and multimedia formats. This book is available in paperback, cloth,
and Adobe eBook formats from Parlor Press on the World Wide Web at
http://www.parlorpress.com. For submission information or to find out about
Parlor Press publications, write to Parlor Press, 816 Robinson St., West Lafayette, Indiana, 47906, or e-mail editor@parlorpress.com.

The WAC Clearinghouse supports teachers of writing across the disciplines.
Hosted by Colorado State University's Composition Program, it brings together four journals, three book series, and resources for teachers who use
writing in their courses. This book will also be available free on the Internet at
The WAC Clearinghouse (http://wac.colostate.edu/).

To Kristen Beth

"I would like to imagine that we could approach the social world the way Aristotle did the natural world, believing that the delights of the senses bear witness to our desire to know, and that our desire to know consists in the pleasure of bringing differences to light."

—*Janet Atwill*

Contents

Tables   xi
Preface   xiii
Acknowledgments   xv
Common Abbreviations   xvii
Community Literacy and the Rhetoric of Local Publics   1

1 *Introduction and Overview*   3
   What This Book Doesn't Do   11

2 *Definitions and Distinctions*   14
   The Local Public Framework   16
      Guiding Metaphor   16
      Context   18
      Tenor of the Discourse   20
      Literacies   21
      Rhetorical Invention   22

3 *Locating Community Literacy Studies*   25
   Two Prior Accounts   26
   Situating the Study of Literacy in
      the Public Realm   28
         Documenting and Theorizing Local Public Discourse   35
         Features of Situated-Public Literacies   39
   Situating the Study of Participatory Democracy   41
         Ideas about Actually Existing Democracy   42
         Rhetorical Interventions to Support
            Democratic Engagement   43

4 *An Impromptu Theater: A Local Public That
   Turns Its Back on Formal Institutions*   55
         Distinctive Features: Dramatic and Spontaneous   55
         The Impromptu Theater in Context: Location, Power,
            and the Integrity of Community Life   56
         Tenor of the Discourse: Edgy and

Competitive, Curbed by Play   *58*
   Performative Literacies   *59*
   Rhetorical Invention: Practice, Modeling, and Feedback   *60*
   Implications   *61*

5 *The Cultural Womb and the Garden: Local Publics That*
Depend on Institutions to Sponsor Them   *64*
   A Cultural Womb: The Local Public in Brandt's
   Literacy in American Lives   *64*
      Distinctive Features: Nurtures and Prepares   *65*
      The Cultural Womb in Context: Location
        and Cultural Agency   *66*
      Tenor of the Discourse: Resourceful   *68*
      Interpretative Literacies   *69*
      Rhetorical Invention: Inspiration, Instruction,
        and Transformation   *70*
      Implications   *71*
   A Garden: The Local Public in Heller's
   Until We Are Strong Together   *74*
      Distinctive Features: Nurtures and Prepares   *74*
      The Garden in Context: Location, Agency,
        and Maturation   *75*
      Tenor of the Discourse: Literary Uplift   *78*
      Belletristic Literacies   *78*
      Rhetorical Invention: Precision at the Point of Utterance   *79*
      Implications   *81*

6 *The Link and Gate: Local Publics That*
Intersect with Public Institutions   *85*
   A Link: The Local Public Sphere in Barton
   and Hamilton's Local Literacies   *85*
      Distinctive Features: Linking Networks Across Domains   *85*
      The Link in Context: Location, Bottom-
        Up Initiative, and Agency   *87*
      Tenor of the Discourse: Hybrid—a Mix of the
        Formal and the Everyday   *89*
      Mobilizing Literacies   *90*
      Rhetorical Invention: Adapting and Retooling   *92*
      Implications   *93*
   A Gate along a Fenceline: The Local Public in
   Cushman's *The Struggle and the Tools*   *96*
      Distinctive Features: Access, Space, and Conflict   *96*
      The Gate in Context: Location and Linguistic Agency   *98*

Tenor of the Discourse: Dueling Dualities   *100*
Institutional Literacies   *100*
Rhetorical Invention: Evaluating Acquired Literacies   *101*
Transferred to New Contexts   *101*
Implications   *103*

7 *The Community-Organizing Effort and the*
Community Think Tank: Local Publics Forged in
Partnership with Formal Institutions   *106*
A Community-Organizing Effort: The Local
Public in Goldblatt's "Alinsky's Reveille: A
Community-Organizing Model for Neighborhood-
Based Literacy Projects"   *107*
Distinctive Features: Complexity and Pleasure   *107*
The Community-Organizing Effort in Context:
Location and Legacy   *108*
Tenor of the Discourse: Bite Tempered by Sweetness   *109*
Consensus-Building Literacies   *110*
Rhetorical Invention: Transforming Problems
into Issues for Action   *112*
Implications   *114*
The Community Think Tank: The Local Public Sphere
in Flower's "Intercultural Knowledge Building: The
Literate Action of a Community Think Tank"   *118*
Distinctive Features: Diversity, Conflict, and Tools   *118*
The Community Think Tank in Context:
Location and Legacy   *120*
Tenor of the Discourse: Prophetic—
Principled and Inventive   *124*
Design and Inquiry-Driven Literacies   *124*
Rhetorical Invention: The Construction of
Negotiated Meaning   *128*
Implications   *129*

8 *The Shadow System: A Local Public that*
Defies Formal Institutions   *137*
Distinctive Features: Mimics and
Shelters Difference   *137*
The Shadow System in Context: Location
and Cultural Imaginary   *138*
Tenor the Discourse: Threatening
and Hyperbolic   *140*
Tactical Literacies   *140*

Rhetorical Invention: Cultural Appropriation   *141*
Implications   *142*

9 *Pedagogical Practices*   *154*
Overview   *157*
Interpretative Pedagogies   *158*
Institutional Pedagogies   *163*
Tactical Pedagogies   *170*
Inquiry-Driven Pedagogies   *175*
Materialist Rhetoric: Realizing Practical
    Outcomes through Consensus   *176*
Intercultural Inquiry: Restructuring Deliberative
    Dialogues around Difference   *178*
Performative Pedagogies   *189*
Conclusion   *198*

10 *Glossary*   *200*

11 *Annotated Bibliography*   *214*

Notes   *252*
Works Cited   *264*
About the Author   *281*
Index   *283*

Tables

Table 1. Prominent relationships between local
publics and formal institutions.   7
Table 2. The local public framework.   16
Table 3. Prominent images of local public life:
A comparative analysis.   23
Table 4. The text-resource-strategy matrix for the
Allotment Association.   90
Table 5. Activities used to acquire, transfer, and
evaluate institutional literacies.   101
Table 6. A comparison of three defiant local publics.   144
Table 7. How students use prominent literacies to go public.   155
Table 8. A comparison of materialist rhetoric and
intercultural inquiry.   177

Preface

Charles Bazerman

Rhetoric, as a discipline, was born in the world to serve worldly needs. Typically these were the needs of power, exercised by the powerful—in court, parliament, political office, and the pulpit. The powerful could afford to pay rhetoricians for advice and to speak on their behalf. The wealthy could hire rhetoricians to educate their children to ensure dynastic power, and powerful institutions could sponsor schooling to provide continuing leadership and bureaucracies. Within such academic settings, rhetoric became a school taught art and an elaborated theoretical subject. However, the poor, the dispossessed, the victims of power, or even just the ordinary working people were left to their own spontaneous rhetorical savvy and carnivalesque resistance to assert their rights. Only rarely did they gain access to the most powerful tools of oratory and language.

Composition was born in the nineteenth-century school and university to teach the writing skills necessary for academic accomplishment and entering elite social roles upon graduation. Yet the increasing democratization of education in the nineteenth and twentieth centuries also brought in more people of various backgrounds and an interest in the needs of all parts of society. Universities often became sites of community involvement and progressivism, starting with the landgrants and famously with the University of Chicago at the time of John Dewey, George Herbert Mead, and Jane Addams. In the Post World War II and Civil Rights eras in the U.S., universities became increasingly engaged with community issues and what became eventually known as urban missions. So perhaps it is not so surprising that composition and rhetoric have engaged with community projects, where ordinary citizens gain public voice. Nonetheless, this return to the public sphere turns the power dynamics of rhetoric on its head and represents a major turn outward from composition's traditional work in preparing students for academic and professional success.

Elenore Long's *Community Literacy and the Rhetoric of Local Publics*—the latest volume in the Reference Guides to Rhetoric and Composition—reviews the major community rhetoric projects that have emerged in recent years, laying out the underlying logic, approaches and methods of each, and illuminating them through a theorized comparison. Long's theoretical view unpacks the underlying metaphors of these projects to understand how each conceives the local public, the participation of individuals and groups, and the relations to larger institutions. In so doing she illuminates what role writing teachers and other communication specialists can take within community organizations and how such projects can serve as a means of community engagement for college writing students.

This volume gives us overview and insight into a major new direction in rhetoric and composition that foretells changes in undergraduate education and a reorientation of the university to the community. This volume brings these movements to a new level of understanding, thoughtfulness, and effectiveness.

Acknowledgments

My heartfelt thanks to Wayne Peck, Joyce Baskins, and everyone at the Community House Church. My greatest joys in life include the projects we have carried out together. I am also indebted to the scholars whose work informs community-literacy studies. Their care as research-ers and their commitments as people have made my task inspiring and pleasurable. Linda and Tim Flower have been steadfast friends of this project—one could ask for no better collaborative planning partners. Linda, thank you for your patience, insight, and encouragement across enumerable drafts.

Maureen Daly Goggin prompted patiently as I shaped the third chapter that locates community-literacy studies in the larger disciplin-ary history. Lorraine Higgins rekindled my interest in communica-tive democracy and offered helpful comments on chapter 5, especially regarding implications that follow when work disappears from urban areas. I am grateful to my entire circle of friends—including Patti Wojahn, Loel Kim, David Fleming, Kirk Branch, and Amanda Young—who contributed all varieties of support and inspiration.

Several professional forums have nourished this project and made a place for it in the discipline. I am grateful to those whose vision and attention to detail have allowed for such fruitful discussion: Frans H. van Eemeren and colleagues sponsored the Fifth Conference of the International Society for the Study of Argumentation where I mapped out the initial grid for this book; Glynda Hull and Kathy Schultz or-ganized the 2004 NCTE assembly for research where colleagues from the Community House in Pittsburgh and I cast digital storytelling as local public practice; Peter Goggin and Maureen Mathison sponsored the annual Western States Rhetoric and Literacy Conference where I tested early and the most recent incantations of a local public rhetoric; Charles Bazerman and Sue McLeod made possible CCCCs sessions dedicated to this and related work. With support from *Reflections: A Journal of Writing, Community Literacy, and Service-Learning* and the

Community Literacy Journal, Eli Goldblatt, Steve Parks, and David Jolliffe organized a symposium in Philadelphia to imagine the future of community-literacy studies.

In all my enthusiasm, my initial version of this project was far too long. You are in for a better read, thanks to Charles Bazerman and his vision for the Reference Guides to Rhetoric and Composition. David Blakesley and Michael Palmquist patiently provided guidance all along the way. Judy Holiday, Sundy Watanabe, Jeffery Grabill and his students in AI 877: Community Literacies put drafts of this manuscript to various uses; their interest and feedback have strengthened this text and fortified my spirit in numerous ways. I am grateful, as well, to Tracy Clark, who copyedited the manuscript.

The administration and my colleagues at Bay Path College provided time and resources to support this project. I am especially indebted to the College's provost, William Sipple; the reference librarian, Sandra Cahillane; student assistants, Andrea English and Stephanie Zeiser; and my dear friend and colleague, Brenda Hardin Abbott.

New colleagues at Eastern Washington University helped me to make time to complete this project while learning a new culture and assuming new professional responsibilities. I am particularly indebted to Logan Greene and Garrett Kenney.

My extended family has sustained me with their companionship, laughter, food, and great stories. John and Hannah Jarvis have adjusted their own lives to make room for this project and celebrated each little step toward its completion. Best of all, now—they say—the time has come to pack it up. Thank you.

Common Abbreviations

AAHE: American Association for Higher Education:
BEV: Black English Vernacular
CCCC: Conference on College Composition and Communication
CLC: Community Literacy Center
CMU: Carnegie Mellon University
DUSTY: Digital Underground Storytelling for Youth
IGLSVL: International Group for the Study of Language
      Standardization and the Vernacularization of Literacy
IPRP: Interprofessional Research Project
IIT: Illinois Institute of Technology
Metro AME: Metropolitan African Methodist Episcopal Church
NLG: New Literacies Group
NLS: New Literacies Studies
NWP: National Writing Project
SRTOL: Students' Right to Their Own Language
SWE: Standard Written English
TWWW: Tenderloin Women's Writing Workshop
UNESCO: United Nations Educational, Scientific and Cultural
      Organization
WFYL: Write For Your Life

Community Literacy and the Rhetoric of Local Publics

1 Introduction and Overview

Over the past twenty years that community-literacy studies has emerged as a distinct area of inquiry, scholars have tested the capacity of rhetorical theory to make a difference in the world outside college walls. Working with community partners, they have prepared students in new ways to carry on responsible, effective, socially aware communication in a variety of workplaces and communities, as well as in school. There is joy in much of this work—the fruit of working with people whom we otherwise would not have known on projects that matter to others as well as to ourselves.

A vibrant array of theoretical perspectives and methods of inquiry infuses this work. The array is due, in part, to the complexity and range of issues that community-literacy studies explores—issues of "real-world" reading and writing, of ethical communication, of cultural border crossing, among others.[1] But the variation is also due to something even more basic. Community literacy requires each of us to make a judgment call. It demands that we venture an educated guess in response to a pressing social question: *How do we engage such issues (of reading and writing, ethics, and border crossing) in ways and in locales that will make a difference?* And it demands that we make that call not only in the theoretical claims we assert in our classrooms and scholarship but also in the theory-driven action we take outside the academy—in what we *do* with others under material, social, political, and economic conditions not of our making or under our control, nor even entirely within our understanding. This is, after all, the very conundrum of human affairs that characterizes rhetoric itself as a deliberative domain calling for productive knowledge (Aristotle, *Nicomachean Ethics* 1139a27–28) and practical wisdom (Isocrates, *Antidosis* 256–57)—the ability to articulate new understandings and to intervene rather than to represent what is already known (Atwill 66–69).

Community-literacy scholars have made this judgment call in a number of ways—for instance, by carefully documenting and sup-

3

porting the literacies of African American women negotiating the
bureaucratic world of social service agencies (Cushman *Struggle*), by
cultivating consensus among community organizers for a shared literacy initiative to support adult learners in North Philadelphia (Goldblatt "Alinsky's Reveille") and by building the rhetorical capacity of
Pittsburgh residents to construct an alternative, inclusive discourse for
deliberating issues of shared concern, such as welfare-to-work policies
and staffing issues at long-term care facilities (Flower "Intercultural
Knowledge").

Despite this variation, however, such responses share a common
theme: we, as everyday people, stand to make a difference by using our
literate repertoires *to go public*.

As expressed in Cornel West's prophetic pragmatism, the promise
of going public is twofold. First, public engagement strives to "accentu-
ate [. . . the] humanity [, . . .] agency, capacity and ability" of ordinary
people "to attenuate the institutional constraints on their life-chances
for surviving and thriving" (*Keeping* 29). This means that opportunities for going public are open to all of us who, as "ordinary people,"
strive "to participate in the decision-making procedures of institutions
that fundamentally regulate [our] lives" (*Keeping* 140). The purpose of
this book is to pull together alternative theoretical accounts of public
engagement, so I won't try to encapsulate them all here. But even a
quick glance at some public-writing textbooks suggests the range of
options available to those looking to go public—from having our say
(Charney and Neuwirth) to researching social issues (Collins) to problem solving in the community (Flower *Problem Solving*). So readers
of this book—including teachers, researchers and students—are, like
myself, ordinary people developing their own literate repertories for
public action.

Second, the promise of public engagement calls readers located in
relative institutional privilege to speak wisely and persuasively for social change. To do so is to acknowledge—as West puts it—that the
"bourgeois liberal and communist illiberal status quos" have "culturally degraded, politically oppressed and economically exploited" some
of us more than others (*Keeping* 29)—another theme in community-
literacy studies. Although the goal of leveraging institutional resources to bring about progressive social change is generally shared across
community-literacy scholars, it, too, affords multiple theoretical perspectives and multiple conceptions of democratic practice.

Among the questions that organize community literacy as a field of study, this question of how ordinary people go public perhaps best indicates community literacy's relevance to rhetoric and composition at large, especially given "the public turn" the discipline has taken over the past two decades (Weisser 1). Granted, individual researchers don't necessarily state their research questions this way.[2] All the same, this interest in how ordinary people go public is an abiding one. It shows up not only in rhetoric textbooks, but also whenever literacy scholars draw on a vocabulary of publicness to convey the rhetorical significance of their observations. It also appears whenever literacy scholars look to public-spheres theorists to help them think through rhetorical conundrums of contemporary life.

The question—*how it is that ordinary people go public?*—carries with it several implications. First, the question represents a shift from the academy and workplace, where so much of composition research has previously focused attention, to the community, itself a hybrid domain at the intersection between private lives and public institutions (Crow and Allan 18). The question is also more narrow in focus than two broader strains of scholarship—work in service learning and action research—that frame community-literacy scholarship in the largest sense to include studies of the more private literacies of individuals, families, and neighborhoods (Cushman, Barbier, Mazak, and Petrone).

This question also raises the issue of *where* it is that ordinary people most often go public. In this book, these spaces are called *local publics*. As a rhetorical construct, the phrase *local publics* fills the gap between descriptive accounts of situated literacy (Barton; Barton, Hamilton, and Ivanič; Street *Literacy*) and more abstract theories of public discourse. In comparison to both dominant *formal* (Barton and Hamilton; Warner) and *adversarial* (Roberts-Miller) publics, the *local* publics of community literacy extend Nancy Fraser's notion of *alternative* publics. Local publics are located in time and place. Their potential (as well as limitations) as hosts for "actually existing democracy" makes them important sites for rhetorical inquiry (Fraser 109). More than any other entity, local publics constitute the *community* of community literacy.

The question also immediately raises the issue of institutional affiliation. Some of the earliest controversy in community-literacy studies focused on the power of institutions to define literacy. In this vein, Jeffery Grabill criticized Wayne Peck, Linda Flower, and Lorraine Higgins, founders of Pittsburgh's Community Literacy Center (CLC), a partnership between Carnegie Mellon University (CMU) and a settlement house called the Community House on the city's North Side.[3] Although Peck, Flower, and Higgins "manag[ed] to define" community literacy for the discipline, Grabill charged them with failing to define community (with all its institutional affiliations) "in any meaningful way" (*Community* 89). Likewise, Eli Goldblatt made institutional sponsorship the focus of "Van Rides in the Dark." "Literacy, like all human activities," wrote Goldblatt, "is practiced within a context of institutions, both institutions whose sponsorship of written language is quite explicit [. . .] or institutions for which written language functions subtly to maintain its solidity in the culture [. . .]" (78). In a hallway conversation at the Conference on College Composition and Communication (CCCC) the year prior to the publication of "Van Rides," Goldblatt gently pointed out to me that the analysis I had just presented insufficiently theorized the issue of institutional sponsorship. At the time, I was coordinating college students serving as writing mentors at the CLC. For me, the revealing relationship was the connection college mentors made between literacy and social justice. In their work supporting urban teen writers at the CLC, they struggled with how best to forge this connection. How to juggle competing priorities (e.g., grammatical correctness, emancipation, free expression, action-oriented problem solving) was a pressing concern for students and an open question in the discipline at large (Long "Intercultural Images").

Since that time, both Grabill (*Community Literacy*) and Goldblatt ("Alinsky's Reveille"; "Van Rides") have stressed the role that institutions play as literacy sponsors, and Deborah Brandt's study of literacy sponsorship has provided theoretical underpinnings for understanding this relationship more fully (*American*). As much light as this work has brought to the issue of sponsorship, it also represents the momentum community-literacy studies has gained while investigating a whole range of problems that arise when literacy is publicly situated. The relationship between local publics and formal institutions is a case in point.

As the following analysis will show, when we ask *how do ordinary people go public?*, the responses we get in return expose a whole range of possible relationships between local public and formal institutions, sponsorship being one among many. So while the studies reviewed under current views (chapters 4 through 8) have each contributed significantly to community-literacy studies, together they also dramatize a complex (and no doubt incomplete) set of relationships between local publics and formal institutions that shape and constrain how ordinary people go public.[4] As table 1 suggests, a local public may turn its back on formal public institutions, or it may rely on one or more such institution to sponsor it. A local public may intersect with a public institution, or be forged in partnership with one. Or a local public may outright defy formal, public institutions.[5]

Table 1. Prominent relationships between local publics and formal institutions.

Literacy Scholar/s	Metaphor for the Local Public	Relation to Formal Institutions
Shirley Brice Heath	an impromptu street theater	the local public turns its back on public institutions
Deborah Brandt; Caroline Heller	organic imagery: a cultural womb and a garden	the local public relies on one or more institution to sponsor it
David Barton and Mary Hamilton; Ellen Cushman	a link and a gate along a fence-line	the local public intersects with a public institution
Eli Goldblatt; Linda Flower	a community-organizing effort and the community think tank	the local public is forged in partnership with a formal institution
Ralph Cintron	a shadow system	the local public defies formal public institutions

Together, the studies reviewed in these chapters portray places where ordinary people develop public voices. But to draw implications from the distinctive features of these discursive spaces, the discourses they circulate, and the literate practices that sustain them, we need some sort of heuristic. The local public framework was designed for the job. It is introduced in chapter 2.

Following the format for the Reference Guides to Rhetoric and Composition, chapter 2 provides key definitions and distinctions. It begins by distinguishing *ordinary people* from those typically depicted going public, namely political leaders and celebrities. Then it provides a rhetorical definition of *community* for the study of community literacy—a definition rooted in the local publics reviewed in this volume. The chapter then defines key elements of the local public framework: the *metaphor* that frames the account of people going public and its distinctive *features;* the *context* (including *location*) that frames the site; the *tenor* of the discourse; the *literacies* that people in the account use to go public; and the process of *rhetorical invention* they use to figure out what to say, to do, and to write. The chapter concludes by previewing images of community literacy. The chapter suggests that learning to read local publics is an engaging intellectual enterprise and a prerequisite to forging mutually respectful community-university partnerships.

Chapter 3 asks the question: *to what disciplinary priorities can this interest in how ordinary people go public be traced?* The chapter argues that the history of community literacy is tied up in efforts to define the *local public* as an object of inquiry and a site for rhetorical intervention. The chapter suggests that what has attracted community-literacy scholars to local publics is the promise they hold of enacting what Flower has called "a rhetoric of engagement" grounded in relationships and focused on rhetorical action (*Community Literacy* 1). Scholars' interests in local publics have coalesced around the connection between vernacular literacies and public life—a connection that contends with the inherent ambiguity of language rights discourse and all the complexity of public-spheres studies. The chapter looks at how the ideals of the Students' Right to Their Own Language (SRTOL) movement pervade research in community literacy and how community-literacy projects test these ideals by situating them in public domains where vernacular literacies have a place at the table.

The book's next section, current views, uses the local public framework as a lens for interpreting a range of positions, arguments, and lines of research related to community literacy and for examining possible opportunities for new research, programs, and applications. To do so, current views features, in turn, a series of images of local public life prominent in the literature.

Chapter 4 features the impromptu street theater in Shirley Brice Heath's ethnography of Trackton, the rural African-American community she studied in the 1970s in the Piedmont Carolinas and described in *Ways with Words: Language, Life, and Work in Communities and Classrooms.* Theatrical imagery is especially attuned to the performative quality of local public discourse. Thus, chapter 4 draws a parallel between the poetic world-making power of style in written text (e.g., the metaphors researchers use to describe local publics) and the "poetic worldmaking" power of performance (Warner 114), such as those Heath observed on Trackton's public stage. The chapter also compares Trackton's public performances to the Native American New Ghost Dance which insinuates local issues into more formal public forums (Lyons).

Chapter 5 features two organic images for local public life: the cultural womb— characterizing the Metropolitan African Methodist Episcopal Church (Metro AME) parish to eight of the African Americans whom Brandt interviewed for *Literacy in American Lives*—and the garden, depicting the Tenderloin Women's Writing Workshop (TWWW) in Caroline Heller's *Until We are Strong Together.* Both images characterize local publics in relation to their sponsoring institutions; thus, the comparison highlights issues of institutional sponsorship and sustainability. The cultural womb and the garden also enact a rhetoric of transformation in which a local public serves as an "inspired context" for literacy learning (Willinsky 153). The chapter shows that in locations of stress and scarcity, such local publics transform lives through spiritual renewal and transform literacies by revamping familiar practices for new purposes. Somewhat ironically, then, this condition of stress and scarcity—what Brandt calls an "economy of efficiency"—contributes both to a local public's vibrancy and its vulnerability. The chapter highlights the need for *mestiza* publics (Anzaldua), capable of supporting the demanding and necessary cultural work of intercultural communication (Fraser 125), intercultural inquiry (Peck, Flower, and Higgins 209), and border crossing (Higgins and Brush 695).

If the cultural womb and the garden featured in chapter 5 use literacy to enact democratic values and practices, the images featured in chapter 6 show just how tenuous the connection between literacy and democracy can be. The chapter features images of local public life at the intersection between private lives and public institutions. *Local Literacies: Reading and Writing in One Community* is an ethnography of Springside, a working-class neighborhood in England, in the 1990s. Here David Barton and Mary Hamilton depict the private-public intersection as a link. They show that while a community group might use its literate repertoire to enact democratic values one moment, the group's practices may violate tenets of democracy the next. In Ellen Cushman's *The Struggle and the Tools: Oral and Literate Strategies in an Inner City Community*, the local public is a gate—the discursive and physical space between the gatekeeper, on the one hand, and the community resident, on the other. Of all the gatekeeping encounters Cushman documents in the industrial city she calls Quayville, only one affords anything resembling democratic access. Indirectly, Cushman's ethnography asks, *what would it take to teach gatekeepers in training to enact professional identities as knowledgeable advocates and fair judges?* (Long "Rhetorical Education").

Chapter 7 features local publics as partnerships between the community and the university: the community-organizing effort in Goldblatt's "Alinsky's Reveille: A Community-Organizing Model for Neighborhood-Based Literacy Projects" and the community think tank in Flower's "Intercultural Knowledge Building: The Literate Action of a Community Think Tank." These images pose two distinct rhetorics for local public life. On the one hand, a rhetoric of consensus guides Goldblatt's recent effort to help a group of community leaders in North Philadelphia formulate a shared strategy for a literacy initiative called Open Doors. Based on the community-organizing discourse of Saul Alinsky, consensus transforms a problem into an issue for collective action. In contrast, the community think tank is, in part, a response to the frustrations Pittsburgh residents have voiced with community-organizing practices (Flower, "Intercultural Knowledge" 250; Flower and Deems 97). For this think tank, the goal for deliberation is not consensus among group members but the transformed understanding of individual participants made possible through the structured process of collaborative inquiry. The comparison highlights the prevalence of conflict in local public life, as well as tools for maximizing its potential in rhetorical invention. Most of all, the chapter asks: *toward what ends do we, as ordinary people, deliberate in local public spheres?* And, if the ultimate rhetorical art is intervention: *what practices are available (or invent-able) to help us ordinary people get there?*

Chapter 8 features a local public that defies formal public institutions: the shadow system in Ralph Cintron's *Angels' Town: Chero Ways, Gang Life and Rhetorics of the Everyday*. The shadow system mimics the commonplaces so important to mainstream institutions—throwing them back onto the mainstream in forms the mainstream itself no longer recognizes. Furthermore, the shadow system shelters as its identity the difference between the mainstream's symbol system, on the one hand, and its own mimicry of that system, on the other. In the chapter, I use the shadow system as a lens to read two studies of defiant local publics perhaps more relevant to readers than the street gangs in Cintron's study: Perry Gilmore's 1991 study of girl "steppers" confronting teachers' judgments about them as learners and Phaedra Pezzullo's 2003 study of the Toxic Link Coalition's (TLC) toxic tour exposing corporations responsible for producing and profiting from carcinogenic chemicals. The chapter highlights how structural features of a guiding metaphor (such as Cintron's shadow system) may make visible complex discursive activity and power relations. The chapter also considers conditions under which a shadow system—which perpetuated the logic of violence in Angelstown—may open up a discursive space for trust, tolerance of ambiguity, and human connection.

Chapter 9 takes students as the primary focus of attention and asks: *how do students go public? As educators trained in rhetorical theory and practice, how can we best support them?* The chapter organizes a set of best pedagogical practices around literacies featured in the previous chapters, including *interpretative pedagogies* that adapt textual interpretation—English departments' stock in trade—to community contexts; *institutional pedagogies* that prepare students for future careers as technical communicators, human service workers, and medical professionals; and *performative pedagogies* that yoke inquiry, wisdom, and action and—as we'll see—also push against the very borders of contemporary rhetorical theory. Culled from exemplary rhetoric courses, research projects, and literacy programs, the practices do not rest in easy relation to one another, but rather pose any number of quandaries for educators. The chapter maps alternatives, indicating the kinds of choices and trade-offs educators must make when supporting students' public action.

Following the format for this series, chapter 10 then provides a glossary of terms, and chapter 11 offers an annotated bibliography of selected texts relevant to community-literacy studies.

What This Book Doesn't Do

This book doesn't address blogs, virtual urbanism, crowd sourcing, or citizen media. Instead, this book focuses on local publics that are at once physical and discursive—places where people go public face to face and soul to soul. There are important political reasons for focusing on local rather than virtual publics as Nancy Welch reminds us:

> Virtual reality is not a sufficient counter to or substitute for increasingly privatized and regulated *geographic space*. While it's true that information technologies and the virtual communities they create played organizing roles in such historic events as the student takeover of Tiananmen Square and the global demonstrations against a second Gulf War, it was the *physical taking* of Tiananmen Square that made possible its *transformation into a space representing democracy* (Mitchell 148). And it was to prevent such a *material transformation* that New York City cops herded thousands of frustrated protestors into pens on February 15, 2003, far from the rally they'd traveled miles to attend. (487–88, emphasis added)

However, this is not to say that work in community-literacy studies resists digital technologies. In fact, community literacy embraces the potential of multimodality—particularly the "praxis of new media"—to create alternative discourses that respond to complex socio-cultural exigencies ("Toward a Praxis" 111; cf. Comstock 49–50; Hull and Katz; Long, Peck, and Baskins). Pittsburgh's CLC has sponsored a number of computer interventions to support various forums for intercultural inquiry (Lawrence; Long, Peck, and Baskins; A. Young and Flower). Similarly, the enormous success of Digital Underground Storytelling for Youth (DUSTY)—University of California at Berkeley's computer-based outreach project—is testament to the synergy that Glynda Hull and her colleagues have harnessed between digital technologies and children's eagerness to compose stories of identity. Concern for social justice that drives *The Struggle and the Tools* has compelled Cushman to design not only interactive software programs for critical literacy educators in K-12 classrooms but also digitally mediated "third spaces" for collaboration among college students, community members, herself and her colleagues ("Toward a Praxis"). Likewise, Grabill designs his technical writing courses to explore how community-based Web-tools can help "to democratize data" ("Written City" 129). Computer supported pedagogical practices are treated in chapter 9.

Ultimately, much of the political philosophy driving current interest in computer-supported public deliberation (e.g., Gastil and Levine) is also relevant to understanding how ordinary people go public. I anticipate that future work in community literacy will explore the complex relation between local democracy and innovative technologies in further detail.

2 Definitions and Distinctions

The question *How is it that ordinary people go public?* is predicated on a prior distinction—that of *ordinary people*. Iris Marion Young included herself among the ordinary residents of Pittsburgh who together agitated for a citizens' review board to monitor police conduct. She opened *Inclusion and Democracy* with a "story of ordinary democracy in action" to illustrate that "more-marginalized citizens with fewer resources and official status can sometimes make up for such inequality with organization and time" (3).[1] Welch, too, is interested in how "ordinary people [. . .] go public" (470, 476). For her, it's the legacy of class struggle that puts most academics and students, their parents and other workers in the same ordinary boat (478–79). Magaly Lavadenz takes *ordinary* further still in her study of transcultural repositioning within immigration raids. *Ordinary* refers not to the status of citizen or authorized worker as defined by the state, but rather to the fact that all of us (our students, ourselves, the community residents with whom we work) are neither political figures, nor celebrities, *and yet*—and here's the important part—we, in our humanity, are full and representative people in the local publics in which we participate.[2] "The public sphere," as David Coogan points out, "does not exist in any meaningful way apart from our own rhetorical investments in it" ("Counterpublics" 462).

Furthermore, the term *ordinary* signals a difference between how ordinary people show up in politicians' and celebrities' public discourse and how we ourselves actually go public. In politicians' public address, the "ordinary person" (Wells 329) is typically "a prop" (330), "the mouthpiece of monologic public policy" (330). Similarly, the ordinary person is cast as the mere recipient of the celebrity's public appeal, as demonstrated in the photo op that Brad Pitt and Angelina Jolie staged for their newborn to turn America's attention to poverty and disease in Namibia (Smith 61). Interested in how ordinary people piece together "scraps of discursive space" to go public, Susan Wells is among those who have oriented rhetorical study toward the public discursive practices of ordinary people (326). She and her students go public, for instance, to appoint a minister, to improve the safety of a neighborhood, to expose incidents of police brutality.

Community literacy has made the enterprise of going public central to our own and our students' rhetorical education. Studies in community literacy ask, what does it take for ordinary people to go public? What constitutes situated-public literacies? How might we, as activist rhetoricians, best work to improve the quality of contemporary public life? By forging mutually respectful institutional partnerships? By structuring intercultural inquiry? Or, by designing forums for deliberation to inform wise action? How can a better understanding of ordinary people going public help us, as educators, to figure out "what [. . .] we want from public writing" and to design educational experiences that college students use to develop their own rhetorical acumen (Wells 325)?

This volume suggests that the *community* of community literacy might be best understood in terms of these discursive sites where ordinary people go public. From a rhetorical perspective, then, *community* refers not to existing geographic locales as the idea of a *neighborhood* would suggest (Barton and Hamilton 15) but to symbolic constructs enacted in time and space around shared exigencies—in other words, *local publics.* People construct these communities—at once discursive and physical entities—around distinct rhetorical agendas that range from socializing children into appropriate language use (e.g., Trackton's street theater) to eliciting stakeholders' perspectives on a shared problem (e.g., Pittsburgh's community think tank) to demanding respect under conditions that yield little of it (e.g., Angelstown's shadow system). And people draw upon a whole family of situated-public literacies, in order to do so.

To study sites such as these, below I suggest a parsimonious framework, not so much an overriding set of terms, but just enough structure to put alternative accounts of people going public in relation to one another. I use this framework to emphasize public features of community literacy not always salient in other standard accounts of literacy, such as "Family and Community Literacies" (Cushman, Barbier, Mazak, and Petrone; Qualls). Nor are these public features necessarily addressed in discussions of everyday literacy (Knobel; cf. Nystrand

and Duffy) or, as Barton and Hamilton observe, when community literacy is framed in terms of minority-group practices (15).[3]

THE LOCAL PUBLIC FRAMEWORK

This chapter introduces the five-point local public framework as a heuristic for comparing alternative accounts of people going public and for considering the implications that follow from them. The point of the framework is not to dissect individual studies as much as to set different kinds of accounts of local public life in relation to one another. We all know better than to compare apples and oranges. In literacy studies, the fruit basket is even more varied, with literacy scholars employing a wide range of research methods—from discourse analysis and cultural critique to action research, including progressive pedagogies and innovative organizational practices. Without deracinating their literate activities from the contexts in which they derive their significance, the framework is my attempt to attend to the rhetorical dynamics at play when ordinary people go public.

Table 2. The local public framework.

Point of Comparison	Brief Definition
1. Guiding Metaphor	the *image* that describes the discursive space where ordinary people go public, including distinctive *features*
2. Context	*location,* as well as other context-specific *factors* that give public literacies their meaning
3. Tenor of the Discourse	*register*—the affective quality of the discourse
4. Literacy	key *practices* that comprise the discourse; how people use writing and words to organize and carry out their purposes for going public
5. Rhetorical Invention	the *generative process* by which people respond to the exigencies that call the local public into being

Guiding Metaphor

Metaphors figure prominently in literacy research describing the discursive sites where the ordinary people go public. As rhetorical devices, these metaphors serve a dramatic function due to their "magical quality, one difficult to describe in discursive academic language" (J. Murphy 6). Metaphors wield the evocative capacity to conjure up discursive space, to call that space into being. Chaïm Perelman and L. Olbrechts-Tyteca called this quality "presence" (116–17); Michael Warner calls it the "world-making" capacity of style (128). Thick descriptions of local public life are stylistic accomplishments in their own right. Through these descriptions, literacy scholars not only conjure up in readers' minds local publics such as Trackton's public stage and Angelstown's shadow system, but in doing so they have also successfully created another type of discursive space for the study of local public rhetoric: a formal public that you and I as readers and writers also help to maintain.

I have identified the guiding metaphors in these researchers' accounts of local public life by reading one of two ways. In some cases, the metaphor is designated by the author as a key conceptual home. This is the case, for instance, for the theater in Heath's *Way with Words,* the link in Barton and Hamilton's *Local Literacies,* and the shadow system in Cintron's *Angels' Town.* In other cases, identifying the core metaphor required a more constructive effort on my part. For instance, Cushman refers the institutional site she studied as a *gatekeeping encounter.* I looked to her analysis to see how a gate operates within such an encounter—to swing shut or to creak open, for instance—and how the image of the gate signals both space beneath and above it, as in the expressions "hitting bottom" and "getting over."

In identifying each guiding metaphor, I sought evidence of each researcher's rhetorical understanding of the local public life he or she observed. As heuristics, the researchers' metaphors work like other such images: to structure and to define "the human conceptual system" (Lakoff and Johnson 6), indicating the "working theories," or internal representations, people build to interpret and to carry out complex discursive phenomena such as teaching, composing, deliberating, and theory building (Flower, *Construction* 260–62).[4] For instance, Cintron uses the metaphor of the shadow system to account for the tension between the political theories he brings to his critical ethnography and what he observes on the streets of Angelstown. Cintron calls this metaphor his interpretative scheme. It functions "heuristically" which, he says, "is how all metaphors work" (*Angels' Town* 176). Because a metaphor suggests similarities between two otherwise dissimilar objects, metaphors reveal "unsuspected connectives" (Burke 90). To identify these connectives, the framework's analysis of metaphor includes both the dominant image—the metaphor itself (such as Cintron's shadow system)—and the metaphor's distinctive features; for instance, that the shadow system *mimics* the system world and *shelters* difference. Likewise, Heath's impromptu theater is *dramatic* and *spontaneous*; Brandt's cultural womb *nurtures* and *prepares*. In connecting their guiding metaphors to such features, the researchers articulate their theories of how local public rhetoric works. For instance, Barton and Hamilton's *link* between private lives and public institutions carries out its rhetorical work by *connecting* domains to networks for the purpose of social action.

Metaphors preview differences in scholars' descriptions of local public life. Four additional elements help to identify and to elaborate key distinctions: the *context* that frames the discourse that people use to go public in a given study, the *tenor* of that discourse, the *literacies* that constitute the discourse, and the process of *rhetorical invention* that generates new local public discourse. To define the first three of these elements, I draw from Brian Street's ideological model of literacy (*Cross-cultural*). In the discussion below, please keep in mind that I am not devising a tool to unearth objective facts but an interpretive framework for making useful distinctions across multiple accounts of ordinary people going public.

Context

Under "context," the framework attends to two factors: first, the issue of location; second, the "broader features of social and cultural life" that give public discursive activity its meaning (Street, *Cross-cultural* 15). To replace the autonomous model that characterized literacy as a discrete entity that could be transported across contexts for similar effect, Street emphasizes that context-specific factors shape specific literacies and make them meaningful. Positioning their work in relation to the ideological model, for instance, Barton and Hamilton entitle their study of literacy in a British working-class neighborhood *Local Literacies: Reading and Writing in One Community*. For Street, new literacy studies should do more than amass numerous case studies of local literacies. His aim? "[U]seful generalizations" (*Cross-cultural* 10).

In fact, one of the most significant generalizations to be gleaned from the study of local literacies is that community literacy's decidedly public orientation gears its practices toward what Kirk Branch refers to as "'the ought to be'"—not only the world as it currently is, but also some future-oriented version of the social world as it could be (18).[5] I believe a rhetorically-centered framework that supports comparisons across accounts of local literacies can enhance our understanding of how different literate practices may "transform local actions into meanings *bound for* or *relevant to* other places" (Brandt and Clinton 349, emphasis added). Attention to location offers a useful vantage point for "bringing [such significant] differences to light" (Atwill 212).

Location. The term *local* has captured the collective imagination of rhetorical scholars for some time (Killingsworth 111). In community-literacy studies *local* is something of a Burkean godterm. Yet depending on whether *local* modifies *knowledge, literacy* or *attitudes,* its connotation can change dramatically. Modifying *knowledge, local* often carries a positive connotation. For instance, Clifford Geertz's depiction of indigenous people's local knowledge carries over to the CLC's strategies for eliciting the local knowledge of community residents (Flower, "Intercultural Knowledge" 258; Higgins and Brush). Modifying *literacy, local* suggests a rather technical distinction; local literacies are situated in domains other than work, school, or government; for instance, the home and the neighborhood (Barton and Hamilton 15). However, Barton and Hamilton chose to document how ordinary people use literacy in their daily lives, in part, because of their social commitment to complicate the "moral panic" that accompanies outcries over falling literacy rates (21). Yet when modifying *attitudes, local* often suggests something parochial, bigoted, backwards, even brutal. Genital mutilation is often referred to as a local tradition (e.g., Kissling and Sippel), and George Bush played to rural Ohio's local attitudes in his speech against same-sex marriage in the summer of 2006 (Gilgoff). Similarly, local attitudes can limit the capacity of a public to invite difference into dialogue. As Cintron observes, "a public sphere cannot 'think' beyond what terrifies it" (*Angels' Town* 194). The local public framework lets us consider implications of these and other connotations of *local* and its variations, *locale* and *location,* within accounts of ordinary people going public.

Foremost, location signals the material conditions that shape how people go public; location indicates the politics of place. Without such attention to location, it would be tempting to say that local public life is primarily a rhetorical activity that circulates discourse—and to leave it at that. Yet attending to location highlights the complex interplay here between situated activity (Chaiklin and Lave) and discursive space (Hauser *Vernacular*). For instance, just try to transport Trackton girls' public performances to the schoolyard in Gilmore's study where girls engage in a similar public performance. The lewd lyrics, rhyme, rhythm, clapping and jumping—key aspects of jump roping and stepping—are the same. But the politics of place make the activities associated with the plaza and the playground quite distinct. Indulging in their lewd lyrics in the safety of their secluded community, Trackton girls cleaned up their lyrics when jumping rope at school. In contrast, the girls in Gilmore's study performed their provocative lyrics on the school grounds in overt defiance of the school's authority, for "doing steps" had been banned. Only in this location did their lyrics and body language assume their full rhetorical force. By attending to location, the local public framework illuminates such differences.

Additional Contextual Factors. Location is only one of the contextual cues that imbue literacies with meaning. For Street, context attends to the ideological forces that were missing from the autonomous model of literacy, including the ways that institutions exercise control and that social hierarchies manage their power (*Cross-cultural* 7). In the local public framework, *context* refers to forces that make local publics viable discursive sites for people to go public. These forces include the *cultural agency* of the black-church-as-institution (Brandt, *American* 107), the *linguistic agency* of community residents (Cushman, *Struggle* 34), and the *cultural imaginary* of Angelstown's political landscape (Cintron, *Angels' Town* 141). As Street has argued, accounts of these forces say as much about the researcher's interpretative lens as they do about external reality (*Cross-cultural* 7). The challenge lies in grappling with how these lenses affect our understanding of situated-public literacies.

Tenor of the Discourse

For the New Literacy Group (NLG), *register*—or tenor—is a linguistic category referring to the more "typified" choices that together constitute the affective qualities of a discourse (Biber 9). Through its tenor, a discourse encodes attitudes, relational cues, and power differentials—often in highly nuanced ways (Besnier 62–65; Street, *Cross-cultural* 2). The tenor of a discourse is shorthand for subtle and often complex aspects of discourse typically implied through performance rather than stated explicitly in prose. Its closest correlative would be the term *tone* when used to describe affective qualities in a piece of writing. However, the difference is that local public discourse transpires in real time and engages people in all their thinking, feeling, reading, writing, doing, valuing complexity. The NLG got interested in describing the tenor of discourses to characterize how situated literacies differ from essayist qualities of standard academic discourse and the "literate activities and output of the intellectual elite" (Street, *Cross-cultural* 2).

Characterizing the tenor of a discourse, as I have in the following chapters, is a constructive act that asks us to imagine that we can hear first hand the real-time interactions that researchers reconstruct by necessity as text. By attending to cues in the researchers' descriptions and commentary, we can contrast, for instance, the *edgy competitive play* of Trackton's impromptu theater to the *literary uplift* of Heller's garden to the *bite—tempered by sweetness*—of Goldblatt's community-organizing effort to the *threatening hyperbole* of Cintron's shadow system. Approaching the tenor of local public discourse in this way may take some getting used to. But I would hope that you will find doing so to be worthwhile, for these registers offer handles (*edgy competitive play* vs. *literary uplift* vs. *threatening hyperbole*) that succinctly capture some of the most significant differences across alternative versions of local public life. Differences in register also emphasize that for an ordinary person to go public, never is it enough simply to decode or encode text; one must also perform specific literacies in the tenor of a given local public.

Literacies

This part of the framework attends to the literacies that ordinary people use to go public. These are the "technical" repertoires affiliated with discursive activity described in a given account (Street, *Cross-cultural* 9). Literacies are *purposeful*—as in Scribner and Cole's definition of literate practices (236). Literacies help *organize* public life—as in Heath's notion of a literate event (386). Literacies employ conventions that people may *transform* to meet the demands of their own rhetorical goals—as in Flower's definition of a literate act (*Construction* 36–37). In sum, *literacies* organize how people carry out their purposes for going public. As Street would advocate, the framework is also attentive to the ways that that oral and written literacies "mix" in different combinations in different contexts (*Cross-cultural* 10).

Rhetorical Invention

The last element in the local public framework is rhetorical invention: how a discourse permits people to respond to exigencies that arise within its discursive space.[6] Rhetorical invention solves "the problem [. . .] all writers face," that of "finding subjects to write about and of developing these subjects" (Lauer 1). Here, I pose not a single definition of rhetorical invention but rather a question: *what's the version of rhetorical invention embedded within a given account of local public life?* The framework lets us identify both the data and the theoretical explanations driving accounts of rhetorical invention across accounts of local public life.

A key way to compare invention's generative responses across local publics is to consider its implications—how rhetorical invention translates into choices, practices, and actions. To get at these implications, I conclude each five-point analysis in chapters 4 through 8 with a set of implications and some commentary. In these sections, I consider implications that a given viewpoint holds for some of the most perplexing issues that vex community-literacy studies—issues such as local democracy, program sustainability, the politics of identity, and institutional sponsorship. I draw connections to viewpoints treated in other chapters and to other relevant studies and theories. Foremost, these implication sections focus on "consequences [. . . for] knowledge making, policymaking, and day to day operations" (Royster and Williams, "History" 564). In doing so, these sections attempt to model one way to "keep[. . .] our intellectual engagements with contentious and complex issues productive" (Royster and Williams, "Reading" 142).

In using the local public framework to review community-literacy studies, I have planned my project to be comprehensive although it obviously is not exhaustive. The measure of the framework's success will be its ability to spur readers to make connections and comparisons of their own.

In part, the framework affords within-type comparisons, as table 3 demonstrates. For instance, both Barton and Hamilton's *Local Litera-*

Table 3. Prominent images of local public life: A comparative analysis.

1. Guiding Metaphor and its Features	2. Context	3. Tenor of the Discourse	4. Literacies	5. Rhetorical Invention
Heath's impromptu theater — It's dramatic and spontaneous	location, power, and integrity	edgy and competitive, curbed by play	performative literacies	practice, modeling, and feedback
Brandt's cultural womb — It nurtures and prepares	location and cultural agency	resourceful	interpretative literacies	inspiration, instruction, and transformation
Heller's garden — It (too) nurtures and prepares	location, agency, and maturation	uplifting	belletristic literacies	precision at the point of utterance
Barton and Hamilton's link — It connects domains to networks	location, bottom-up initiative, and agency	hybrid—a mix of the formal and the everyday	mobilizing literacies	adapting and retooling
Cushman's gate along a fenceline — It creates a space for access and conflict	location and linguistic agency	dueling dualities	institutional literacies	evaluating effects of acquired literacies transferred to new contexts
Goldblatt's community-organizing effort — It's complex and pleasurable	location and legacy	biting—tempered by sweetness	consensus-building literacies	a three-part process for transforming problems into issues for action
Flower's community think tank — Its diversity builds in conflict that requires tools	location and legacy	prophetic—principled and inventive	design literacies and inquiry-driven literacies	explicit instruction in strategic problem solving
Cintron's shadow system — It mimics and shelters difference	location and cultural imaginary	threatening and hyperbolic	tactical literacies	cultural appropriation

cies and Cushman's *The Struggle and the Tools* portray the local public as the discursive space where private and public spheres intersect. To depict this intersection, Barton and Hamilton invoke the image of a *link* and stress movement between the private-public binary; Cushman, invokes a *gate* and stresses the binary's outright collapse. By implication, Cushman's gatekeeping encounter makes salient political dynamics that the link does not. Because gatekeeping encounters are sites of intense political struggle, the *institutional literacies* required to navigate such spaces are inherently political tools.

The framework also supports readers' connections to other studies. For instance, a reader could use Barton and Hamilton's working theory of a link to frame Gail Weinstein-Shr's portrait of Chou Chang, a "literacy and cultural broker" for other Hmong immigrants who like himself are trying to negotiate "urban bureaucracy" in downtown Philadelphia (283). Additionally, a reader may consider how other studies extend implications that follow from those reviewed here; for instance, how Lavadenz extends Cushman's analysis of institutional literacies by describing the immigration *raid* (designed to expose illegal immigrants) as the extreme gatekeeping *encounter.*

Like many other artifacts from community-literacy studies, the meaning and function of the local public framework reside not only in the definitions of its terms but also in relation to the larger history of efforts in rhetoric and composition to span the distance between the situated and the public. The next chapter recounts this history as a response to two of the most pressing questions that the field of rhetoric and composition has faced over the past thirty years: *How do ordinary people best exercise their language rights? And how does local democratic discourse actually work?* To that history, we now turn.

3 Locating Community Literacy Studies

To what can we trace this interest in how ordinary people go public? How did it come to pass that community-literacy studies put a new unit of analysis—the local public—on the table in order to pursue this interest? Topics come and go all the time in academic fields, so what about this one let it take hold? What roles have sites such as Pittsburgh's CLC played in the history of community literacy, particularly in relation to building the kinds of observation-based theories and practices that scholars have needed to get this line of inquiry off the ground? These are some of the questions that the previous chapters raise.

In response to these questions, this chapter argues that the history of community literacy is tied up in efforts to define the *local public* as an object of inquiry and a site for rhetorical intervention. What has attracted community-literacy scholars to local publics is the promise they hold of enacting (never perfectly, always provisionally, and sometimes never that) what Flower has called "a rhetoric of engagement" grounded in relationships and focused on rhetorical action (*Community Literacy* 1).

As you would expect, the ethical visions that inspire community-literacy scholars' interest in local publics vary. Flower anchors her vision in Reinhold Niebuhr's "'ethic of love and justice' [. . .] a "spirit of stubborn generosity [. . . that] acknowledges the undeniable—the social and economic substructures of power, racism, of identity that will not be erased by goodwill" ("Negotiating" 51, 60). Coogan anchors his vision in West's "'love ethic' that is neither sentimental nor culturally separatist" ("Counterpublics" 463). Affiliated with Karl Marx, Cushman's vision upholds "reciprocal relations" as a standard for "ethical action in the research paradigm to facilitate social change" (*Struggle* 28). Rooted in Ernest Bloch's utopian ideal, Paula Mathieu's street-based literacy projects enact "hope"—a gesture that seeks to move out of abstractions about a better world toward actions devised to change the current world (*Tactics* 18). Inspired by Alinsky, Goldblatt's vision is "the promise of true mutual benefits for postsecondary schools and their off-campus partners" ("Alinsky's Reveille" 294).

For all the differences in their language, politics, and theoretical orientations, these scholars are drawn to the potential of local publics to dismantle university/"white" privilege and to reconfigure writing instruction outside the academic classroom in terms of mutual learning, linguistic and cultural diversity, and rhetorical action. In sum, scholars' interests in local publics have coalesced around the connection between vernacular literacies and public life—a connection that contends with the inherent ambiguity of language rights discourse and all the complexity of public-spheres studies.

Two Prior Accounts

People have been writing in their communities for several hundreds of years (Howard).[1] Yet compared to invention—the topic of the first book in this series—with its two-thousand-year history, the history of the discipline's interest in community literacy is strikingly brief, transpiring over the last few decades. Significant portions of this history have already been told. In *Moving Beyond Academic Discourse: Composition Studies and the Public Sphere*, published in 2002, Christian Weisser positioned community literacy in terms of larger social then public turns in the field at large. One of the earliest visionaries was Michael Halloran who in 1975 and then in 1982 sounded the call to revitalize rhetorical education by reclaiming the classical attention to public discourse. In relation to this call, Weisser mapped a now familiar disciplinary history in which cognitivism, expressivism, and social constructionism gave way to one another respectively and then to the radical pedagogy of Paulo Freire and to Freiristas' "activism in the academy" (116). In relation to this history, Weisser identified community-literacy programs as valuable sites where college students develop their capacities for going public (48).

More recently, in the third chapter of *Community Literacy and the Rhetoric of Engagement*, Flower has recounted the historical context of the CLC as it relates to the development of cognitive rhetoric. The CLC was an experiment in the rhetoric of engagement, the practice of learning to "speak with others [. . .] for something" as an engaged response to collaborative inquiry (79). Flower's account positions the CLC in relation to some of the same process-movement, cognition/society debates that Weisser detailed, but for Flower the promise of this disciplinary discussion has lain not in the power of cultural critique to inform public pedagogies (where Weisser took his history) but in the discipline's capacity to develop working theories to articulate rhetorics of performance capable of supporting both personal and public discovery and change (R. Young, Becker and Pike). That, for Flower, is the power of Freire's pedagogy—its contribution as a working theory of politically charged literate action and reflection. Likewise, for Flower what is especially valuable about the renewed interest in Aristotelian and sophistic rhetorics is that they restore traditions of *praxis* (theory and action) and *phronesis* (contingent judgment) that can be employed to meet the contemporary demands of intercultural inquiry for productive working relationships and wise action.

As Flower explains, the CLC was founded in 1989 as an attempt to enact a theory-driven, context-sensitive rhetoric, grounded in the legacy of the African American freedom struggle, in the commitments of social activism as embodied in the settlement house tradition, and in the problem-solving orientation of cognitive rhetoric (Flower *Community Literacy*). Based on Wayne Peck's observations of the inventive, transactional purposes to which the everyday people in his neighborhood put literacy, the CLC tested four principles of literate social action: a dedication to social change and action; support of intercultural inquiry and collaboration; a commitment to strategies for collaboration, planning, argument, and reflection that are intentionally taught and deliberately negotiated; and a commitment to a mutually beneficial community-university partnership that supports joint inquiry (Peck, Flower, and Higgins 207–18). The CLC posed "[t]he question [of] how to create an atmosphere of respect, a commitment to equality, and an acknowledgement of the multiple forms of expertise at the table" (210). In response, the CLC envisaged the alternative public discourse of the community problem-solving dialogue—what Flower has termed more recently a *vernacular* local public (Flower "Can You Build"; Flower, "Intercultural Knowledge" 252; Higgins, Long, and Flower 16–18).

Over the years that community literacy was coming into its own, scholars outside rhetoric and composition sounded two calls that would shape the direction of community-literacy studies. One of these calls urged literacy scholars to situate the study of literacy in the public realm in an effort to study language rights; the other call urged public-sphere scholars to test their theoretical propositions in the crucible of "actually existing democracy" in order to build a more nuanced understanding of the limits and potential of democratic practices (Fraser 109). While literacy scholars and public-spheres theorists responded to these calls within their own disciplinary arenas, community literacy emerged as another site of inquiry, one attentive to the new scholarship in both sociolinguistics and public-spheres studies. As a constructive response to these two calls, community-literacy studies has coalesced in a distinctive way around the democratic potential of vernacular local publics. In this account, I locate community-literacy studies in its academic/disciplinary context at the same time that I make a case for community literacy as a distinctive area of scholarship that integrates literacy and public-spheres theories to study how ordinary people go public and to design interventions that help them to do so more effectively within and across complex discursive spaces.

SITUATING THE STUDY OF LITERACY IN THE PUBLIC REALM

Over time, the call to situate the study of literacy in the public realm would come to mean studying people using literacy in a multiplicity of decidedly public domains—not commercial nor academic ones, but institutional sites representing versions of some greater good, such as the medical system designed to promote health or human service agencies organized to strengthen the larger "social fabric" (Cushman, *Struggle* 45). Eventually, this call would direct literacy scholars to conduct research in the community. In sociolinguistic parlance, community designates that subset of the public domain mediating between "the private sphere of home and family [. . . and] the impersonal institutions of the wider society"; thus, community is the realm that ordinary people most readily experience as "public life" (Crow and Allen 1). In the 1970s, it was a new idea to situate the study of literacy in any locale whatsoever—and it was toward this effort that the call was first sounded.

The call to move the study of situated literacies into the public realm was international in scope. It began as a critique of assumptions about literacy so pervasive and bold that they governed most notably the international, multi-organizational, multi-million-dollar initiative that the United Nations Educational, Scientific and Cultural Organization (UNESCO) sponsored in the 1950s to eradicate illiteracy world wide (Le Page 4): the vernacularization project.[2] Today, literacy scholars use the phrase the *autonomous model of literacy* to encapsulate these assumptions. In short, the autonomous model took literacy to be a generalizable skill that fostered levels of abstract thinking and critical analysis unavailable to the oral mind (Goody; Havelock; Ong). The model assumed that, as a generalizable skill, literacy could be packaged and transported from one setting to another for equal effect. It drove the overstated claims of the great divide: that literate people are more intellectually agile (for instance, able to separate fact from myth and to glean abstract principles from concrete experience) than people who do not read and write. The model also supported the view that a country needs to cross a certain threshold of literacy in order to ensure the functioning of its institutions and to achieve economic autonomy (Le Page 9). According to this model, everyday people "went public" to the extent that they developed the literate skills necessary to participate in the economic mainstream of their countries. Thus, the vernacularization project (which aimed to teach people in developing countries to read and write in their mother tongues) was a means toward an end—the most efficient means, that is, to teach people to function in a given country's standard language.[3]

Among the first to call for and conduct research to interrogate the claims of the autonomous model were Sylvia Scribner and Michael Cole. From 1973 to 1978 they directed the Vai Literacy Project in Liberia. Rather than describing general features of literacy, Scribner and Cole found it necessary to refer to literate practices, defined as "a recurrent, goal-directed sequence of activities using a particular technology and particular systems of knowledge" (236). Situated as they were within specific domains of activity, literate practices—from letter writing to reciting the Qu'ran to "doing school"—let the Vai accomplish different things in different contexts for different purposes, but these practices didn't add up to sweeping changes in cognitive ability or socioeconomic status.

Freire was another early, outspoken critic of UNESCO's conception of literacy—and one of the first to situate the study of literacy in the public realm. First expressed in his dissertation in 1959, his ideas caught international attention with the publication of *Pedagogy of the Oppressed* in 1970. Working in Brazil and later for UNESCO under exile in Chile, he critiqued teaching literacy as a technical skill and focused instead on literacy learning as a critical act of emancipatory engagement. Interrogating the purposes of literacy instruction, Freire challenged the assumption driving the UNESCO 1953 monograph that the ultimate purpose of literacy instruction was to "bring about conformity to [. . .] the present system"—a position that got him exiled from his home country (Gerbault 147). Instead, Freire promoted education as "'the practice of freedom,' the means by which men and women deal critically and creatively with reality and discover how to participate in the transformation of their world" (Shaull 16). His pedagogy called for circle facilitators to introduce vernacular literacy to the extent that it addressed the problems that members of the circle had posed. It would be hard to overstate Freire's influence on rhetoric and composition. Looking back on the discipline in 2002, Weisser contended: "[Freire's] work—most notably *The Pedagogy of the Oppressed* [. . .]—is directly responsible for the discipline's current focus on public writing" (37).

The critique of the autonomous model instigated numerous historical studies, such as David Cressy's "The Environment for Literacy: Accomplishment and Context in Seventeenth Century England and New England," published in 1983.[4] These historical reviews indicated that rather than triggering economic development, literacy flourishes in contexts where other "favourable factors" such as health and economic well-being do, too (Carrington 84).

By the mid-1980s, problems with the autonomous model of literacy—primarily, its insufficient empirical grounds—gave rise to New Literacy Studies (NLS) that focused on "the role of literacy practices in reproducing or challenging structure of power and domination" (Street, *Cross-cultural* 7). One of the strongest advocates of the ideological model and the research supporting it is Street who in 1984 published *Literacy in Theory and Practice* based on his fieldwork in Iran in the 1970s. Arguing that anthropology offered a better framework for studying literacy than formal linguistics, Street pushed literacy scholars to use ethnographic methods to study "the site of tension between authority and power on the one hand and resistance and creativity on the other" (*Cross-cultural* 8). During the second half of the 1980s, the NLG advocated studying literacies in the social and cultural contexts in which they actually occur—for instance, a village in Papua

New Guinea (Kulick and Stroud), a fishing boat in Alaska (Reder and Wikelund), or a high school in North Philadelphia (Camitta).

Throughout the 1990s, the NLG continued to launch numerous cross-cultural comparisons (Street Cross-cultural; Tabouret-Keller et al.) and inspired similar studies of minority-group practices here in the United States—work that continues today (e.g., Anderson, Kendrick, Rogers, and Smythe; Farr, *Latino Language*; Farr, *Racheros*; Joyce Harris, Kamhi, and Pollock; Kells, Balester, and Villanueva; Moss *Community Text*; Moss *Literacy Across Communities*; Zantella). Such research has highlighted that literacy helps shape ethnic, gender, and religious identities by structuring and sustaining the institutional relationships that engage these identities (Street *Cross-cultural*).

By the 1990s, the NLG's *ideological model of literacy* had replaced the autonomous model in most literacy scholarship (Hull and Schultz). The ideological model defined literacy as a constellation of local, situated practices (Barton, Hamilton, and Ivanič) that are shaped by institutional power (Street *Literacy*) and responsive to changes across time and place (Tusting). In a 2000 retrospective, Karin Tusting characterized the claims of the ideological model:

- Literacy is best understood as a set of social practices; they can be inferred from events which are mediated by written texts.
- Different literacies are associated with different domains of life.
- Literacy practices are patterned by social institutions and power relationships. Thus, some literacies are more dominant, visible, and influential than others.
- Literacy practices are purposeful, embedded in social goals and cultural practices.
- Literacy practices change and new ones are frequently acquired through the process of informal learning and sense making as well as formal education. (38–41)

The NLG and its ideological model were instrumental in advocating the study of situated literacies. The strength of the ideological model is its ability to "connect[. . .] microanalyses of language and literacy use with macroanalyses of discourse and power" (Schultz and Hull 23).

The effort to locate the study of literacy in decidedly *public* domains came about in the 1990s primarily as a result of two research projects, led—not surprisingly—by researchers affiliated with the NLG: the Lancaster Literacy Project (conducted by David Barton, Mary Hamilton, and associates) and the re-evaluation of UNESCO's 1953 vernacularization project, led by Andrée Tabouret-Keller in association with the International Group for the Study of Language Standardization and the Vernacularization of Literacy (IGLSVL). Conducted in the first half of 1990s, these two landmark research projects moved the study of situated literacies into public domains, and they did so not by studying formal public discourse, but by identifying local discursive sites where ordinary people went public.

Barton and Hamilton conducted the Lancaster Literacy Project 1990 to 1996 and published the results in 1998 under the title *Local Literacies: Reading and Writing in One Community*. Here Barton and Hamilton used the term "domain" to refer to the "structured, patterned contexts within which literacy is used and learned" (10).[5] In keeping with the NLG, they observed that the literacies which people of Lancaster practiced in the domain of the home were different from those they practiced in the neighborhood, and different still from literacies required within the academy, workplace, or formal public institution such as the courtroom or doctor's office. The differences were due, in large part, to the distinctive social purposes that organize these domains. But Barton and Hamilton were especially interested in the domain of community; thus, reports of a neighborhood activist named Shirley caught their attention. Interviews with Shirley revealed that in her informal but efficacious social role as local-public liaison, Shirley used a mix of vernacular and more formal literacies to go public, spanning the space between the informal and formal, the private and public.

At this same time, an international group of literacy scholars, under the acronym IGLSVL, joined forces to re-evaluate the 1953 UNESCO vernacularization project that had proclaimed vernacular literacy to be a human right. When their research results were published in 1997, Tabouret-Keller sounded the call for more literacy scholars to situate their studies in the public realm. To consider this call, imagine yourself a member of the IGLSVL that met in Sèvres, France, in 1992 to re-evaluate UNESCO's earlier project. You and your colleagues represent vernacularization projects from all over the world—"former colonies of Britain and France, but also in Europe, the Americas, East, South, and South-East Asia and in Oceanic Australia" (Le Page 6). For your contribution to the research symposium, you need to identify the consequences of the 1953 UNESCO monograph on the corner of the globe where you have been conducting your sociolinguistic research. Your colleagues would be doing the same for theirs. It's not just that forty years have passed. Time itself would have made your job quite straight forward: you would have measured the effect of the vernacularization policies on your region and identified any constraints that thwarted their effectiveness—or conditions that made for their success. But that's not what frames your research problem. The point is that over the past forty years, you and your colleagues have rejected the formal linguistics, as well as the great divide theory, that motivated the 1953 UNESCO monograph. You no longer see languages as discrete entities that more or less respect the boundaries of nation states. Instead, you have come to understand languages falling along "linguistic continua focused from place to place and generation to generation around social group nodes, and labeled accordingly" (Le Page 4).[6] Likewise, you no longer assign agency to language as the UNESCO monograph had. Instead, as a colleague put it: "It is no longer very meaningful to say that languages are capable of doing things, such as being used for education; people do things—languages are abstractions from what people do, and language is in a symbiotic relationship with other social processes" (Le Page 6). Given this shift in perspective—given the humility that has replaced UNESCO's ethnocentric confidence—the question is, *what do you now consider noteworthy to report back to your colleagues?*

From here, we no longer need to hypothesize. Published in 1997, the IGLSVL's research proceedings *Vernacular Literacy: A Re-Evaluation* recorded observations the group considered noteworthy. For example, Jean-Michel Charpentier described a group of singers in Melanesia who had devised an improvisational pidgin to "exalt the existence and the genius of a group that had previously remained unexpressed" (242). The singers could have sung in their regional local language. But that vernacular was already used for folk songs. Instead, the invented pidgin let the singers reach a larger audience (Charpentier 242).[7] Referring to the singer's decision to employ a pidgin over a regional vernacular, Charpentier noted that the pidgin allowed the singers to call into being a "new semantic field" that made an "outward-turn[. . .]" (242).[8] Pushing the capacity of sociolinguistic terminology to express rhetorical ideas of audience and reach, commentary like Charpentier's referred to the rhetorical space of a local public; his phrase "new semantic field" suggests an invented, local discursive space and the "outward turn" refers to the singers' public orientation.

Throughout *Vernacular Literacy: A Re-Evaluation,* what the sociolinguists noted were accounts of "ordinary people" finding "genuine utility" in literacy (whether standard, vernacular, or some inventive mix) as it proved useful "for those aspects of social and political life with which they are concerned" (Tabouret-Keller 327). In fact, this descriptor becomes the group's boldest claim concerning where and how it is that people exercise their language rights. In her conclusion to the report, Andrée Tabouret-Keller offered not broad, propositional claims about literacy or language rights.[9] Instead, she concluded that people best exercise their language rights by using language to pool literate resources in order to address pressing social and public issues (327).

Here in the United States, the call to situate the study of literacy in the public realm has also been framed in terms of language rights. In rhetoric and composition, the clearest example is the 1974 Students' Right to Their Own Language (SRTOL) resolution "affirm[ing] the students' right to their own patterns and varieties of language" (*Students' Right* 1).[10] Most basically, the SRTOL resolution encapsulated the field's commitment to respond to and to make room for the growing number of "Blacks, Browns, women and other historically marginalized groups" who appeared in mainstream colleges in the 1960s and 1970s (Smitherman, "CCCC's Role" 354). The SRTOL recognized the existential centrality and linguistic legitimacy of the discourses that students bring with them to composition classrooms—vernacular literacies like Black English Vernacular (BEV) or, more generally, what the linguistics in the UNESCO project would have called one's *mother tongue.* In calling attention to the ways that classroom practices have institutionalized racial and class-based biases, the SRTOL also raised the possibility of reconfiguring educational spaces and institutional relationships to allow for reciprocity and mutual learning among writers who come from different cultural backgrounds and occupy different social locations (Smitherman, "CCCC's Role" 354).[11] When the profession passed the resolution back in 1974, the unspoken question was how those in rhetoric and composition would promote linguistic and rhetorical diversity in "public and professional settings" (Bruch and Marback 664).

The SRTOL resolution spoke for compelling social ideals—most notably human dignity, improved literacy education, and fair and equitable institutional practices. The challenge was how educators in an academic discipline would work within their spheres of influence to make public life more inclusive—a challenge that continues to engage some of the field's most active scholars (e.g., Bean et al.; Bruch and Marback; Busch and Ball; Canagarajah "Place"; Gilyard Race; Gilyard *Voices;* Joyce Harris, Kamhi and Pollock; Kells; Kinloch; Marzluf; Parks; Tollefson; Smitherman "CCCC's Role"; Wible).

As an heir of the SRTOL, community-literacy studies has instantiated the movement's ideals by documenting two possibilities for situating vernacular literacies in public domains. The first possibility emphasizes students and other ordinary people *employing* vernacular literacies in public spaces. The second designs and tests rhetorical interventions to help students and other ordinary people use their vernacular literacies as resources for public *engagement*, building together new knowledge about shared issues.

Documenting and Theorizing Local Public Discourse

In rhetoric and composition, researchers have documented ordinary people using vernacular discourses to go public in arenas more fluid and permeable than the sites that Graham Crow and Graham Allen describe as formal publics. And vernacular discourse still gets the job done here, and arguably more effectively than more sedimented practices (Cushman Struggle; Moss Community Text). Cushman documented this comparative advantage, for example, when an African American admissions counselor switched to BEV to signal to a nervous young admissions candidate that she could do the same—whereby inviting her to set some of the terms of the admissions interview (*Struggle* 187). Likewise, in "Negotiating the Meaning of Difference," Flower observed that in crafting their public documents, teen writers at the CLC often used the help of writing mentors to devise text conventions for encoding BEV to address rhetorical goals (for dialogue, say, or commentary) that Standard Written English (SWE) alone could not have conveyed nearly as effectively (Flower, Long, and Higgins 229–53). Likewise, Barton and Hamilton attributed the success of the newsletters that Shirley wrote and distributed around her neighborhood to her skillful integration of vernacular and formal discourses (253).

Descriptive research has verified that such instances are not as rare as prescriptive standards would suggest (Higgins). Such research can be grouped into two categories:

1) ethnographies and other descriptive accounts of minority group practices. These accounts are typically concerned with documenting a whole range of group practices and, thus, draw upon a language of publicness to the extent necessary to describe distinct features within the larger set of group practices.

2) ethnographies that deliberately *set out to study* situated literacies *in the public realm.*

In the first set of ethnographies, researchers didn't set out to study public discourse but drew upon a language of publicness in order to describe and to interpret what they observed over the course of their studies. We can see this dynamic in *Ways with Words*, published in 1983. A language of publicness (in this case, coded in the theatrical language of public stage performances) let Heath contrast the language-learning rituals in Trackton with those of the neighboring white community of Roadville, but describing language-learning rituals, not public discourse, was Heath's first priority.

Likewise, when launching *Until We are Strong Together,* published in 1997, Heller sought a personally and professionally meaningful research project (10). So she positioned her ethnography within a women's writing workshop in San Francisco's Tenderloin District. At first glance, the workshop seemed to be expressivist in nature, emphasizing belletristic genres for personal expression. However, she soon found that the workshop's sponsors were committed to developing the writers' public voices. So as we will see in chapter 5, Heller employed a language of publicness to the extent necessary to describe specific public features within the workshop's overall orientation; for instance, workshop members represented the "larger public" (143) and neighborhood poetry readings created "public forums" (103).

Likewise, Beverly Moss and Deborah Brandt had other fish to fry besides documenting public discourses in their analyses of African American churches. In *A Community Text Arises,* published in 2002, Moss set out to document the intertextual composing process by which congregations and pastors co-created sermons as community texts. Moss drew upon a language of publicness to describe worship service as a "public" event (see also Moss, "Pew" 209). Published the previous year, Brandt's study of the African American church was part of a larger study entitled *Literacy in American Lives* analyzing how ordinary people born between 1895 and 1985 in the U.S. have learned to read and write. In both cases, Moss and Brandt drew upon a language of publicness in order to convey the significance of the church as public institution that circulates practices for personal and social transformation. While Moss explicitly classified her work as community literacy, Brandt did not. Either way, in documenting situated-public literacies, their work participated in the constructive process by which scholars both piqued disciplinary interest in how it is that ordinary people go public and also contributed scholarship to a growing body of literature exploring this question.

Meanwhile, another set of descriptive studies within rhetoric and composition identified from the outset the public realm as pertinent to their research, and deliberately situated their studies of literacy there. Among the first to carry out this line of research was Wayne Peck in his 1991 study of Bob, Althea, Buzz, and Barbara—community residents whom he documented "composing for action" (1). Based on the case studies of these writers, Peck defined the complex and persistent nature of the rhetorical situation that would come to define community literacy as a rhetorical act of shared deliberation and problem solving:

> Whether the occasion for literate practice be a dispute with city housing officials, such as in the case of Bob, or a person trying to turn his life around by writing an action plan, such as the case of Buzz, community literate practices emerge as existential responses to problems that carry real consequences for the writers. Either Bob wins his case before the city or he loses his house and must go live in a neighborhood shelter. Either Buzz composes a workable plan for his life or he must move from the shelter to live on the streets. Community literacy practices are rooted in the life struggles of urban residents and are best understood as transactions or responses of people addressing dilemmas through writing. (20)

Peck's observation that community literacy is a literate response to pressing social and existential exigencies is not only relevant to Barton and Hamilton's Lancaster Literacy Project, but it also provides a tighter frame than the sociolinguistic one that Tabouret-Keller used to describe the situations in which "ordinary people" in the IGLSVL's study practiced their language rights. The women in Dakar who assumed responsibility for their household finances (Tabouret-Keller 324), the farmers in North Cameroon who responded to newly mandated land-management practices (Gerbault 183), the Portuguese immigrants in France who invented a vernacular *immigrais* to aid communication under hostile social conditions (Gardner-Chloros 216)—in these instances everyday people pooled their literate resources to respond to pervasive and complex manifestations of poverty and disenfranchisement that UNESCO has long attempted to eradicate. Likewise, it was the rhetorical nature of such community problems that compelled Lorraine Higgins and Lisa Brush to position their research of personal narratives in the public realm. Their 2006 study "Writing the Wrongs of Welfare" examined "how subordinated rhetors [former and current welfare recipients] might enter into the public record their tacit and frequently discounted knowledge about poverty and welfare" (697).

As Peck's study indicates, as scholars in rhetoric and composition situated literacy studies in the public realm, their scholarship also developed theories of local public discourse. This is even the case, for instance, for scholars who positioned their work as a deliberate departure from some of the earlier community-literacy scholarship. In the first chapter of *Angels' Town,* Cintron noted the insufficiencies of sociolinguistic theory to get at "the broader cultural examination [he] aspired to" (10). Thus, he called his 1997 analysis of street life in an industrial city outside Chicago a "critical ethnography" by which he "bec[ame] a rhetorician of public culture" and "Heath as a theoretical lens [was] replaced by Michel de Certeau" (10). Throughout *Angels' Town,* Cintron drew upon de Certeau's *The Practice of Everyday Life* to account for the repetitive and unconscious aspects of everyday life that fuel how culture is both produced and consumed. Likewise, Cushman framed *The Struggle and the Tools* within the same French political philosophy, quoting, for instance, de Certeau's *The Practice of Everyday Life* in its opening lines. Focused on the private-public nature of the gatekeeping encounter, Cushman developed a theory of dueling dualities by which everyday people's hidden transcripts spar with the public transcript to unleash the noisy wrangling between political binaries. In important ways, European political philosophy has let rhetoricians infuse their observations of literacy in the public realm with NLG's concern for issues of power and ideology. By drawing on political philosophies such as de Certeau's, literacy scholars have helped to characterize community literacy as a distinctive multivocal, multimodal local public discourse.

Features of Situated-Public Literacies

Taken together, studies of literacy have identified distinctive features of the situated-public literacies that people use to go public. These studies confirm that—as Tabouret-Keller observed—although the vernacular-vs.-standard distinction carries important information, other features may be more instrumental in helping ordinary people go public. Some of these most prominent features are described below.

Situated-public literacies are performative. Heath needed a language of public performance to describe what was distinctive about the situated literacies she observed in Trackton. Here, youngsters' street performances called a public into being around the rituals that defined community life—and in the process, children learned their community's ways with words. Performance is a "magic[al . . .] verbal art" capable of conjuring up discursive space, explains ethnographer Richard Gelb (323). Performance transforms passersby into members of a public who bear witness to performers laying claim to the integrity of their own lives as well as to their rightful share of resources needed to sustain those lives (Gilmore 79–80). Performance links the material and the symbolic (Cintron, Afterword 381), often challenging the status quo by mixing humor and critique for political, as well as dramatic, effect (Farr and Barajas 23).

Situated-public literacies are also collaborative. This feature means that situated-public literacies need to be nurtured in supportive environments like the women's writing workshop in Heller's *Until We Are Strong Together* or the workshop for Mexican immigrant mothers in Janise Hurtig's "Resisting Assimilation." These and other ethnographic studies of literacy workshops highlight the importance of facilitators who support the nascent ideas of inexperienced writers. Just as importantly, they identify the invaluable role that these same writers play for one another as readers and members of a local public, taking one another's ideas seriously and responding to them with respectful candor. To the extent that community-literacy scholars share a common *crie de coeur,* I would think it's their shared commitment to collabo-

ration (in any number of configurations) as a joint response to socio-
political mechanisms that otherwise exclude ordinary people from the
processes of public dialogue and decision making. Collaboration is a
means by which ordinary people make their voices heard. Collaborative also refers to the complex ways that multiple readers and writers,
speakers and listeners may move among interchangeable roles within
complex networks to co-create literate texts (Moss Community Text;
Comstock 59).

Situated-public literacies often strike a problem-posing stance. It
was Freire who most eloquently articulated the humanizing consequences that follow from theorizing local public discourse in praxis. In
Pedagogy of the Oppressed, Freire advocated problem-posing teams (or
culture circles) where participants learned to read the world as a site of
colonialism and class struggle. Freire's method motivated "members of
the community to exchange ideas, to understand a specific problem, to
find one or more solutions to it, and to determine a programme with
a timetable, using specific materials" (Gerbault 153). Freire's pedagogy
has informed ethnographic efforts to document situated-public literacies (Sleeter and Bernal 240–58). Its problem-posing feature is prominent in the adaptations that re-invent for American classrooms Freire's
pedagogy designed for resilient peasants (Finn; Shor and Pari). The
problem-posing feature of situated-public literacies has also compelled
scholars to augment Freirian pedagogy with additional problem-solving rhetorics, including John Dewey's civic ideals (Coogan, "Community Literacy" 106); Alinsky's community-organizing principles
(Coogan, "Service Learning"; Faber; Goldblatt "Alinsky's Reveille")
and Flower's social-cognitive rhetoric (Peck, Flower, and Higgins;
Flower "Talking Across Difference").

Situated-public literacies also tend to be sponsored—that is, affiliated with institutional sponsors that circulate not only texts but practices for interpreting and composing texts (Brandt *American*; Brandt
Involvement). Brandt calls this circulatory process sponsorship—the
process by which large-scale economic forces [. . .] set the routes and
determine the worldly worth of [. . . a given] literacy (*American* 20).
Sponsorship helps account for how knowledge is distributed within
organizations (Hull "Hearing Other Voices") and households (Moll
and González), how people navigate social networks (Farr *"En Los Dos
Idiomas"*), and how institutional design can promote social change
(Grabill *Community Literacy*).

Finally, situated-public literacies often comprise alternative discourses affiliated with no single homeplace or public institution. Alternative discourses may be an inventive hybrid (Barton and Hamilton 122) that laces together discourses of the street and school, policy talk and political activism (Peck, Flower, and Higgins 210). In other situations, the alternative discourse may be a "hidden transcript" in direct tension with the standards and assumptions of a public institution's bureaucracy (Cushman, *Struggle* 139) or a city newspaper's petty bourgeois bias (Cintron, *Angels' Town* 193). Alternative discourses support transcultural repositioning, the "self-conscious[. . .]" process by which members of minority culture move among "different languages and dialects, different social classes, different culture and artistic forms" (Guerra 8). As such, alternative discourses support strategic border crossing, at once linguistic, symbolic, literal, and political (Lavadenz 109).

SITUATING THE STUDY OF PARTICIPATORY DEMOCRACY

As literacy scholars took issue with the dominant autonomous model of literacy, in a similar fashion, public-spheres scholars have critiqued the dominant, abstract, and idealized (though skewed) version of how democratic discourse works. Most notably, in 1990, Fraser sounded the call for the study of "actually existing democracy" (109).[12]

Fraser sought to complicate the abstract democratic theory that Jürgen Habermas issued in *The Structural Transformation of the Public Sphere: An Inquiry into a Category of Bourgeois Society,* published in German in 1962 and circulated in English by the Massachusetts Institute of Technology in 1989. In *The Structural Transformation of the Public Sphere,* Habermas described the method (deliberating claims and adjudicating evidence) by which private citizens (propertied men) set aside (bracketed) their individual interests and differences in order to discuss the most pressing issues of their day (the common good). Habermas identified a method by which public talk supersedes force or coercion in efforts to determine matters of public concern. He also designated a discursive space (*the public sphere*) separate from that of commerce or the state where people participate in democratic public life through talk. What Fraser objected to were the exclusionary aspects of the Enlightenment-era, bourgeois public sphere that informed Habermas's theory. In "Rethinking the Public Sphere," published in

1990, Fraser argued that this sphere restricted the access of "women, workers, peoples of color, and gays and lesbians" (123). She argued that a better model would configure the public sphere not as singular but multiple, and would recognize that in democratic deliberation differences are not bracketed but rather inform the very terms of discussion. She called scholars to attend to the conditions that thwart or make possible intercultural communication (121).

In 1999, Gerard Hauser added that it's not enough to situate studies of actually existing democracy in contemporary, large-scale media-driven conceptions of the public—what this volume refers to as *formal publics*. These conceptions tend to limit the participation of ordinary people to the voting booth, opinion poll, and jury box (*Vernacular* 190–91). When scholars assume public life pertains only to large-scale politics of the state, it's easy not only to view the populace as apathetic (Eliasoph 1), but also to sever the study of democracy from "the dynamic context in which democracy is experienced and lived" (Hauser, "Rhetorical Democracy" 3). Instead, Hauser called for scholars to take an "empirical attitude" toward the "untidy communicative practices" that shape local vernacular public life (*Vernacular* 275).

Ideas about Actually Existing Democracy

In heeding the call to situate the study of participatory democracy in actual practice, public-spheres scholars have contributed to our field's understanding of local public discourse. Instead of theorizing about "*the* public sphere" where citizens bracket their differences and follow the rules and style of rational-critical argument in order to deliberate over common concerns, Fraser identified a multiplicity of alternative publics "formed under conditions of dominance and subordination" (127). Because late-capitalist societies like the United States fall short of their democratic ideals, alternative or counter publics are immensely important. Not only do they offer safe havens to minority groups who within these spaces can develop and articulate their shared interests and identities, but they also persuade the dominant culture to think and behave differently about issues that affect the counterpublic's members. Fraser credited feminist alternative subalterns, for example, with making domestic abuse a public, rather than solely familial, issue.

In *Vernacular Voices*, Hauser clarified that it is vernacular voices—the "street-level give-and-take of contrary viewpoints"—that promote discussion and provide insights that matter most to public discourse, not the opinions of "institutional actors" nor some abstract standards of logic, disinterest, or rationality (89). These vernacular voices make pubic discourse more interesting, lively—and, yes, untidy—than Habermas's idealized versions. Scholars can't make valid claims about public discourse without tapping into how everyday people—those "not privy to official sites or are marginalized"—engage in "society's multilogue on issues that impact their lives" (276).

The problem-solving dimension of democratic discourse carries real consequences, for example, for designing treatment programs for pregnant addicts or writing (or obstructing) laws to recognize the plurality of family forms. This was Iris Young's point in *Inclusion and Democracy,* published in 2002. She argued that public discourse affects the very quality of our lives, the terms by which we know our existence and exercise our citizenship.

In *Publics and Counterpublics,* first published in 2002, Warner distinguished counterpublics from publics according to the discourses each circulates. Warner claimed counterpublics circulate politically charged alternatives to rational-critical discourse that call attention to the exclusionary politics of the dominant culture. In order to maximize their oppositional identity-building capacity, these counterpublics circulate countervalent, performative discourses that the public mainstream may consider hostile and indecorous.

In *Democracy Matters: Winning the Fight Against Imperialism,* published in 2005, West cautioned that given the force with which imperialism and materialism threaten American democracy, going public requires of ordinary people nothing short of a tragicomic commitment to hope (16). West commended a deeply critical and intensely energetic "vision of everyday people renouncing self-interest and creating a web of caring under harsh American circumstances" (95).

Rhetorical Interventions to Support Democratic Engagement

Rhetorical interventions serve as sites for situated theory-building that test, refine, and extend ideas from public-spheres studies. These interventions also scaffold public engagement—often by drawing on vernacular discourses as a resource for deliberation. Rhetorical interventions tend to fall into three groups: activist educational initiatives in the community, pedagogical practices in college courses, and techne for designing local publics—particularly as partnerships between community organizations and universities. In practice, these interventions are often integrally connected. Take Pittsburgh's CLC, for example. As a collaborative, it was intentionally designed to serve both community and university interests. Likewise, its design supported activist educational initiatives like INFORM and other literacy projects; furthermore, specific classroom pedagogies prepared college students to work as writing mentors with urban teens in these literacy projects (Peck, Flower, and Higgins). For the sake of clarity, however, in the analysis that follows, I separate interventions into these three categories.

Activist Educational Initiatives. Activist educational initiatives are community-based literacy projects that support mutual learning among participants and writing that "makes a difference" (Stock and Swenson 157). These projects are part of a long history of university-outreach programs that attempt to respond to the social and economic conditions of neighborhoods beyond the borders of (especially urban) universities (Hull and Zacher). Community-literacy initiatives, however, have introduced a distinctive focus on transactional writing that draws upon learners' local knowledge and supports the rhetorical action of participants. Exemplars include the following:

ArtShow (1989–1999). Youth-based arts programs in New York, Boston, rural California, and Kentucky engaged young people through the arts in social entrepreneurship and community-building. For example, in a project called TeenTalk, youth worked with subject area experts to develop knowledge-rich scripts which the youth performed to draw audiences into focused discussions on such topics as illegal drug use, parental neglect, and sexual abuse (Heath and Smyth; McLaughlin, Irby, and Langman).[13]

CLC Projects and Derivatives (1989-). Affiliated with Pittsburgh's CLC, the Community House Learning and Technology Center, and CMU's Center for Community Outreach, these projects build intercultural working relationships and use writing to support personal and public inquiry and deliberation (Flower "Intercultural Knowledge"; Flower "Negotiating"; Flower "Talking Across Difference"; Long "Community Literacy"; Long, Peck, and Baskins; Peck, Flower, and Higgins). Such projects include the following:

ARGUE: an inquiry-driven project using problem-solving strategies to address controversial open questions around such issues as landlord-tenant relations, drugs, and school suspension.

DIGITAL STORYTELLING: a group of computer-supported initiatives (e.g., STRUGGLE and Voices from the GLBT Community) helping youth, adults, and faith-based organizations to use digital tools to tell their own stories on their own terms.

HANDS-ON PRODUCTIONS: a literacy project using video and multimedia tools to dramatize teens' perspectives on a broad range of issues, including school reform, teen stress, and risk and respect.

INFORM: a literacy project bringing urban teens and college students together to take action on urban issues. Over the course of each 10-week project, teen-mentor pairs draft articles for a newsletter and host a problem-solving dialogue with other stakeholders, including city officials and other members of the community.

Carnegie Mellon's Community-University Think Tank: a culturally diverse body of problem solvers committed to bringing wider perspectives and collaborative action to urban issues. The think tank creates a structured dialogue in which people from Pittsburgh's urban community—representing community residents, business, regional development, social service, and education—meet to construct and to evaluate workable solutions to workplace and worklife problems.

Write for Your Life (1994-). Housed in Michigan State University's Writing Center, the Write For Your Life (WFYL) project supports a consortium of teachers in Michigan, Wisconsin, New York, Georgia, Texas, Minnesota, Oklahoma, Maryland, Massachusetts, and Pennsylvania as they develop curriculum that students use to examine local issues that influence student health, literacy, and learning. Though the program started several years earlier, WFYL began to flourish in 1994 when its curriculum started asking students not only to research local issues that mattered to them, but to write and to implement proposals for social action that addressed these issues. Over more than a decade and around the country, students have implemented numerous proposals to improve the quality of life in their communities—for instance, by testing regional water quality, instituting cross-generational mentoring programs, and implementing recycling campaigns. Like DUSTY (below), WFYL has roots in the National Writing Project (NWP), a nationwide professional development program for teachers.[14] Within the history of the NWP, WFYL represents the effort—under Dixie Goswami's leadership with the Bread Loaf Teacher Network—to move classroom instruction from expressivist objectives to transactional ones through which "students' writing can accomplish beneficial social work" (Stock and Swenson 155; see also Benson and Christian).

New City Writing Institute (1998-). New City Writing supports a collaborative network among Philadelphia schools and community organizations. With support from Temple University, the institute "focus[es . . .] on community-based writing and reading programs that lead to publications as well as educational ventures whereby schoolteachers, neighborhood people, and university-related people can learn together" (Goldblatt, "Alinsky's Reveille" 283). The institute supports New City Press which publishes documents, including a magazine called *Open City,* that feature local writers and the perspectives and interests of specific communities in the area, ranging from disabilities activists to rural farm workers who work just west of the city. The institute also supports arts initiatives throughout the city, particularly with African American and Asian communities (Parks and Goldblatt).

Digital Underground Storytelling for Youth, or DUSTY, (2001-). DUSTY is University of California at Berkeley's computer-based outreach project. It began in the basement of a community center in West Oakland and now operates in several public schools. With partners worldwide—from Norway to India—DUSTY connects youth through their digital work across racial, linguistic, cultural, geographic, and political borders. Using digital technologies, youth produce stories in which they position "themselves as agents in and authors of their lives locally and globally" (Hull, "Transforming Literacy" 40). The program takes as its central question, "how [should educators]

transform schooling and its principle activity and means—literacy—
so as to engage young people and sustain their participation?" (Hull
and Zacher par. 16). DUSTY responds to this question by offering
youth the opportunity to communicate via multiple modalities (Hull
and James; Hull and Katz).

Such initiatives stake claims about how vernacular discourse contributes to public discourse—but not the same claim. Take the WFYL
curriculum, for instance. It has learners start with what they know and
how they would typically talk about issues among their peers. Over
time, the curriculum directs them toward wider funds of knowledge
and more formal textual expectations to produce competitive proposals that meet professional standards (Stock and Swenson 159).

The CLC projects take a different tack by making room for the
rhetorical power that urban teens bring to the table. Flower poses this
goal as a question that turns on the meaning of literacy:

> How can a literacy program that works with black
> youth, for instance, balance this presumption [what
> is it?] with an awareness of the indirect but analytical
> tradition of African-American vernacular, the logical
> structures embedded in street talk (Labov 1972), or
> the rich expressive literate practices such as signifying
> (Gates 1988; Lee 1993), in which white volunteers
> find they are illiterate (Flower 1996)? (Flower, "Part-
> ners" 97)[15]

DUSTY also emphasizes communicating across borders. But here,
learners not only draw from vernacular discourses to describe their
social worlds, but they also trade in a wide spectrum of geographic,
spatial, and multi-modal genres through which they construct "tel-
lable" selves (Hull, "Transforming Literacy" 33). In fact, youth often
trade among these genres and discourses much more skillfully than
the participating academics. Through such initiatives, vernacular discourses infuse situated-public literacies, and learners themselves in-
stantiate legitimate public alternatives to rational-critical models of
deliberation.[16]

Pedagogical Practices. Pedagogical practices refers to interventions designed to help college students participate in local public life. When

Thomas Deans published *Writing Partnerships* in 2000, what distinguished community-literacy pedagogy was the emphasis on "writing *with* the community" in contrast to other service-learning pedagogies supporting college students writing *in* or *for* the community. Years later, it is possible to distinguish at least five distinct kinds of pedagogies that fall under the category. (For an extended discussion, see chapter 9.)

Interpretative pedagogies: students venture somewhere new, building relationships to confront and to revise familiar stereotypes (e.g., Canagarajah "Safe Houses"; Coogan "Counterpublics"; Goldblatt "Van Rides").

Institutional pedagogies: students learn professional research methods to elicit and to represent the interests and expertise of community residents (e.g., Grabill and Simmons; Swan).

Tactical pedagogies: students learn to circulate their own public writing that challenges the status quo. These often boisterous public acts activate shadow systems that mimic and critique the dominant culture (e.g., Mathieu *Tactics;* Pough; Welch).

Inquiry-driven pedagogies: students learn to deliberate pressing social issues with community partners; they circulate documents that serve as catalysts for social change (e.g., Coogan "Service"; Flower "Literate Action"; Flower and Heath; Long "Rhetoric"; see also www.cmu.edu/thinktank/docs/29.pdf.pdf).

Performative pedagogies: students learn to engage as rhetors with others to gain the practical wisdom required to build inclusive communities for effective problem solving (e.g., Coogan "Sophists"; Flower Community Literacy; Lyons; Simmons and Grabill).

Taken together, these pedagogical practices stress that for college students, going public entails not only crafting one's own public arguments (Charney and Neuwirth), but also assessing one's institutional position and from that position listening to and representing the expertise, interests, and agency of others (Flower *Community Literacy;* Simmons and Grabill; Swan).

Techne for Designing Local Publics. Historically, the kinds of problems that have brought universities and communities together are the tenacious, structural issues of poverty, illiteracy, and social fragmentation. In response to problems of this magnitude, universities have often assumed their expertise, research agendas, and curricula could be readily exported to the community. Not so. History is rife with examples of failed experiments and disappointed working relationships. Conversely, community practices have their own limits that can shut down active inquiry into complex problems. One of the central challenges of designing local publics is figuring out ways to encourage participants to suspend default strategies that have thwarted community-university partnerships in the past so that participants may put their differences into generative dialogue and productive working relationships that support rhetorical action. As a model for personal and public intercultural inquiry, Pittsburgh's CLC drew upon the pragmatism of Dewey and upon the principles of cognitive rhetoric to design problem-solving strategies for eliciting situated knowledge, engaging difference in dialogue, and evaluating options as tools for collaborative rhetorical action.

In 1997, when Flower argued for making collaborative inquiry central to service-learning initiatives, she said the point isn't for universities to deny their power, skills, and agency ("Partners"). Rather, the challenge lies in figuring out how to offer these resources to community partners in ways that are genuinely useful. Writing in the Service-Learning in the Disciplines series published by the American Association for Higher Education (AAHE), she emphasized collaborative inquiry grounded in "the logic of prophetic pragmatism and problem solving" (101). She laid out a plan by which university faculty teaching "'ordinary classes'"—not necessarily those involved in "a long-term stable collaboration such as the CLC"—can sponsor community problem-solving dialogues. Such dialogues "bring together students, faculty, community leaders, and everyday people [. . .] around the kind of issue that is both (1) an open question with no single answer, and (2) a problem with immediate and local impact on lives" (105).

If Peck, Flower, and Higgins defined the central challenge and promise of community literacy (Grabill, *Community* 89), in a series of subsequent publications, scholars cast their own interpretations of the most pressing challenges that such partnerships pose and the techne— or rhetorical interventions—that would allow activist rhetoricians to respond deliberately and wisely to these challenges.

Writing *Community Literacy and the Politics of Change* in 2001, Grabill argued that the most effective rhetorical intervention would attend to issues of institutional power. Invoking the ideological model of literacy, Grabill emphasized that institutions have power, and through this power they imbue literacies with their meaning and social value. So the most responsive community-literacy program would ask community residents to help shape the programs in which they wish to participate. Drawing on Iris Young's political philosophy, Grabill designed an intervention called participatory institutional design to support a "group-differentiated participatory public" (I. Young qtd. in Grabill, *Community Literacy* 123).[17] Drawing on his background in usability testing and human-centered design principles, Grabill commended community leaders at the Harborside Community Center in Boston for designing and hosting forums for client involvement during which participants themselves named the literacies and kinds of instruction that would be meaningful and efficacious for them. Grabill commends participatory institutional design as a systematic approach for drawing out "the expertise of participants, particularly those thought to lack such expertise" (119).

In 2002, Brenton Faber published *Community Action and Organizational Change.* He argued that if universities are to reclaim their relevance "to the publics and constituents they represent, serve and support" (5), university researchers need to work as change agents "forming academic and community alliances" (13). Such change agents could effect the greatest change by supporting stories, particularly the narratives organizations tell about the work they do and the purposes they serve. When such stories are intact, organizations may use them to launch practices that "challenge oppressive practices" and "work towards [. . .] positive social change" (11). Faber stresses that as "critic, consultant, and [. . .] community activist," the change agent "play[s] a self-conscious, direct role in change [. . . and has] a real stake in the projects" of the partnering organization (12–13). Like the observation-based theory behind the CLC's approach to rhetorical problem-solving, Faber's rhetorical intervention is an *"empirical-yet-activist discourse of change and community action"* (6, emphasis added).

Also in 2002, Linda Flower and Julia Deems directly addressed the key question that Habermas's theory of the public sphere had raised: *how does difference figure into democratic deliberation?* Should it be bracketed, as Habermas suggested? Suppressed in search of a common good? If participants *do* put their differences on the table, how can these differences serve as a resource for intercultural knowledge building, rather than the source of competition and strife? "Conflict in Community Collaboration" reports findings from a literacy project called ARGUE that brought together a group of landlords and tenants. With Lorraine Higgins as project leader, the participants addressed a set of related concerns, ranging from irresponsible tenants and negligent, insensitive landlords to unkempt and abandoned buildings that eroded property values and neighbors' sense of safety. The project introduced a rhetorical intervention called collaborative planning which committed participants "on the one hand, to articulating conflict— vigorously representing a competing perspective on inner city landlords or tenants—and on the other, to supporting and developing each other's position in planning and writing a useful document" (99). Unlike strategies that forge consensus, collaborative planning provided a method for "identifying and elaborating on new and unheard positions" (104). The intervention structured and supported negotiated meaning making, placing "writers within the midst of multiple, social, cultural and linguistic forces [that] introduce competing attitudes, values, and bodies of knowledge" (107).

But how would a writing teacher or program administrator go about forging partnerships in the first place? Peck, Flower, Higgins, and Deems described a partnership several years in the making. Grabill recommended his design principles to existing organizations—a United Way organization and other community centers. Faber marketed himself as a change-management consultant to organizations actively seeking his services and looking to change. How could university types—aware of the complex terrain on which they are about to tread—initiate such partnerships? Two studies, published in 2005 and 2006, respectively, depicted activist rhetoricians in the process of public making, using rhetorical interventions to chart their way through complicated rhetorical terrain and then commending their interventions to others. Though Goldblatt and Coogan set their sites on different priorities within the partnership-building process, each offered a rhetorical intervention for building consensus among university and community partners.

In "Alinsky's Reveille: A Community-Organizing Model for Neighborhood-Based Literacy Projects," Goldblatt asked, *how can university partners leverage the resources that a university has to offer without con-*

trolling the terms of agreement? As a knowledge activist, Goldblatt nurtured a neighborhood-based initiative to serve the mutual benefit of community and university partners. The knowledge activist enacts a "deeper level" of Alinsky's community organizing technique in which partners "talk through conflict and negotiate [. . .] tensions" in order to reach consensus regarding future joint action (Goldblatt, "Alinsky's Reveille" 289). The knowledge activist becomes an active/activist listener who builds relationships with community leaders and studies their understanding of a community's needs. With Goldblatt's patient guidance, members of the Open Doors Collaborative identified a shared problem from which they developed a two-part strategy for providing literacy instruction to adult non-native English speakers in North Philadelphia.

What motivated Coogan's "Service Learning and Social Change: The Case for Materialist Rhetoric" was the need to locate current arguments in their larger historical and political context. In a partnership with a community organization in a Chicago neighborhood called Bronzeville, he served as a rhetorical analyst mobilizing ideological fragments in an effort to forge consensus among disparate parties (see also Coogan "Public Rhetoric"). Coogan based his techne on Michael McGee's materialist rhetoric in which ideographs "represent in condensed form the normative, collective commitments of the members of a public, and they typically appear in public argumentation as the necessary motivations or justifications for action performed in the name of the public" (Condit and Lucaites qtd. in Coogan, "Service" 670).[18] To make this concept of ideographs more concrete, one need look no farther than community-literacy studies. Within this body of scholarship, <local>, <public>, and <literacy> operate as ideographs— "icebergs" indicative of larger arguments and ideologies (Coogan, "Service" 670). One of the tasks of this book is to map how, as ideographs, <local> and <public> have assumed their "formative power to contain our commitments" (Coogan, "Service" 670). In fact, <local> was one of the ideographs that wielded tremendous rhetorical power in the public arguments over school reform in Bronzeville. When tethered to <control>, however, it harkened back to an earlier era of fractious local politics and dissipated contemporary public support. In contrast, when associated with <responsibility>, <local> assumed an altogether different, more positive valence "persuading parents [and other stakeholders] to take a more active role in [local] children's education" (Coogan, "Service" 688). Coogan found his and his students' efforts to mobilize action to improve local public schools far more successful once they had conducted a materialist rhetorical analysis.

If Goldblatt and Coogan show how systematic interventions can help community partners build knowledge and consensus, two recent publications challenge the field's understanding of techne as it relates to community literacy: Mathieus's *Tactics of Hope: The Public Turn in English Composition* and Branch's *"Eyes on the Ought to Be": What We Teach When We Teach About Literacy*, published in 2005 and 2007, respectively.

Mathieu's sensitivity to academic hubris leads her to distinguish sustained, systematic—or strategic—approaches for public making from a tactical approach that "devis[es] timely and spatially appropriate relationships in the streets" (20). Grounded in the work of de Certeau, *Tactics of Hope: The Public Turn in English Composition* offers a postmodern reading of rhetorical techne. Mathieu urges university types to consider "questions of time, space, credibility, knowledge, and success" (21)—or "Who speaks? Who pays?" (66). These questions are designed to spark tactics of hope—rhetorically responsive actions grounded in humility, "radical patience," and courage (47). "[C]lever uses of time" erupt in the politically charged spirit of the moment and often influence public opinion in ways that not only defy easy prediction and measurement but are themselves "mysterious and unknowable" (48).

Branch prefers the term *métis* over *techne* to describe the dynamism characteristic of the Highlander Folk School that Myles Horton founded in 1932 with a colleague named Don West.[19] Among its achievements, the school practiced crisis education that subverted Jim Crow laws by teaching African Americans to read and write. In response to its unwavering commitment to building a more democratic society, the school understood its practices to be revisable and its ends in sight to be provisional. Branch explains: "The 'crisis moment' was an educational tool that provided motivation and direction, but it did not provide the ends of the educational process, ends which were always fluid, always growing" (152). Consequently, the "Highlander's project could never have predetermined shape, one of the reasons that Horton was famously dismissive of identifying a Highlander method. [. . . T]he basis of Highlander's program [. . .] came from a dynamic relationship between current conditions and future goals" (167). For Branch, the legacy of Horton's crisis education inspires a trickster consciousness that "use[s] hunger and cunning [. . .] to work in the service of covert, situationally grounded, and always constrained action" (189).

Just as descriptive studies of community literacy have documented ordinary people interjecting their vernacular discourses into public spaces, rhetorical interventions—including Mathieu's tactics of hope and Branch's trickster consciousness—have drawn upon vernacular literacies as resources for public engagement. This feature is perhaps most explicit in the rhetorical model for community literacy that Higgins, Long, and Flower described in their 2006 article, "Community Literacy: A Rhetorical Model for Personal and Public Inquiry." In commending practices that enact a vernacular local public, this model of community literacy doesn't privilege vernacular discourses; rather, it makes sure they have a place at the table. The model responds to an issue central to public-spheres studies: "how to deal with the volatile presence of diversity" within deliberative democracy (Higgins, Long, and Flower 29). In addressing this question, the model creates a distinctive kind of counterpublic. Rather than cultivating and safeguarding oppositional identities in the ways that Warner associates with larger-scale counterpublics, a community-literacy counterpublic "aspire[s] to an intercultural, cross-hierarchy composition" (29). This distinctive kind of counterpublic is "less about building oppositional identities than about using difference to articulate silenced perspectives. Rather than dichotomize groups, it challenges the normative exclusionary practices of public talk" (29). The model also circulates distinctive texts that enact a new, inclusive practice for public discourse—one in which vernacular discourses articulate with policy discourse, regional talk, academic analysis, personal testimonials, and narrative to create an alternative discourse for local public deliberation. Through such texts, a rhetorical model of community literacy supports public transformation by modeling and dramatizing "an alternative kind of dialogue in which marginalized voices bring significant expertise to solving a shared problem" (31).

As this retrospective suggests, the history of community literacy is still in the making. The next chapter features Heath's *Ways with Words: Language, Life and Work in Communities and Classrooms* where performative literacies bring an impromptu street theater into being. A classic study of situated literacies, *Ways with Words* continues to offer important implications for current views in community-literacy studies.

4 An Impromptu Theater: A Local Public That Turns Its Back on Formal Institutions

In Heath's *Ways with Words,* the local public is a street theater where impromptu performances teach children socially appropriate uses of language and reinforce the social hierarchy of a tightly knit community. The image of an impromptu theater organizes Heath's analysis of community life in 1970s Trackton, an African American neighborhood in the Piedmont Carolinas. On the local public stage, the "way with words" that mattered were not the practices associated with schooling. Instead, performances entertained Trackton's residents with competitive verbal play even as they prepared children to survive in a world that adults knew to be unpredictable and unfair.

Distinctive Features: Dramatic and Spontaneous

In Trackton, the local public was a dramatic performance, one that burst spontaneously onto an improvised stage.

Dramatic. On Trackton's plaza, "actors" in both the "permanent cast" and "chorus" performed "roles" complete with "cues" and "lines." They made their "entrances and exits" within "scenes" as performances played out across "sets." In addition to the leading roles, the responsive "chorus" and the interactive "audience" intensified the drama of each performance (Heath 72, 79).

Spontaneous. Trackton's public performances ignited whenever conditions were right. Consider, for instance, conditions that sparked the ritualized performance in which wage earners returned home on payday with treats to distribute among expectant children. Specific conditions—the scheduled paycheck, the willingness of working residents to cash their checks and stop for groceries on the way home, the preparation of those who awaited their return, the anticipation that intensified as each minute passed—each of these conditions was required in order for a particular performance of "the distribution routine" to burst forth on stage (Heath 97). As this example shows, time (in this case, payday) and place (the plaza or porch) were necessary, but insufficient, for creating the local public. Also vital were the community's actors, prepared and willing to perform various roles—leading roles, yes, but also that of a discerning, responsive audience and chorus. Trackton's local public came into being in the moment that these necessary conditions were met.

Heath directs us to look outdoors for such performances. Beyond that, performances could have cropped up in several alternative locations, the plaza being the most central but not the only candidate for a public stage. And several performances could have ignited simultaneously, or a particularly dramatic show may have sparked subsequent performances elsewhere. After the burst of creative energy, each stage returned to its original state, whether a porch, yard, or plaza. In this context, spontaneity suggests fluidity and synergy. This is not to say that schemas and repertoires weren't involved, for they structured these performances just as they do the impromptu performances in nightclubs and subway stations (Bennett 106). Rather, the impromptu street theater brings to mind the creative flash of joint story telling and competitive verbal play that ignite as people go about their day-to-day lives.

THE IMPROMPTU THEATER IN CONTEXT: LOCATION, POWER, AND THE INTEGRITY OF COMMUNITY LIFE

In Trackton, the plaza was a "public area" (Heath 79) and its discourse—from story telling to yo-mama insults to hand-clapping playsongs—"public performances" (81). The descriptor *public* distinguishes Trackton's literacy events from those of the neighboring white community where language learning was the private endeavor of individual households. But Trackton's location, its circuits of power, and its integrity as a community distinct from nearby public institutions also qualified Trackton as a distinct local public.

Location. Trackton's geographic location helped to create a local public distinct from the public institutions in the nearby town of Gateway. Given the "good stone's throw" that measured the road running between Trackton and Gateway, location separated and distinguished Trackton from town (Heath 47). At the center of the neighborhood, Trackton's plaza invited residents to turn their attention to one another and away from the demands in town. The plaza's public performances were not about preparing children for life outside the neighborhood where as adults they would likely go to look for work but rather about asserting their places in the social hierarchy of the neighborhood.

Location also distinguished Trackton's local public discourse from the discourses of the institutions in town. Because of the political and economic history behind its geographic borders, Trackton's location separated residents from the town's political processes, decision-making, policies, and procedures (Heath 62). Thus, location signaled differences in how residents used words at home and in town. For instance, the problem-solving orientation of the town's banks, housing office, and real estate firms would have stipulated that upon learning that her house had been condemned, Aunt Bertha would have immediately gone to town to start searching for another house and financing its purchase. But performances on Trackton's public stage were compelling in their own right, providing Aunt Bertha with the ready option to spend her time, instead, in the company of her neighbors, leaving "everyday challenges of current life" to sort themselves out (66).

Power. The politics of Trackton were different from the politics of the town's public institutions where power plays and contests referred to election campaigns and where it took appointments and paperwork to infiltrate the bureaucracy associated with state and federal social programs. Though Trackton's politics also involved status, control, rewards and penalties, the dynamics were not institutional but informal. On Trackton's public stage, performances were challenges, and challenges measured youngsters' abilities to "outwit, outtalk, or outact their aggressors" (Heath 84).

Public performances reinforced power relations among residents in Trackton, relations stratified by age and gender. For instance, it was the prerogative of the preschool boys to perform on stage; girls practiced their roles on its periphery (Heath 95). Public performances continued to grant boys power as they grew older by extending public roles to them. A young man's social status was tied to his ability to assert his own identity and to position others in relation to it—as a teenager named Darret did when he told a toddler named Teegie, "'You gonna be all right, boy, you be just like me'" (80). Expectations for girls' performances were more limited and limiting, endorsing a certain kind of "girl talk" as a requisite for becoming "good 'mamas'" (98).

Integrity of Community Life. Trackton's impromptu theater recognized and preserved the internal integrity of community life distinct from the nearby town and its public institutions. Rather than drawing attention to the gap between Trackton residents' home discourse and the demands of public institutions, the theater underscored the integrity of the habits, preferences, and practices that defined social life in Trackton and made the plaza its center stage. In a community where the ability to struggle, to make do, and to survive was judged more valuable than traipsing into town to fill out forms for some ambiguous bureaucratic process, public performances affirmed the integrity of the community itself as well as the identities, roles, and social positions of residents within it. Public performances permitted the residents of Trackton to assert themselves as a "closed community" (Heath 63), distinguishing themselves from the sometimes "snobbish ways" of the neighboring African American townspeople (62).

TENOR OF THE DISCOURSE: EDGY AND COMPETITIVE, CURBED BY PLAY

Trackton's public discourse had an edgy quality to it. Even though public performances were largely entertaining—the "hostility, disrespect, and aggressive behavior" only "feigned" (Heath 81)—the tension is palpable in Heath's descriptions. The edginess is most evident in the ritualized insults and accusations characterizing boy talk but was also true of girls' fussing, reprimanding those who violated various social codes. Verbal competition tested youngsters' discursive adaptability and flexibility. "[M]eanings of a particular word, phrase, or set of actions [. . .] are often neither literal or predictable" (84). Thus, public performances tested the performer's ability to respond spontaneously to subtle and changing contextual cues, intensifying the competitive edge of verbal play (79).

Residents used verbal play to assert their place in Trackton's social hierarchy. Given its premise of winners and losers, competition gave children the chance to practice responding to the nuances of a challenger's assertions. Indirection and competition were part of a tradition designed to initiate children into an unstable and unpredictable world where one's survival was often based on the ability to improvise. Conversely, to violate the codes of discourse was to risk a public shaming that struck to the core of a person's identity, a threat that ran throughout not only childhood but also adulthood. Thus, the tenor of the discourse maintained rules that reinforced residents' social standings.

Performative Literacies

Three distinct oral practices characterized Trackton's public stage performances: boys' public-stage challenges, in all their variations; two kinds of girl talk, fussing and playsongs; and story telling, especially among elderly matriarchs.

- *Boys' Public-Stage Challenges.*[1] These "put-downs" combined aggressive words and gestures to provoke other boys to respond with retorts of their own (Heath 80). Challenges could take the forms of teasing, defying, bossing, begging, arguing, babying, scolding, boasting, insulting and ridiculing (85). Used to gauge quickness and intelligence, challenges were embedded within other rituals—for instance, determining how treats were allocated within the distribution routine.
- *Girl Talk.* Girls accessed the public stage primarily through their participation within two practices: fussing games and playsongs. Through fussing games, girls berated someone of lower social status for violating an aspect of the social code—say, not showing due care when slinging a baby across one's hip. Playsongs used rhythm and rhyme to structure and to sequence patterned games, including handclap games and jump-rope playsongs.
- *Matriarchs' Story Telling.* Story telling involved ritualized narratives marked by repetition and a "lilting chant-like quality" (Heath 65). Recounted primarily by the elderly, these stories reinforced a shared sense of pride in past accomplishments and

acceptance of life circumstances, including stories of the living and working conditions that elderly residents had encountered growing up further south. Stories emphasized "the fact that there were some good things back then in spite of the hardships" (65). Miss Bee's story of her childhood featured a wood cabin, cracks in floorboards, and chickens visible between these cracks.

Trackton's residents used these literacies both to call into being and to access their local public.

Rhetorical Invention: Practice, Modeling, and Feedback

Given the emphasis on repeated practice, modeling, and feedback, Trackton children's inventive processes parallel other descriptions of children's language learning (e.g., Halliday 24), but embedded in the rich description of a specific, rural African-American community.

Repeated practice. Public life provided Trackton's boys with repeated opportunities to practice countering verbal insults and accusations. In a similar vein, older siblings noted the value of repeated practice when they attempted to compensate for the infrequent invitations issued to their younger sisters to participate in public discourse. Girls were "not excluded from this scene, [. . .] but they [were] rarely given parts to play and almost never full-stage performance opportunities" (Heath 79). However, because they were disconnected from the promise of an audience's "rewarding response" (86), "these sessions rarely last[ed] longer than a few minutes, since the younger child quickly los[t] interest" (96). As the older siblings knew, practice makes a difference. Without it, girls "ha[d] a much smaller store of experiences from which to draw" (96). Those boys judged to be best at public discourse were given the most opportunities to continue to practice and, thus, to hone—even as they demonstrated—their performative prowess. Consequently, those who practiced most also became most adept at handling their public roles.

Modeling. Children learned their roles by watching other Trackton players perform theirs. Sometimes, the modeling was made quite explicit, with an older sibling, for instance, cuing the learner to mimic the modeled behavior, as in the prompt "'[S]ay——, say it like I do'"

(Heath 96). But more often, boys learned the art of the counterchallenge by watching their challengers' moves and tactics.

Feedback. How did young actors on Trackton's public stage assess the adequacy of their own performances? Through feedback, often in the forms of laughter, applause and verbal praise but also packaged as "food, affection, and gifts" (Heath 82). In countering public-stage challenges, some combination of "a verbal and nonverbal put-down" typically elicited enthusiastic responses from audiences (80). But feedback wasn't consistent. Instead, adults used indirection and inconsistency as tools for developing children's inventional capacities, especially their ability to discern judgments from subtle contextual cues.

Through invention, children discovered not only what to say but how to handle the kinesis of the entire performance (Heath 81). Catching a child in the throes of invention—in this case, thinking on his feet—was often the very point of a challenger instigating a public performance. Practice and learning "t[ook] place on stage" (86), rather than offstage in preparation for a performance as strategies for rhetorical planning typically suggest. Performances tested whether young performers had the wherewithal to assess and to respond instantaneously to an audience's multiple demands.

Implications

1. *Local publics are simultaneously discursive as well as physical spaces.*

A local public need not have some pre-existent status as a physical entity—as in the case of a New England town hall that holds regularly scheduled town meetings. As the distribution routine demonstrates, local publics burst into being virtually anywhere in Trackton—as along as the necessary conditions were met. Yet Trackton's location also constrained and configured what went on there. Location separated Trackton from town, not only geographically but also ideologically, privileging residents' own priorities and values.

2. *With integrity of its own, a local public can be a welcome alternative to public institutional spaces that people find hostile and alienating.*

Heath illustrates one way that a local public supports a community's integrity; Scott Lyons's New Ghost Dance, another. On Trackton's public stage, integrity meant that performers like Darret—rather than, say, the institutions in Gateway—set the terms for public discourse. This measure of integrity is also central to Lyons's analysis of the rhetorical sovereignty of Native Americans for whom the ultimate hostile public institution was the boarding school that stripped native children of their culture, language, and practices and often humiliated and brutally punished them for refusing to fulfill their teachers' demands.

But Lyons replaces a closed community's hierarchical public performance with that of the intercultural New Ghost Dance. The difference means that the New Ghost Dance sets "at least some" of the terms of debate (Lyons 462). That is, rather than reinforcing rigid borders, the New Ghost Dance allows issues that bubble up in local publics to find their way into more formal arenas. The benefit of this apparent compromise rests in its outcomes. Consider, for instance, the Supreme Court's upholding of native people's "right to hunt and fish on ceded land" and the federal Trademark Trial and Appeal Board's "disrecognition of the Washington Redskins trademark" (466). Crediting the victories' local origins, Lyons writes: "Both initiatives arose from the grassroots, each in their own way fought over questions of land and identity, and the ultimate outcome of both was an honoring of 'a whole way of life'" (466).

3. Expressions of researchers' working theories of local public discourse, the metaphors used to describe local publics carry important theoretical implications.

Heath compared Trackton's local public life to a theater, where actors performed roles across scenes and acts. Theatrical imagery dominates descriptions in public-spheres studies, as well. Fraser, for instance, explains that "'[t]he idea of the public sphere' [. . .] designates a *theater* in modern societies in which political participation is enacted through the medium of talk" (110, emphasis added). This chapter suggests theatrical imagery is particularly well suited to describing the performative aspects of public literacies. However, it follows from Catherine Prendergast's reading of *Ways with Words* that the image does not sufficiently illuminate political dynamics between and among the other publics with which a local public inevitably interacts.

Foremost, Prendergast has taken issue with Heath's characterization of Trackton as a closed community ("Race" 48–50).[2] Prendergast argues that this description isn't so much untrue but insufficient. Using critical race theory to revisit *Ways with Words*, Prendergast argues that

Trackton was a closed community not because it was free of racism, nor because it was isolated from the neighboring white community (for it was not), nor even so residents could take a break from racism's grasp. Rather, the fact that Trackton was a closed community is testament to the multi-generational mechanism of racism that shaped the history of these Piedmont mill communities and—by implication—that continues to shape racist public opinion and educational practice.[3] Prendergast argues that at the time of Heath's study Trackton was already socialized into the discourse of racism. For this reason, adults found it necessary to teach children "[s]trategies for dealing with the basic inconsistencies and inherent contradictions" that constitute "the experience of double-consciousness" (Prendergast 48), the paradox "in which people of color have to believe simultaneously that they have a right to participate equally in society and that rights are whatever people in power say they are" (49). Comparing Trackton's public discourse to a theatrical performance captures many of its distinctive qualities, but not its race relations with other Piedmont communities.

4. Performative discourse is especially adept at public making.

In *Publics and Counterpublics,* Warner uses the phrase "world making" to refer to the capacity of certain discourses "to bring a public into being" (129). It is this world-making capacity that Heath captures in her choice of dramatic imagery. Public stage challenges, for instance, created a crucible in which children developed signature styles such as Darret's "smart-cat strut," capable of calling into being a public space and drawing others into the public stage performance. Dramatic performance—what Warner calls "corporally expressive performances" (147) and what Heath calls "public [. . .] stage performance" (79)—creates a discursive reality that is more dimensional, more compelling, and more provocative than any text could create or any textual analysis could suggest. In choosing theatrical imagery to characterize and interpret Trackton's public qualities, Heath highlights the capacity of Trackton's discourse to make its own world. When it comes to world making, performative practices are far more effective than venerated academic texts or the "straight talk" rewarded in Roadville (294–310), both of which value extended, consistent, and predictable discourse. Heath makes clear that some communities cultivate this world-making capacity better than others.

5 The Cultural Womb and the Garden: Local Publics That Depend on Institutions to Sponsor Them

Some local publics depend on institutional sponsors and use these institutional affiliations to create "inspired contexts" for literacy learning that operate in locations of stress and scarcity (Willinsky 153). As inspired contexts, these local publics employ democratic practices to nurture participants within their walls and to prepare them for literate social action outside them. But what makes an inspired context for literacy learning a decidedly *public* achievement—albeit, a local one? The answer lies within the rhetoric of transformation that such sites enact. To explore the rhetoric of transformation and its relation to public life, this chapter compares an African American congregation in south central Wisconsin to a women's writing workshop in the Tenderloin District of San Francisco.

A Cultural Womb: The Local Public in Brandt's *Literacy in American Lives*

In *Literacy in American Lives,* the local public is a cultural womb that nurtures the whole person, even as it prepares members for social activism outside its borders.[1] This image describes Metro AME, eight of whose members participated in Brandt's study of "how ordinary people learned to read and write" over the course of the 20th century (*American* 2). The image of the cultural womb describes the black church at large and also Metro AME as an individual congregation. The image evokes not the biological womb supporting the lone fetus but the political space safeguarding a colonized people. As such, the cultural womb evokes the political significance of what bell hooks calls "homeplace" (41)—whether the slave hut or the meetinghouse—where "colonized people can project an alternative future partly on the basis of a place beyond domination" (I. Young, *Body* 160).[2]

Distinctive Features: Nurtures and Prepares

As an image of local public life, the cultural womb first reclaims nurturing as a potentially political act of meaning making. The image then pairs nurturing with preparation for social action outside its walls.

Nurtures. Nurturing is a key feature of the African American church at large, and of Metro AME, in particular.[3] Organic and holistic, the cultural womb suggests a place that nourishes the many dimensions and phases of human development. Unlike a school that prioritizes the intellectual development of its students or a Boys and Girls Club that prioritizes social or physical aspects, the image of the cultural womb attends to the full range of human needs. In the context of the African American church, the act of nurturing members from cradle to grave—in art, music and politics, for instance, as well as theology—has had political, as well as spiritual, implications. In various forms of "cultural support and uplift" (Brandt, *American* 118), nourishment has played a "compensatory role [. . .] in providing against poverty and government neglect" (114).

Prepares. Along with nurturing its members, the cultural womb also prepares them for social activism, both by teaching members to read and write and also by tying literate practices to "values of self-determination and social activism [. . .]" (Brandt, *American* 110).[4] In other words, preparation links literacy to democratic values of access and participation. Historically, church-based democratic practices have prepared members to protest mainstream systems of exclusion and oppression and to bear witness to the liberatory power of literacy—a tool that otherwise had been "turned as a weapon against their liberties" (106). At Metro AME, democratic values infused the incentives for literacy learning that the congregation offered its members. "Bible reading for members [. . .] served as both a channel for developing religious consciousness and for enacting and demonstrating that consciousness" (135).

The Cultural Womb in Context: Location and Cultural Agency

As an institution, the African American church must continue to exist in material spaces such as Metro AME in order to sustain its institutional identity and legacy as a catalyst for social change.

Location. As a local public, location matters to Metro AME because the material space of the church shapes the congregation's discursive practices which in turn support a distinctive institutional identity. In their interviews with Brandt, members of Metro AME made clear that their congregation functioned as "a geography of hope" (Hull and James 255). In fact, it made little sense to talk about their participation in the congregation without referring to the church building as a site with a sanctuary, classrooms, libraries, and kitchens. These physical spaces host distinctive practices and relationships that parishioners use to uphold the black church's legacy.

Cultural Agency. Claims that attribute agency to publics are controversial. In defining formal publics, Warner, for instance, argues that claims attributing agency to formal publics are fictitious, grounded in images of people reading texts to arrive at a joint decision (123). In contrast, the local public as a cultural womb banks an understanding of agency not in terms of decision making but in terms of an increase in a distinct social phenomenon (in this case, literacy rates) under conditions that would predict a shortage or reduction of the phenomenon. Cultural agency suggests ways that individual local publics may articulate with other institutions and practices in order to change social conditions.

One of the first to apply Stuart Hall's theory of articulation to literacy studies was John Trimbur. In a 1993 review of Mike Rose's *Lives on the Boundary,* Trimbur drew on the concept of articulation to assert that there is not "a fixed or necessary correspondence between literate practices and social formation" (48). He argued that rather than being predetermined, the effect or role of literacy in lived experience must always wait to be articulated as "particular ideologies, political subjects, cultural practices, and social movements and institutions" are uttered and combined within specific moments of history (42). Metro AME illustrates how a local public may participate in acts of articulation through its institutional affiliation which endorses specific literacies and incentives for members to use them.

Extending Trimbur's analysis of literacy and institutional articulation, Brandt grounds her claim of the African American church as cultural agent in the distinction between economies of excess and efficiency. Brandt notes that the rise in African American literacy rates between Reconstruction and the modern civil rights movement complicates the thesis developed in the first three chapters of *Literacy in American Lives*, where she explores conditions of excess (109). In interpreting results from her research, she found that a theory of excess could account for the fact "that in twentieth-century America, opportunities for literacy became increasingly reliant on economic sponsorship and increasingly vulnerable to the lack of it" (*American* 107). However, a theory of excess could not account for the increased literacy rates among African Americans between Reconstruction and the modern civil rights movement, for these rates increased "in the *absence* of broad-based economic and political subsidy and the presence of so much social hostility" (107, emphasis added).

To account for the rise of literacy rates within an economy of efficiency, Brandt sought "the presence of a system for human development long identified with African American society, sets of sponsorship networks that provided political and cultural support to members (*American* 107). The system she identified is the African American church, a self-help system within which Metro AME continues to participate through the "incentives" it offers its members for "critical reading and writing" (118).

In sum, Brandt grants agency less to people and more to the church as an institution. As readers well know, agency is a contentious issue in rhetorical studies (cf. Geisler; Hull and Katz). Traditionally, the term has been used to refer to people.[5] Metro AME's institutional membership affords us a different perspective. Through its affiliation with a larger institution and its practices, the African American church is first among a small set of institutions whose practices have earned the distinct status as a cultural agent.[6] The church has achieved the status of cultural agent because of the cumulative effect of individual congregations like Metro AME extending opportunities and incentives to their members for literacy and literacy learning.

To a reader accustomed to thinking about agency in terms of people, Brandt's description would seem to personify local publics. Note below Brandt's use of personification to explain how something as apparently vague as a local public's institutional practices could carry out something as consequential as acts of cultural agency:

> The framework of this chapter borrows from a body of sociological literature [. . .] who have identified a core set of *cultural agents* within African American society who have been most *responsible* for racial survival since the days of slavery. In the face of economic and political exclusion, these *agents circulated resources and nurtured skills,* including literacy, all within what several sociologists have identified as a core set of cultural values. (*American* 107, emphasis added)

In charting the postmodern turn from the personal to the institutional, Brandt illuminates how the African American church has circulated resources—an outcome achieved *in situ* as local political acts of nurturing that have challenged the anonymity that has come to characterize so much of contemporary inner-city public life.

Brandt's figurative language suggests the magnitude of influence that local publics—here, individual congregations—can exercise when measured in terms of the cumulative effect of their institutional practices—in this case, the practice of providing incentives for reading and writing. Referring to the composite effect of individual congregations in promoting African Americans' literacy learning, Brandt writes: "these concentrated *sites of sponsorship* were *the deep wells* that *fed* a steady *rise* in literacy and education *rates* among African Americans in the first half of the twentieth century" (*American* 107, emphasis added). In this description, local publics are wells that feed. This imagery directs the reader's attention away from parishioners (those whom we may expect the wells of a church to sustain) toward the large socio-political trend: "a steady rise in literacy and education rates among African Americans in the first half of the twentieth century" (107). Metro AME demonstrates how a local public's institutional affiliation, including the associated discursive practices, may articulate with other institutions and practices to constitute cultural agency.

Tenor of the Discourse: Resourceful

Resourcefulness distinguishes the discourse of Metro AME as a local public—its capacity to make something new from what has been around awhile (Brandt, *American* 8). For years, parishioners of Metro

AME had relied on familiar practices to participate in their congregations, for instance, to offer extemporaneous prayers, to respond to a pastor's biblical exegesis, or to develop Sunday school lessons. Then, in walked a new pastor, requiring them to produce a new literate practice called *the talk,* researched presentations on biblical texts to be composed for delivery at evening meetings and special church services. The genre of the talk was as unfamiliar to parishioners as it was characteristic of the new pastor's method of leadership. And the demand for it caused parishioners some initial stress. In my experience, someone would have surely balked, "That's not how we've always done it." Instead, however, accustomed to working in an economy of efficiency, the parishioners "held onto, stretched, circulated and recirculated, altered and realtered" what they had been doing in church all those years (Brandt, *American* 109).[7] They transformed these tried and true literacies into the new practice that the pastor asked of them.

Interpretative Literacies

Interpretative literacies organized how members of Metro AME participated in the life of the church. In addition to their exegetical functions, these literacies also structured parishioners' engagement with one another in what Brandt has previously termed "pure acts of human involvement" (*Involvement* 6).

- *The talk:* Parishioners delivered these presentations on biblical texts at evening meetings and special church services designed to involve lay members more than the typical Sunday service. Although the name of the talk, as a genre, focuses on the oral aspect of its delivery, this practice also required practitioners to engage actively in reading and writing.
- *Textual interpretation:* Members participated in these pastor-initiated lessons by reading and listening in order to draw analogies between their own lives and the biblical text and to debate rival interpretations of the biblical text.
- *Extemporaneous petitions:* Prayers could be offered orally or in writing. Oral prayers were offered spontaneously at a designated point in the church service. Written prayers were recorded on notecards or other small pieces of paper and placed inside a "burden box"—a place to deposit worries, prayers, commu-

nions, and other private thoughts in written form" (Brandt, *American* 113).

- *Sunday school lessons:* Sunday school teachers read teaching materials to prepare for Sunday school class and often used writing to record their plans. In delivering these lessons, they also relied on literacy, including oral performances of bible stories.
- *Meeting literacies:* Members used reading and writing to participate on various committees, including the stewardship and finance committees.

Familiar or new, these interpretative literacies invited parishioners to engage actively with texts, with one another, and in the life of the church.

Rhetorical Invention: Inspiration, Instruction, and Transformation

Rhetorical invention at Metro AME involved spiritual inspiration, pastoral instruction, and transformation.

Inspiration. Sometimes, ideas for talks came to parishioners in moments of inspiration. Parishioner June Birch, for instance, "recalled having an idea for a talk come to her as she looked at herself one day in a mirror" (Brandt, *American* 117). She explained: "'I just got in a quiet spot and things *just came to me,* and I started writing it on the paper'" (117, emphasis added). Later, Birch reorganized and edited her prose, but only after first capturing the flash of inspiration: "'[W]hen thoughts were coming to me, I'd just jot them down'" (117).

Instruction. The pastor also provided instruction to parishioners as they prepared their talks. In the planning phase, he provided relevant textual resources. He also coached the delivery of their presentations. By providing "feedback and correction" in this manner, the pastor assumed his role as both "'a preacher and a teacher' among his practitioners" (Brandt, *American* 118).

Transformation. Rhetorical invention also includes the process parishioners used to transform church-based literacies for new, often secular, purposes. Two accounts from *Literacy in American Lives* are especially illuminating, those of Metro AME member Francis Hawkins and Jordan Grant, both of whom recounted having transformed church-based literacies to meet their own rhetorical goals. At the time of her interviews with Brandt, Hawkins was using her limited salary as a classroom teacher's aide to build a home library featuring black history books, since the holdings at her children's school libraries were so limited. Hawkins's home library paralleled in important ways the church library at Metro AME, and it protested childhood memories of exclusion from her hometown public library. Brandt interprets this library as an act of rhetorical transformation. Through the library, Hawkins "*instantiates* in daily practice [. . .] *integrated values* of faith, advancement, liberation, and survival that were remarkably similar to the *earliest formulations* of the AME church doctrine" (Brandt, *American* 119, 120–21, emphasis added).

Similarly, as an affirmative action officer, Jordan Grant transformed his father's sermonic style to "writ[e] an action plan and training manuals in a field that never existed before" (Brandt, *American* 141). Describing Grant's capacity for transformation, Brandt writes: "For Grant, developing as a writer in the second half of the twentieth century entailed *amalgamating* and *transforming* these traditional resources [including his father's sermons] to respond to—and contribute to—a period of tremendous political and cultural change" (138, emphasis added).

Implications

1. *A local public enacts its institutional membership by providing opportunities and incentives for participants to use literacy in ways that support the interests of the sponsoring institution; however, participants may put literacies to whatever purposes they see fit.*

A local public provides incentives that take reading and writing in one direction.[8] However, resourceful participants may direct those literacies toward purposes of their own. Consequently, a local public is a crossroads of (at least) two literacy systems. The first is the institutional system through which the institution enacts cultural agency—circulating the particular literacy practices it endorses. This system is the easier of the two to trace. The second system is what people do with their literate repertoires—performances that are often less predictable though also highly constrained.[9]

Yet just because resourceful writers can try to transform institutional literacies for their own purposes, institutional sponsors aren't exempt from the responsibility to support the needs and interests of their participants. This is Grabill's claim in *Community Literacy Programs and the Politics of Change*, where he argues that sponsors of adult literacy programs should implement a participatory design so that the literacies a program sponsors coincide with participants' motivations for enrolling in the program in the first place (199).

2. *The same inspired context for literacy learning may participate in different economies and for different effects for different writers.*

I'm thinking here of Cara and Chaz, two teen writers at the CLC in the early 1990s. Cara had lots of support beneath her; the literacy project was a bonus between various after-school programs and before college. In contrast, Chaz was caught in gang crossfire. His mother finally moved to a suburb north of town to extricate him from gang territory. In material terms, the location of the literacy project was the same for both writers: 801 Union Place; however, the teens experienced the literacy project differently. This difference was most marked in the circumstances of Cara and Chaz, but could be said of other teens in the community-literacy project, as well. I don't know how to calculate that difference, but I do know that the stress that Chaz was under was an injustice perpetrated by an unequal distribution of resources. We all missed out because of it, especially Chaz. To the extent that the CLC could serve as an inspired context—or an urban sanctuary (McLaughlin, Irby, and Langman)—its hospitality was a political act that defied social injustice. But this nurturing was also inadequate to circumstances that framed Chaz's existence as an urban teenager. This comparison between Cara and Chaz suggests that economies of efficiency and excess may converge in people's lives—and do so differently within different life experiences—further complicating our explanatory accounts as literacy scholars and our understanding of how economic conditions play out in the lives of our students.

3. *Local publics participate in a larger social movement by sponsoring, as part of their institutional membership, ways of reading and writing that on a local level circulate a whole host of resources, including the moral consciousness, texts, and practices that sustain the movement itself.*

Warner argues that formal publics function in order to circulate texts (123). The previous five-point analysis suggests, however, that for local publics, circulating texts may be a small part of their larger function. When they operate within a larger institutional structure, local publics may also sponsor ways of reading and writing that circulate other resources on the local level—resources including a moral consciousness and a set of practices for enacting that consciousness. Such was the cumulative effect of African American congregations like Metro AME that over the past century have sponsored literacy within the context of the church's values of "resistance, freedom, self-determination, and collective uplift" and in conjunction with the civil rights movement and the black press (Brandt, *American* 108). The literate heritage of the African American church prepared ordinary people to participate locally in the civil rights movement, whereby securing the movement's "manifestations and successes" in the American public at large.[10]

Furthermore, local publics may circulate not only texts, but also literate practices. These are social routines for literacy "propelled into new directions by new or intensifying pressures for its use" (Brandt, *American* 9). Brandt credits the black church with circulating the resources that made the civil rights possible: "Especially significant were the efforts to transform historically church-based resources, ranging from ethical power to oratorical power to organizational power, into projects of secular activism" (142). Everyday literate practices that supported the civil rights movement were "text-based routines for liberatory action" (138), routines structured according to "formats" and rhetorical "stances" that circulated within and across religious congregations and other groups supporting the movement (137). The literate practice of protest writing serves as the chief example of such text-based routines, structuring both "the release of anger and the exercise of rights and self-determination" (137). Brandt documents that the practice of protest circulated into other local forums beyond the church, including "countless local settings in the push to end discrimination in employment, housing, commerce and education" (133). Thus, the efficacy of local publics may be best measured in terms of their capacity not to inform specific decisions but to alter the discursive landscape itself by challenging the moral consciousness of ordinary people and by structuring a range of literate practices that people can use to enact that consciousness.[11] In sum, then, local publics can alter how people think about pressing social issues and broaden the range of literate practices that people use to enact their new understandings. Metro AME served this dual function for its parishioners—a two-part purpose that, as we see next, the TWWW also served for its members.

A Garden: The Local Public in Heller's
Until We Are Strong Together

In *Until We Are Strong Together*, the local public is a garden that—like the cultural womb—nurtures people within it and prepares people for social action outside its borders. The image of the garden organizes Heller's description of a women's writing workshop sponsored from 1987 to 1993 by the Tenderloin Reflection and Education Center (TREC), dedicated to serving residents and the homeless in the Tenderloin District, one of the most economically distressed neighborhoods of San Francisco.

Distinctive Features: Nurtures and Prepares

As a garden that nurtures and prepares, the workshop invited participants to "'create something true'" and "put it into the world" (Heller 5).

Nurtures. The image of a garden highlights the nurturing qualities of the writers' workshop. In the extended metaphor, the workshop is a garden; the writers' investments in the meaning of their own lives and in each other, its soil. The garden offered to grow something for which the women yearned: the "'wish to be at home'" (Heller 131). That offer was realized through a process that transformed a disorganized set of strangers into a productive group of writers: "The soil of our individual places was being transformed into something that contained us all" (132). This transformation was cultivated through the writers' acts of nurturing, "a tenderness rare even for them" (132). The metaphor equates opportunity, time, and attention with the elemental qualities of sunlight, soil, and water. What grew in this garden was meaning, the significance of one's own life and of the group's collective experience.

Like Brandt, Heller attributes the nurturing quality of the TWWW to its democratic values and practices. Summarizing her interview with the director of the workshop's sponsoring organization, Heller writes: "It is the fundamental principle of the Tenderloin Reflection and Education Center that a true *democracy* is contingent upon all *citizens* developing clear, precise, and powerful *voices*" (Heller 8, emphasis added). Within this conception of democracy, voice is the ability to speak of one's experiences with clarity and conviction, a process that requires rehearsing and refining one's insights with others—thus, the need for such workshops (i.e., local publics) as the TWWW.

Prepares. As a womb implies birth, a garden implies harvest. A fruit harvested from the writers' workshop was social action, the capacity to address larger publics. Heller dramatizes the process. Initially, the members told stories to forge relationships with one another. Over time and because of the "investment in bringing their sense of place to their neighbors," they engaged also in political issues that mattered to them: "fairness, equality, justice, authority, power" (Heller 162). By nurturing the writers' voices, the workshop came to constitute a public in its own right; the workshop also prepared the writers to speak about their experiences in more formal arenas.

The Garden in Context: Location, Agency, and Maturation

Heller attributes the viability of the workshop to three main forces: its *location* that created a distinctive discursive as well as physical space; the *agency* of the workshop (as a "centripetal force") to sponsor literacies that, in turn, fostered the agency of the women writers; and the *maturation* of the workshop.

Location. On the one hand, the workshop was portable. Over its lifespan, the workshop met in a storefront, a hotel lobby, and a church basement. Heller celebrates all three as "sites for visibility and self-creation" (18). But as a discursive space, the workshop was transportable only so long as its defining vision, relationships, and discursive practices stayed more or less intact. So when it became necessary to relocate the workshop, TREC's director invested the intellectual and manual labor to do so—everything from planning and fund raising to assembling and disassembling the aluminum folding chairs (8).

Yet its physical location was not immaterial to the workshop's success. Location served a heuristic value. "The [hotel's] *picture windows,* opening to a view of the busiest drinking and drug-sale corner in the Tenderloin, *served to connect* the writers' workshop to the neighborhood in which it met [. . .]" (Heller 9, emphasis added). Framing even personal prose within this larger context, the workshop's location prompted writers toward socially relevant insights. Toward this end, TREC sponsored cultural events, at which TWWW writers "would take to the podium [. . .] to read their work publicly" (29). TREC sponsored these events "to maintain an *ongoing link between* the writers taking part in the [. . .] *workshops* and the *broader Tenderloin neighborhood*" (Heller 29, emphasis added).

Agency. As we saw earlier, Brandt's portrait of the black church as a cultural agent is compelling in large part because of the status and stability that institutional membership grants places like Metro AME. In contrast, the TWWW operated outside a strong institutional framework. True, the workshop was sponsored by a social service agency—TREC. True, too, the Freirian commitments of the agency's director framed the goals of the workshop (Heller 8). Surely, then, Brandt and Grabill would agree that TREC served as the workshop's official *sponsor*. But while its Freirian orientation positioned the workshop within a larger liberatory tradition and TREC provided immediate funding, in material terms neither the Freirian tradition nor TREC could come even close to providing the institutional stability that the black church as an institution offers individual congregations. On what grounds, then, does Heller attribute agency to the TWWW to justify its description as "'the centripetal force' [. . .] the force [. . .] that propelled the calm" (132)? To borrow Brandt's language, the answer lies in the workshop's capacity to sponsor literacies that circulated resources in an economy of efficiency.

Over its six years, the workshop itself achieved the role of sponsor resonant with Brandt's description of black churches. As Brandt describes the African American church as a consolidating force, "promot[ing] integration over fragmentation, persistence over change, remembering over forgetting" (*American* 112), similarly, Heller describes the TWWW as a centripetal force, "calming and consolidating narratives of place and order amidst a fragmented backdrop of chaos and disorder" (122). Likewise, as the church distributed a wide range of resources including literacy to compensate for poverty and racism, the TWWW offered a wide range of resources to its participants. Some resources were distributed within the workshop's sessions themselves—a direct consequence of its design and delivery. Heller calls these resources "levels of supports" and includes in a longer list the following especially relevant to the study of literacy:

- Boosting identity and self-esteem—as people, as writers, and as a public presence [. . .]
- Sharing information and resources [. . .]

- Building skills as writers through writing [and] critique, including forming definitions of oneself as a writer and engaging in complex examinations of language. (Heller 17)

Other resources became tangible as writers from the workshop adapted what they were learning in the workshop to address new rhetorical demands: for example, to hold a landlord accountable to fixing a broken elevator or to fight the sale of property that foreshadowed one's own eviction (Heller 58). Because of the workshop, the writers "found renewed certainty as effective agents in their lives" (19). The workshop provided "a launching place for the writers to take increased action to better their lives" (58).

Maturation. Heller also attributes the TWWW's vitality as a public forum to the maturation of the group itself. First, as the group matured, the women's writing took a decidedly public turn. Heller writes: "The *longer* I was with the Tenderloin Women Writers Workshop, the more I noticed participants in the group critiquing American life [. . .]. In *later months and years,* stories and poems [. . .] engendered conversations *denser and richer* with invigorating analyses of varied social problems" (17, 54, emphasis added). Spawned from their personal writing, the women's public writing took the forms of cultural critique, social commentary, and problem analysis. For Heller the distinction between personal and public writing is neither a false distinction nor a fixed dichotomy but a web of meaning explored more intensely over the course of the workshop's life cycle (101).

Second, maturation accounts for the workshop's capacity to respond to the diversity of its participants and the conflicts that came with it. The group's diversity brought a host of discourse styles, dialects, and personalities to the workshop that introduced a set of power relations that led to interpersonal conflict (66). Accounting for the decision of a participant named Francis to leave the group, Heller evokes organic imagery: "[T]he workshop wasn't *yet solid* or secure enough in its footing, in its formative identity, *to absorb* her struggle" (66, emphasis added). Over time, however, the workshop matured to become more adept at responding to conflict. As evidence, Heller points to the group's capacity to deal with conflict. "In fact, *later years* provided *growing evidence* of the group's capacity to resolve complicated conflicts" (67, emphasis added). According to Heller, this maturation cultivated a more robust "sense of community that didn't just 'accept' diversity, but whose very vitality was built upon it" (57).

Tenor of the Discourse: Literary Uplift

Literary uplift refers to the capacity of the workshop's discourse to "reassure [. . . writers] that they had lived lives that were of value and that could be—through the precision of their own words—felt, understood, and remembered by others" (Heller 18). Literary uplift was achieved through the covenant between readers and writer: as readers, the women served "as witnesses" for the claims they, as writers, made "for the richness of their complicated experiences" (18). To suggest the spiritual power of this uplift, Heller compares the tenor of the workshop's discourse to that of a life history course for elderly Jewish immigrants "who found renewed meaning in their lives by publicly 're-creating' themselves" (19).

Belletristic Literacies

The TWWW was a creative writing workshop. As such, writers worked primarily with literary genres. Although mirror stories and workshop discourse also structured the give-and-take of the workshop sessions, foremost the workshop put standard literary genres to the task of constructing local public discourse.[12] Below are some examples:

- *Journal entries:* Frances's "stream-of-consciousness piece described her search for a good night's sleep amid the troubled characters, chronic noise, and disruptions that form the background of her life" (Heller 30).
- *Poems:* Margaret's poem "described her method of backing up four flights of stairs while hauling her wheelchair up to her apartment in a building with a broken elevator" (53).
- *Novels:* Mary's *Doyon* was "a portrait of her homeland, her vanishing tribe in northern Alaska, of memories she would not abandon" (22).
- *Short stories:* Mary's "The Night of Indin Bilijohn" was a tribute to the anomy of Native Americans living in the Tenderloin. "'They're at sea, totally at sea'" (22).
- *Plays and other cultural performances:* Salima's play depicted "[t]he claustrophobic feel of [a one-room] apartment and the

conflict between [twin boys] and their unemployed stepfather"
(20, 53).

- *Articles:* Essays included Laraine's "Homeless Women, Don't
  Give Up! Get Up!" which "examine[d] the many forces that
  prevent homeless women from attaining productive lives, the
  countless issues that make "'having a nice day' for some a rare
  achievement" (94).
- *Satire:* Nikki's "Liberal Anonymous" urged readers to bridge
  "distances between races and classes" even as it "poke[d] fun" at
  her effort to do so (92).

Writers also explored experimental genres, including Leona's "what-
chamacallit," a piece of free verse which prompted the group to "explore[. . .] definitions of poetry as well as those of other literary genres"
(60) and "a script" in which Virginia "performed the order of her home,
the signs by which she knew herself and by which she could imagine
becoming known to others" (122). They also wrote many "self narra-
tions," including Maria's autobiographical novel, *The Life and Times of
Ruby Brooklyn* and Salima's autobiographical play, *Ain't I Right, Too,*
"tell[ing] the story of her childhood and its impact on her later life"
(Heller 111).

Two kinds of "public platforms" provided venues for getting the
women's writing "out there" (Heller 26): public readings where writers
performed their texts orally, such as the TREC-sponsored "Celebrat-
ing Beauty in the Tenderloin" (20); and publication in the neighborhood newsletters, newspapers, and TREC's anthology, *Goddesses We
Ain't.* Through these platforms, the women writers achieved "public
voice and visibility" (19).

Rhetorical Invention: Precision at the Point of Utterance

The TWWW celebrated the "precision" of the writers' insights. Thus,
rhetorical invention was a matter of "shaping at the point of utterance"
(Britton 61) as writers expressed "what they had experienced, what
they knew, what they had 'looked at unflinchingly'" (Heller 145).[13]
The writers and workshop facilitators paid attention to invention indirectly. As the writers read and responded to one another's drafts, they
swapped helpful hints along the way, often in the form of what they
described as habits and obsessions. Heller also credits the facilitators'

guidelines and personal investments for cultivating the precision of the women's prose and poetry.

Habits. Journal writing and "scribbling thoughts down on paper, no matter how these thoughts came out" were habitual approaches to prewriting that the writers commended to one another, particularly as an antidote to writer's block (Heller 61). Sometimes, the exchange of habits yielded "revelations," epiphanies that freed a writer to approach writing in a new way. Yet these conversations were also met with resistance, as writers sought to have their own personal styles and habits validated. For instance, Maria asserted, "'You see, I never change anything'" (59) to support her contention that approaches to writing were entirely personal, so a habit that one writer commended enthusiastically would likely not work for her (59).

Obsessions. Writers sometimes commended to the other writers the rituals they practiced with zealous passion, including revision and editing.

- *Revision fever:* The practice of revision was hotly contested among the writers. Mary commended it with almost religious fervor: "'I rewrite incessantly. Part of my madness is to rewrite. I think it's awfully fun!'" (Heller 59); others found revision offensive, as if the practice itself questioned their skill as writers (59).
- *Nitpicking:* Surface-level editing directed writers' attention to the "precise language" they used to "express their thinking" (149). In this regard, the practice engaged women in the art of invention, "pushing [. . .] them to know what they didn't *know* they knew" (149).

Facilitators' Leadership. The workshop's facilitators offered standard writing guidelines and invested personally in the women's insights and experiences to encourage the writers to express insights with bold clarity:

- *Standard guidelines:* Facilitators encouraged writers "to offer surprises, conflicts, and contradictions" and "to trust in themselves as strong and insightful narrators" (Heller 145).

- *Nonstandard investment:* The facilitators' personal investments in the workshop created "a covenant of care" that motivated the writers to tell with precision and depth "the truth of one's personal, social, and political experience" (14). This investment is perhaps best demonstrated in the portrait of facilitators listening "with an engagement and urgency many teachers reserve for talking" (147).

The facilitators cultivated the TWWW as an inspired context for literacy learning. Just as a parishioner at Metro AME referred to the pastor as both a "'preacher and a teacher'" (Brandt, *American* 118), so, too, the TWWW facilitators graced writing instruction with a spiritual presence, "less [. . . a] pedagogical technique [. . .] than [. . . a] pedagogical *feeling*" (Heller 149).

Implications

1. *Economic efficiency does not cause people to be able to transform their literate repertoires from one purpose to another; instead, inspired contexts cultivate this capacity in conditions of scarcity and stress to compensate for the toll that poverty and other forms of social neglect take on people's lives, including otherwise diminished opportunities for literacy learning.*

One's capacity to transform a literate repertoire for a new purpose depends on having a repertoire to turn to—a repertoire of one's own, yes, but likely also a network of literacy sponsors (Brandt, *American* 114). Yet as William Julius Wilson reminds us, work isn't the only thing to have disappeared from much of contemporary urban life. When work disappears, so, too, do other social institutions, such as churches and community organizations that sponsor literacy. Consider, for instance, the writers in Higgins and Brush's study, entitled "Writing the Wrongs of Welfare." These writers found the task of transforming their personal stories for public ends so intellectually and emotionally demanding that they likely would not have succeeded in writing their documents, had it not been for the support of capable and attentive writing mentors (70). In this regard, Hawkins and Grant in Brandt's study and TallMountain in Heller's were better positioned to use literacy to cope with new pressures in their lives than the women in Higgins and Brush's literacy project, for as Brandt and Heller document, Hawkins's, Grant's, and TallMountain's literate repertoires had been nourished along the way.

2. The garden depicts local public discourse as gritty and grounded, associating expertise with personal experience and yielding insights often missing from mainstream public discourse.

TWWW participants and facilitators found their work satisfying because in their attention to detail, clarity, and precision, the writers' texts offered pertinent truths about American life clearly lacking from larger national discussions. Yet it is often difficult for local knowledge to go public, as several recent studies of community literacy document. Susan Swan encountered this problem in a capstone course for public policy students. The community residents whom the students interviewed offered crucial insights about the conditions that could make or break a proposed urban renewal project. However, the students couldn't figure out how to incorporate this vital information into the professional genre they were assigned to write. Instead, they relied on the expert opinion of published professionals to evaluate the plan and came up with a recommendation that overlooked the residents' well grounded concerns. Similarly, in Higgins and Brush's study, the writers—all of whom were previous and current welfare recipients—had important insights to share with welfare policy makers about welfare reform. Eliciting the writers' local knowledge in text was the purpose of the community-literacy project. Higgins and Brush leave for a future study how such local knowledge might actually go public to circulate within larger public deliberations.

3. Storytelling has an important function in local public discourse, making the cultural values and social knowledge that shape personal experience compelling and accessible to readers and listeners.

Can personal narrative carry out the rhetorical work of public persuasion? Susan Jarratt cautions that expressive pedagogies are insufficient for teaching students "how to argue about public issues—making the turn from the personal back out to the public" (121). Yet narrative—central to many literary genres—may be more attuned to some of the demands of contemporary public rhetoric than its old stand-by, argument (I. Young, *Intersecting Voices* 73). Iris Young argues that prominent rational-critical model of deliberation is too restrictive. Instead, she promotes a communicative model of inclusive democracy. This model draws on "a plurality of perspectives, speaking styles, and ways of expressing the particulars of social situation as well as the general applicability of principles" (*Intersecting* 73). Within the model, narrative plays a central role:

- First, narrative reveals [. . .] particular experiences [. . .] that cannot be shared by those situated differently but that they must understand in order to do justice to the others.
- Second, narrative reveals a source of values, culture and meaning.
- Finally, narrative not only exhibits experiences and values from the point of view of the subjects [who] have and hold them. It also reveals a total social knowledge from the point of view of that social position. (72–73)

Young's model dismisses neither the vitality of the TWWW stories, nor the legitimacy of Jarratt's critique. Young suggests that being able to narrate a compelling personal story may be a helpful, even necessary, first step to fostering "enlarged thought," the moral imagination that makes possible "understanding across differences" (I. Young, *Intersecting* 52).

To make this challenge more concrete, recall the eight former and current welfare recipients in Higgins and Brush's study. They drew from their personal experiences on welfare to craft public narratives that could inform public policy decisions. In order to present publicly persuasive narratives, their texts had to acknowledge stereotypes that reign in the dominant discourse about them (including the welfare queen and deadbeat dad) without forfeiting their own dignity and agency—or dismissing their own culpability in their life circumstances. To do so, for instance, Nikki chose to write her narrative in the third person, a stance that provided her some distance on an earlier era in her life when she accepted public assistance; Jule accounted for her three children's three fathers by portraying herself as sexually naïve as a young woman, but not promiscuous or deceptive. As rhetors, these writers had to provide signposts that skeptical (even hostile) interlocutors would find familiar without themselves succumbing to degrading innuendo and insults. The writers were most successful when they made explicit the choices, values, and circumstances that had governed their decisions—hidden logics typically ignored or dismissed in larger public discussions regarding welfare reform.

Narrative's place in public discourse raises at least two additional issues for local publics: how local publics situate the practice of story telling and how comfortable literacy leaders feel offering explicit instruction within those local publics. As a creative writing workshop, the TWWW took an indirect approach to linking story telling to these additional rhetorical demands. In contrast, Higgins and Brush integrated rhetorical problem-solving strategies and other scaffolds into the design of their community-literacy project in order to maximize the project's effectiveness.

4. *The capacity for a local public to sustain its discourse depends, in part, on the viability of its sponsoring institution.*

The comparison between Brandt's and Heller's local publics stresses the vulnerability of local publics that operate with only tenuous or temporary institutional sponsorship. Metro AME was directly affiliated with a larger institution. Through this affiliation, Metro AME gathered strength and efficacy to nurture its members and to prepare them for social engagement. The TWWW also nurtured and prepared its participants. Yet it was positioned far more precariously as a special project of TREC. Consequently, the workshop disbanded when resources dried up (Heller 9).

The comparison also suggests that it's not always appropriate to assess a local public's merit in terms of its sustainability (though strategies for sustainability are one of the first concerns a funding officer will raise to a community group that seeks funding). First, the TWWW was never designed to last over time. Implicit in the organic model was a sense of the workshop's life expectancy. In fact, the TWWW survived twice as long as predicted—a daunting accomplishment given the social forces pressing down on many of its participants. Second, over the course of its existence, the TWWW certainly made important contributions in its own right—including the (documented and undocumented) ways its writers benefited from their participation in the workshop and the ways the writers' insights intensified public discussion and enacted communicative democracy within the Tenderloin District from 1987 to 1993. Through Heller's published research project, the TWWW also continues to make significant social contributions as a source of scholarship in community-literacy studies.

6 The Link and Gate: Local Publics That Intersect with Public Institutions

Local tends in the direction of the private and personal, *public* toward the social and official. This chapter focuses on the discursive space where the two intersect. Here, each phrase modifies the other, the term *local* qualifying *public* to refer to the informal the accessible, and *public* qualifying *local* to suggest the communal and shared. To depict this intersection, Barton and Hamilton evoke the image of a link and stress movement between the private-public binary; Cushman evokes a gate and stresses its outright collapse.

A LINK: THE LOCAL PUBLIC SPHERE IN BARTON AND HAMILTON'S *LOCAL LITERACIES*

In *Local Literacies,* the local public is a link connecting private lives to public institutions for the purpose of social action. *Local Literacies* is an ethnography of a neighborhood called Springside in Lancaster, England, where in the 1990s, working-class residents forged links to protect the land rights of local gardeners, to advocate for children with dyslexia, and to protest the emission of noxious gases. According to Barton and Hamilton, links can be forged by community groups— as illustrated when a group of gardeners protested the city council's plan to sell public allotments to bolster the city's diminished budget. Individuals can forge links, too, as the community resident named Shirley did while "'fighting injustices, [. . .] making changes, [. . . and] getting things done'" (Barton and Hamilton 100–01).

Distinctive Features: Linking Networks Across Domains

The link as local public depends on three concepts: *domains,* the contexts structuring specific literate practices; *links,* connections forged in literate practice; and *networks,* the social relationships that make forging the links possible and purposeful.

Domains. Domains are the contexts—such as the home, the workplace, and school—that structure and regulate specific kinds of activity. Through their institutional affiliations, domains organize how people spend their time and for what purposes. Some domains are more private and others more public, depending on the degree to which one or more "socially powerful institution" has jurisdiction over a given domain (Barton and Hamilton 10). The home is the most private domain and, thus, the most tolerant of literate activity that is creative, variant, and inventive. Public domains are affiliated with more formal institutions that adjudicate not only procedures and documentation practices but also penalties for violating these rules. Contrast, for instance, the consequences of omitting an item from a grocery list versus from a tax form.

Links. Links connect domains for the purpose of social action. The link "mediates [. . .] between the private sphere of family and household and the public sphere of impersonal formal organizations" (Barton and Hamilton 16). A link can be a noun: "[L]inks were motivated by personal concerns" (x). *To link* is a verb. Adept at linking private lives to public institutions, Shirley:

- liaised between members of the community and local media
- liaised between residents and the office
- crossed boundaries
- mobilized personal networks for public ends
- linked people with resources
- crossed between domains.

Unlike a bridge that exists whether or not a car is on it, links between private lives and public institutions are more tenuous, more like a neurological synapse that must continue to be fired in order to exist. Constituted in literacy, links permit people first to connect their private lives to public institutions and then to preserve the connection in attempt to take some kind of social action.

Network. Networks are the social relations that link people and their activities within and across domains.[1] The image of a network highlights the social relationships people forge and the power relations they negotiate, as they use literacy to carry out a shared goal. Like the domains they occupy, networks can be characterized along the private-public continuum. What was remarkable about Shirley was her ability to mobilize people in and across public as well as private networks "to get things done in the community" (Barton and Hamilton 16). Shirley had networks of friends and associates in her immediate neighborhood of Springside with whom she shared interests and history. Some whom she knew informally—from sharing knitting patterns and exchanging books—joined her efforts to organize a dyslexia association to advocate for children who had difficulty learning in school. People in that network introduced her to still others, including those who later joined Shirley's efforts to protest a neighborhood revitalization plan that residents found discriminatory. The concept of a network connotes not simply pairs or small groups of people working in relation to one another but an ever-growing set of interrelated connections. Networks offer the possibility of dynamic, yet-to-be-constructed points of contact where ordinary people can connect their private lives to public institutions.

The Link in Context: Location, Bottom-Up Initiative, and Agency

Links, domains, and networks raise important questions: *Where are local publics actually located? Who (or what) has the capacity to forge them?* Answers to these questions depend on location, bottom-up initiative, and agency—contextual factors that make a link a viable local public.

Location. In part, *local* refers to Springside's physical location. As suggested in the study's subtitle, *Reading and Writing in One Community,* the term *local* in *Local Literacies* refers to the study of practices associated with a specific time and place. The authors commit two chapters to tracing the economic, political, and social history of Lancaster, England, along with its geography and demographics, in order to situate the neighborhood of Springside within this history. They do so because the various details of the locale (ranging from its history as a milltown, to the location of the public library, to the function of a roundabout in the roadway as a site for homemade banners and flyers) affect how people use literacy in their day-to-day lives.

The literal and local also evoke the theoretical and global. In both the introduction and conclusion to *Local Literacies,* Barton and Hamilton connect their study of local literacies to global trends and theoretical issues. Consider, for instance, the literal-theoretical connection they draw regarding the Allotment Association's effort to stop the city council from selling its garden plots. The situation had both literal implications for the lettuce-consumption of the gardeners and theoretical implications for public-spheres studies. Most immediately at stake was the literal loss of fresh garden produce, including the cost of this loss to household budgets. In theoretical terms, this translated into the "loss of *communally owned open space*" (218, emphasis added). The incident raised questions about both the legality of city council's plans and the residents' claims to the land itself. Resolution would depend on the residents' access to the literate resources required to exercise their right to public land when the land right itself was contested. At issue was whether the gardeners would have the wherewithal to create a discursive space capable of linking their Allotment Association to the city council (a formal public institution) in attempt to restrict the council's intent.

Bottom-Up Initiative. To constitute a viable local public, a link needs to emerge from the private/personal and connect to the public/institutional. Links forged in the opposite direction were doomed to fail. In Springside, community residents were suspicious of initiatives that formal institutions (such as an established political party or a government agency) instigated. The Housing Project Association (HPA) serves as a case in point. At the time of Barton and Hamilton's study, the British government had established community organizations called HPAs to increase local support for a comprehensive urban renewal plan. Merging public and private interests—what Barton and Hamilton refer to as the "very hybridity" of the organization—"was very much part of national government policy at the time" (222); therefore, the project manager "was committed to the community involvement aspect of his work" (222). However, because Springside's HPA imported its agenda and decision-making practices from the government office, many residents were suspicious of it, for "local participation was grafted onto an organization which had been set up without the consultation or informed consent of the residents and which *ultimately they did not control*" (228, emphasis added). Most local residents were unwilling to invest their resources—especially their literate resources—in this organization.

Agency. Local Literacies credits groups and individuals with the capacity to forge local publics. Community groups serve as liaisons between individuals and public institutions, as in the case of the Dyslexia Association serving as a "go-between for parents and schools, usually where parents have identified a problem with their child's literacy that they are finding hard to get the school to recognize or deal with" (104).

Likewise, individuals can mediate between private networks and public institutions. Shirley, for instance, took an "active stance in bridging the public and private spheres in her neighborhood [. . . by] act[ing] as a catalyst in community activities and [. . .] represent[ing] the interests of others" (Barton and Hamilton 109). Issues of her newsletter created "text worlds" that situated residents in positions of influence over representatives of more public domains (109). For instance, Shirley wrote editorials to "try to bring local people together to influence the Council to do things in the neighborhood: whether it is introducing traffic calming measures, getting children's play space, defending allotment land, or getting more resources for building work" (109).

But even when credited with taking strategic action, Shirley was not acting alone. She wrote in order to forge connections with others in her neighborhood networks, urging them to join the effort to pool relevant resources (such as access to a fax machine or word processor) and expertise (such as knowledge of legal proceedings) to take relevant action to protect or to enhance the quality of their community life (such as increased access to home improvement grants).

Tenor of the Discourse: Hybrid—a Mix of the Formal and the Everyday

The discourse that links public and private domains is hybrid in quality, a mix of the formal and the everyday. Links mix the more public and official, on the one hand, and the more private and personal, on the other. The quintessential hybrid genre is the newsletter: "[N]ewsletters [. . .] are a kind of *public writing* that has no fixed, official format and is, therefore influenced a great deal by [. . .] *personal style and purposes* [. . .]" (Barton and Hamilton 107, emphasis added). As editor of such a newsletter, Shirley commingled the dominant and the vernacular, making "public points," for instance, by "using personal examples" (107). The result was a hybrid, one that drew from informal and formal discourses in hopes of humoring, goading, and persuading readers to join the group's efforts to "get things done" (109). When groups, rather than individuals, forge links, the discourse is still hybrid, but often even more varied because more people are contributing to the mix. Take, for example, the Allotment Association. The group's efforts to stop the city council were a mix of literacies that individuals had learned (observed or overheard) on the job, in school, or through prior experience with community organizations (219).

Mobilizing Literacies

Mobilizing literacies coordinate the texts, resources, and strategies that people bring to a shared problem. They emerge from the people's response to the situation, rather than from a pre-existent blueprint imposed from above, like the process the Labour Party attempted to impose to get a foothold in Springside. Situational constraints assign mobilizing literacies their purpose and meaning. For instance, literacies such as the taking and reading of meeting minutes may help a group prepare for subsequent social action—but this isn't the effect of all minutes. Mobilizing literacies, such as letter writing, can serve any number of functions depending on the purpose of the group. Contrast, for instance, letters that invite lapsed members to renew their membership with a letter-writing campaign to governmental representatives in protest of the emission of noxious gasses. The text-resource-strategy matrix for the Allotment Association is described in table 4:

Table 4. The text-resource-strategy matrix for the Allotment Association. Reprinted with permission. David Barton and Mary Hamilton. *Local Literacies: Reading and Writing in One Community.* London: Routledge, 1998.

Strategies, resources and texts: elements of literate practices

The strategies used to solve the problem

This is what people did:

gather and distribute information in the local community
mobilize local people
petition among allotment holders
hold general meetings to agree on what to do

> *form an action committee to implement decisions and to*
>   *negotiate on behalf of the community*
> *hold letter-writing campaign to influential people*
> *start press campaign in local radio and newspapers*
> *influence local officials by oral persuasion*

The resources used

These included material objects, skills, knowledge, time and ideas, money, meetings and space:

> *legal literacy knowledge of trainee solicitor*
> *use of word processor, photocopier*
> *local library*
> *accounting skills*
> *money raised by fund-raising*
> *local contacts in the Council*
> *skills in dealing with the media*
> *skills of persuasion and argumentation*
> *organizing skills—offering structure and being able to work*
>   *with others*
> *design skills—combining words and graphics on signs, posters etc.*

The textual resources involved in these practices

The following texts were used:

> *letters of various kinds, including official*
> *maps (for understanding the compromise plan)*
> *historical records of the Allotment Association (to see how land*
>   *was used and tenure changed over time) and more general*
>   *history of allotments*
> *legal documents*
> *newspaper articles*
> *petition*
> *newsletter to the local community*
> *posters*
> *press release*

Mobilizing literacies are the eclectic mix of literacies that ordinary people use opportunistically for the purpose of social action. They are not individual property (even though individuals contribute different literacies to a group effort) but rather a community resource for enhancing the quality of local life.

Rhetorical Invention: Adapting and Retooling

In *Local Literacy*, rhetorical invention is largely a process of adapting and retooling, both for group members trying to solve a shared problem and for an individual writing independently.

Group Invention. In the tidiest of rhetorical situations, groups selected among options or recombined available literate strategies. However, when the exigency created new or unclear demands, residents' uncertainty about what was required and how to accomplish it made rhetorical invention a far more daunting task than choosing among a preconfigured set of options. Under these circumstances, groups improvised and adjusted their approach based on what went wrong or proved ineffective. For instance, when Springside's gardeners realized they needed to act as a formal Allotment Association to protect their land rights, they constructed a problem-solving process under pressure and over the course of several meetings. This process involved "search[ing] out and draw[ing] upon" different funds of community knowledge, including the history of similar disputes, the group's legal rights, and the decision-making process through which their claim would be reviewed (Barton and Hamilton 220). The precise process is not documented; Barton and Hamilton refer to it more generally as trial and error, a process of "constant reinvention" (226). The daunting challenge for the group was how to manage all this diverse input.

Individual Invention. Shirley offers a closer view of an individual's invention processes. Even when choosing among available alternatives, she often adjusted familiar rhetorical tools to make them suit the situation at hand. As editor of the residence association newsletter, for instance, Shirley drew on her past experience and expertise but adjusted her literate repertoire to suit her more public role. Sometimes, the adaptation could be quite straightforward. Many situations required Shirley to shift her channel of communication from oral to written— something she reported doing easily. The rhetorical moves Shirley made in her newsletter editorials, for example, "dr[e]w heavily on the discursive conventions of addressing a meeting orally" (Barton and Hamilton 109). As evidence, consider that Shirley often used humor in her newsletter to introduce serious issues—a strategy she knew to work well at community meetings. Other situations required Shirley to make deliberate changes to her discursive strategies. To account for her composing process, Shirley observed that she drew from personal experience, but she was also aware of altering what she had done in the past or what she was accustomed to doing in her private life in light of more public demands.

Implications

1. *Not only do individuals have difficulty connecting private lives to public institutions; groups also struggle.*

Although Shirley was able to sustain her commitment to literate social action, she couldn't always transfer her enthusiasm and commitment to others. Likewise, groups in Springside struggled to forge links to public institutions. Figuring out how to proceed required a lot of time and energy. Describing the Allotment Association's process of figuring out how to fight city council, Barton and Hamilton write: "[C]hoices have to be carefully weighed up. [. . .] People were uncertain about what to do and considerable time was spent in meetings discussing the value of different strategies" (225). The group's decision-making process was also riddled with tension, and the less committed members left the group because of it. Furthermore, there was no guarantee that a group's decision-making process would be up to the task at hand. Describing the limits of a group's networks, Barton and Hamilton write: "Networks [. . .] may not provide expertise in the ways that are needed at a particular time" (254).

2. *Forging the link in the first place is hard work, but even more difficult is sustaining the required literate activity so that the connection has some chance of advocating the desired social change.*

This implication extends the first. Granted, connecting private lives to a public institution is hard work in its own right, yet sustaining those connections is even more difficult. For instance, Janice, another participant in Barton and Hamilton's study, organized a protest to oppose an increase in the area poll tax. However, she couldn't sustain the momentum that an initial march instigated because she didn't know how to work with public institutions responsible for the tax or how to network with other relevant local organizations. "Janice [. . .] had strong informal networks but very little experience of dealing with official agencies or formal organizations; she did not know what to do after her initial action, even though organizations existed with which she could have linked, notably the anti-poll-tax union" (Barton and Hamilton 228).

3. *The organic quality of community groups that makes them inventive, spontaneous, and responsive (and, thus, so interesting to literacy scholars) also makes the links they try to forge to public institutions especially vulnerable to established institutional power.*

Community groups that are "vernacular and local" are likely to be sites of creative and inventive literate activity (Barton and Hamilton 226). This inventiveness often correlates with a lack of financial resources, as well as a lack of expertise regarding the dominant practices of public institutions. Moreover, it is unlikely that everyday people receive any formal education or explicit training in the literacies or roles required to forge links to public institutions. Importantly, this includes lack of training in "working together in groups to solve disputes" (228). Thus, the disequilibrium between private lives and public institutions makes any link that a group or individual is able to forge vulnerable to a public instruction's bureaucratic and technical literacies and other dominant practices. In Springside, this disequilibrium set in relief other sources of vulnerability for local publics, namely the agendas, values, and practices of dominant domains that encroach upon local life.

This tension raises another question: *how are we, as rhetoricians, to understand the value of efforts like Shirley's to use literacy to improve daily life?* As Catherine Squires argues in "Rethinking the Black Public Sphere: An Alternative Vocabulary for Multiple Public Spheres," it may be a mistake to conflate a public's capacity to circulate texts with the rhetorical efficacy of those texts. However, community-literacy scholars tend to be deeply committed to the possibility of community literacy to "support civil action" (Grabill, "Written City" 138) while intensely aware of literacy's "radical insufficiencies" (Mathieu 75).

4. *Links between private lives and public institutions aren't necessarily sites of democratic practice.*

Unlike the organic imagery in the previous chapter, the link suggests that the relationship between literacy and democracy is an uneasy one. Data from Springside led Barton and Hamilton to conclude: "Literacy has a role in democratic practice, yet literate practices are not necessarily democratic in their own right. Neither can they, on their own, promote democracy" (228). In each documented instance of a local organization behaving democratically, they observe that "it was not literacy in itself which was democratic; it was the practices" (229).

Another factor complicating the literacy-democracy equation is the constructive, hybrid nature of links. At the moment when a local community group is poised to connect to public institutions, its practices are often under construction. Thus, just as the possibility for democratic practice exists, so too exists the possibility for restriction and exclusion. This tension is evident in Barton and Hamilton's description of the Allotment Association's annual meetings where, on the one hand, "[t]he record-keeping and the minutes *ensure a democratic accountability,* both to the people at the meeting and to the larger membership of the organization" (229, emphasis added). On the other, however, when it came to viewing the organization's financial records, the bank statement was "proffered" in such a way that residents couldn't ask to see it *"without appearing to be rude"* (229, emphasis added). Literacy itself can complicate democratic processes. "Literacy in its administrative, bureaucratic forms without accountability can be limiting, alienating, and stifling" (Barton and Hamilton 228).

Barton and Hamilton commend processes of democratic literacy "where people have competence in and retain control over [. . .] decision-making processes" (230). Here their ethnography takes a prescriptive turn. They caution that to make good on its democratic commitments, a group's leadership must take responsibility for making resources available, including access to information (228). By implication, such a group needs to acknowledge that members will bring a wide range of vernacular literacies to bear not only on their own participation, but also on their expectations of others in the group. This dynamic is likely to increase the potential for conflict and the need for negotiation and wise leadership.

Thus far, this chapter has depicted the local public as a link where working-class residents like Shirley make contact with public institutions to improve the quality of their lives and life of their community. But what if Barton and Hamilton had been researching the local literacies of the "poor" and "marginalized" (Barton and Hamilton 64)? Would they have needed a different image to do justice to their observations of local publics? Cushman, author of *The Struggle and the*

Tools: Oral and Literate Strategies in an Inner City Community, maintains they would. Such circumstances call for an image attuned to
power differentials between community residents and representatives
of public institutions. Like Barton and Hamilton's image of a link
connecting domains across networks, Cushman's image of a gate depicts encounters as the borderland between private and public spheres
(Cushman, *Struggle* 124). But the gatekeeping encounter highlights
political contingencies at play within this borderland and the intensely
political linguistic skill required to navigate such space.

A Gate along a Fenceline: The Local Public in Cushman's *The Struggle and the Tools*

In *The Struggle and the Tools,* the local public is a gate along a fenceline
that can creak open to allow entry or remain shut to restrict access.
Cushman uses this image to describe the local public life of the two
families she studied from 1993 to 1996 in an industrial city in the
northeastern United States, a city she calls Quayville.

Distinctive Features: Access, Space, and Conflict

In the gatekeeping encounter, the local public is the point of contact
between the African American inner-city residents in Cushman's study
and representatives of various public institutions. The phrase *public
institution* here refers to the wide range of social service agencies that
distribute resources in inner cities, including regional branches of the
Department of Social Services, the Housing Authority, and Housing
and Urban Development. The phrase also includes the criminal justice
system. Representatives of philanthropic and religious organizations
such as Urban Ministries are also included in Cushman's group of
institutional workers who operate public institutions, as are landlords
themselves, the final decision makers in community members' search
for housing.

Access. The significance of a closed gate is obvious: access denied. In
this case, the gate and the gatekeeper are barriers between the community resident and the resources she seeks. But a closed gate also suggests—however obliquely—the possibility of an opening, permission
to access the resources on the other side.

Space. A gatekeeping encounter is a rhetorical space. At its best, it invites the community resident to use her community-based literacy skills to negotiate with respect and mutuality fair access to opportunities and equitable distribution of resources. Of all the literacy events that Cushman studied, this version of a local public space was clearly instantiated just once when a young woman named Raejone met with Mr. Villups, a college admissions counselor, to discuss the prospects of enrolling in the state university he represented. Because of the mutuality of their exchange, Cushman credits the exchange with "open[ing] up more opportunities" (Cushman, *Struggle* 187).

A gate also implies the space beneath it, "the rock bottom" which one "hits" under dire circumstances (Cushman, *Struggle* 88). The image of a gatekeeping encounter indicates how high the stakes are for community residents. For a mother of young children, hitting rock bottom means not only "falling through the cracks" yourself, but taking others with you. Women in Cushman's study struggled to negotiate gatekeeping encounters to provide for their dependents. They achieved status in their community by developing the linguistic savvy required to do so.

Conflict. The gate marks contact between two cultures' conflicting value systems. On one side of the gate is the culture of community residents, African Americans living in Quayville's inner city, people who privilege privacy, self-help, and collaboration among kith and kin. On the side of the gate is the institutional culture of gatekeepers. For all the good intentions grounding many social programs, the ideology governing the social service industry is often patronizing, assuming that "poor people, especially poor Black people [are] passive, disorganized, and apathetic" (Cushman, *Struggle* 47). Unlike Shirley whose social-action projects added something extra to her life, the urban poor in Cushman's study constantly negotiated gatekeepers because public institutions intervened in the most basic aspects of their daily lives, from where they lived and what they ate to the living conditions of their children, their marital status, and their eligibility for job-training and higher education. The flipside of this relationship is that—like the bereavement counselors in John McKnight's *Community and Its Counterfeits*—gatekeepers have a parasitic relationship to the residents they serve. Like McKnight, Quayville residents indicted caseworkers for keeping themselves employed by ensuring that the problems that sent community residents in search of their services were never entirely resolved.

The Gate in Context: Location and Linguistic Agency

To be a viable local public, the gatekeeping encounter requires a location; it also depends upon community residents' linguistic agency.

Location. Location pushes certain local publics into the fore (over the possibility of others) because of the historical forces that shape the contours of daily life. In Quayville, daily life is marked by the struggle for employment and housing, "twentieth-century material struggles" that stem from Quayville's position within a larger national history, involving "the Second Great Migration, the displacement of Blacks through Urban Removal, the movement of jobs to the suburbs" (*Struggle* 44–45). In response to the destructive consequences of these events, in the 1960s and 1970s the federal government and philanthropic organizations created social programs to alleviate the suffering of the poor. Though funding for these programs has ebbed and flowed under various governmental administrations, these agencies have continued to control important resources in Quayville—thus, the prevalence of institutional representatives in the lives of the residents whom Cushman studied. As the vortex where political, historical, and economic conditions meet, location determines the local publics that matter most in people's lives and the literacies people use to work within these spaces.

Location is also a central site for "daily politics" (Cushman, *Struggle* 239). "[A]ll political endeavors take place in the daily," Cushman writes (5). As an object of analysis, the gatekeeping encounter permits Cushman to "locate every interaction and literacy event [. . .] in the broadest types of social structures" (5). Because of its position within social structures, a gatekeeping encounter captures a "foundational form of politics" (239). Each gatekeeping encounter has political significance in its own right, independent of its capacity to bring about any large-scale outcome or "massive changes in consciousness" (239). That's because a gatekeeping encounter encompasses the "particulars of daily politics, the commonplace victories and defeats, the subtle and overt challenges" associated with its location (239).

Location also connects gatekeeping encounters to the situated knowledge of community residents—both their perspectives and their local cultural values. Every gatekeeping encounter has the potential to respect or to violate the local knowledge and cultural values of a community resident. In his admissions interview with Raejone, Mr. Villups cues his respect for Raejone's perspective on what it means and takes to earn a college degree. In contrast, during a sting operation to shut down a drug ring in Raejone's neighborhood, representatives from both the police station and the regional office of the National Association for the Advancement of Colored People failed to recognize the validity of local perspectives. The community police program failed on two counts. First, institutional representatives failed to show respect for local perspectives, revealing instead their own "paternalistic attitudes" (106). Second, the program was insufficient to the task of curtailing drug activity—precisely because it failed to reflect the "complexity of the situation," knowledge that local perspectives could have provided. Used to describe the gatekeeping encounter, *local* in the phrase *local public* connotes people's ideological struggle to have their perspectives and expertise respected within the material struggle for resources (3).

Linguistic Agency. More than any other factor, what makes gatekeeping encounters viable local publics is the linguistic agency that community residents exercise within them. In Quayville, residents exercised agency through the linguistic strategies they chose to use in gatekeeping encounters and then by assessing the efficacy of those choices. Consider Salliemae's decision to supplement her housing applications with a list of references that had been typed on a computer and printed. Linguistic agency emphasizes that Salliemae's decision was a choice among alternatives—say, not to bother with a list, to write it out long hand, to mention the names on the list to the landlord orally, to select some names for the list by omitting other candidates, or to describe those on the list with certain attributes but not others. Linguistic agency highlights that such choices are tied to their social functions. In this case, Salliemae wanted to use the list of references to challenge the conclusion that a landlord would draw from reading her housing application alone: that since she collected welfare, she didn't work. By including the names of co-workers at the Department of Dependent Services on her list of references, Salliemae cultivated a rhetorical space for landlords to "ask her about her unique situation," which included working as a child-care provider and her goals to finish her General

Equivalency Degree (*Struggle* 161). In Cushman's working theory of local public life, agency is a linguistic phenomenon. To have agency is to be a "savvy negotiator [. . .] of highly nuanced, everyday interactions with wider society's institutional representatives" (2).

Tenor of the Discourse: Dueling Dualities

To hear what's really going on in Quayville's gatekeeping encounters, we'd need a special audio-recorder that could simultaneously record two frequencies: one broadcasting the signal for the *public transcript*; the other, the *hidden transcript*. Listening to both frequencies, we'd hear "dueling dualities"—the wrestling, the wrangling, the tension between the gatekeepers' public "structuring ideology," on the one hand, and the "counterhegemonic ideology" that residents keep private, on the other (Cushman, *Struggle* 139).

Hidden transcripts challenge the superiority of the public transcript. "[I]n the hidden transcripts," Cushman writes, "we see that individuals critique, question, seek paths around, and attempt to subvert the racist and classist ways these institutions work" (*Struggle* 96). Using hidden transcripts to call public transcripts up short, residents were able "to both mollify and rebuke, play into and off of, adopt and adapt, placate and challenge, conform and undermine, accommodate and resist" (227–28). [D]ueling dualities is the noise of "daily politics" (239).[2] In moments of such wrangling, neither the gatekeeper nor the resident has the upper hand. It's not that Social Structure wins out or that Personal Agency triumphs. Instead, the dueling dualities unleash the noisy collapse of political binaries: "micro/macro, agency/structure; power to/power over; confrontation/ denunciation; resistance/ oppression" (*Struggle* 3).

Institutional Literacies

Institutional literacies both create the discursive space of the gatekeeping encounter and provide people the means to navigate through it. First are the literacies one uses *to acquire* institutional tools. Next are the literacies one *transfers* from one's toolkit to the situation at hand. Third are the literacies used *to evaluate* what went awry during a gatekeeping encounter in order to retool for the next encounter (Cushman, *Struggle* 231). Categories include both oral and text-based literacies (123). They are interdependent, each category "informed by the other two" (231).

Together, these literacies form a "cyclic process" that lets residents continually hone their linguistic repertoires of institutional discourse (4).

Table 5. Activities used to acquire, transfer, and evaluate institutional literacies. Reprinted by permission from *The Struggle and the Tools: Oral and Literate Strategies in an Inner City Community* by Ellen Cushman, the State University of New York Press @ 1998, State University of New York.

Acquiring	Transferring	Evaluating
• questioned the literate artifact before them • modeled ways to transfer knowledge • collectively problem-solved • constructed the mundane as problematic • critically reflected on past experiences and future plans • found people who could teach them more skills • collected literate resources	• bent semantics to index two different value systems • flattered authority of gatekeeper • selected pronoun of solidarity • named and acted upon linguistic shortcoming • compared writing against successful model • crafted linguistic representations of themselves • code-switched when thought appropriate for situation	• assessed the utility of language strategies • considered other linguistic tactics • questioned ethics of using one strategy vs. another • determined why interaction went awry • intervened on someone's behalf if necessary • altered linguistic strategies that worked poorly • considered language and politics of situation

Many factors complicate the interactions between institutional workers and community members: power relations are asymmetrical (Cushman, *Struggle* 68), social service institutions are internetworked (187), and people's subject positions are multidimensional (23). But these factors intensify rather than undercut the importance of residents' reading, writing, speaking, and listening skills.

Rhetorical Invention: Evaluating Acquired Literacies
Transferred to New Contexts

As institutional literacy defines it, rhetorical invention permits a person to revamp linguistic tools available for transfer in hopes of handling the challenges of a gatekeeping encounter more strategically next time. Rhetorical invention promotes a meta-awareness residents use to consider "(1) when and how to resist a gatekeeper who is being unduly harsh; (2) which language styles they should have used given who was present and their authority; and (3) when and how to intervene in those gatekeeping situations that go poorly" (Cushman, *Struggle* 205). Rhetorical invention is a political act and the crux of residents' linguistic agency.

Residents participated in rhetorical invention differently, depending on their age and gender. Because they were inexperienced in negotiations with institutional workers, children were expected to listen to adults talk about altercations with landlords or social workers, but not to interrupt or to interject with their own perspectives. Adults' renditions of their interactions with gatekeepers became "case studies of collective and collected knowledge" about "linguistic and political struggles within wider society's institutions" (Cushman, *Struggle* 189). Kitchens, front steps, and community centers became "local classrooms [. . .] where adults taught through example and youths learned through watching and listening" (106). Such gatekeeping instruction was usually indirect, with children picking up what they needed to know by listening to adults analyze "all sorts of letters, bills, and receipts" that warned of unwelcome institutional interference.

Both boy and girl teens were likely to resist the stance adults promoted in institutional literacy lessons; however, resistance toward institutional discourse and the hypocrisies it represents was a luxury that few teens could afford for long. The transition from adolescence to adulthood was usually a rather sudden one, brought about by "moving out of the parents' home, pregnancy, employment, or graduating from high school" (125). Adulthood positioned teens in a new relationship to "the social networks the individuals could draw upon for resources and support" (125). To cope with the pressures of their new responsibilities, young adults drew upon previous language lessons: "When teens suddenly shift into the roles of young adults, they quickly learn to *play a deeper game with* their language, language they've *acquired* and *learned* in the community" (125, emphasis added). By the time men and women reached adulthood, they assumed diametrically opposed positions in relation to language learning. Men refused to hone the linguistic savvy required, for instance, to appear before a caseworker to apply for welfare, opting rather to preserve their personal integrity, often by working the underground economy. Women, however, were responsible to provide for their children and other dependents. They valued institutional literacy as a means for doing so. Learning to speak White English was a means toward an end. For adult women, learning institutional literacy also meant learning to quiet one's own resistant impulses in order to take care of those who depended on them.

Implications

1. *Local publics invoke democracy when they open up a space for community residents to advocate for their own interests on their own terms.*

The relationship between local publics and democracy is a contested one. The cultural womb and the garden depict an easy relationship between literacy and democracy that nurtures participants and prepares them for social action. The link, on the other hand, makes democratic practice more tenuous because of the very nature of literate activity that can evoke democratic values one minute and uncut them the next. Cushman provides a deeper analysis. She argues public institutions were indeed founded on "democratic values" (*Struggle* 226), "established out of a concern for the well-being of citizens who were hungry, unemployed, homeless or living in dilapidated housing, or who lacked access to higher education" (223). Because of these democratic tenets, Cushman argues that public servants should "strike a balance between the role of judge and advocate in ways that promote social and political equality" (184). However, gatekeeping encounters are fraught with difficulties that compromise democratic values. Along with the policies that the gatekeepers oversee and the bureaucratic forms and procedures used to maintain them, the reigning ideology invokes "insidious attitudes" toward welfare recipients and public-housing residents (48). Yet as weary as the residents became of the "mire of requirements, codes, and insidious attitudes," they tenaciously maintained belief in "the *promise always present* in public institutions" (19, emphasis added). The obligation Cushman places on the gatekeeper is to meet the community resident half way.

2. *A respectful local public wouldn't attempt to eradicate hidden transcripts, but rather to create a productive tension among participants' values, knowledge, and priorities.*

The gatekeeping encounter offers a strikingly different approach to conflict than the TWWW garden that absorbed interpersonal conflict as it celebrated the group's diversity. A respectful encounter wouldn't attempt to eradicate hidden transcripts but rather would recognize the legitimate differences between the participants' social locations. Referring to Raejone's encounter with the college admissions counselor, Mr. Villups, Cushman writes: "My data show that both community residents and gatekeepers can actually communicate effectively, *mutually indexing* the *shared task* of providing and accessing resources" (9, emphasis added). Using West's notion of prophetic pragmatism, we could conclude that ordinary people like those in Cushman's study act "prophetically" when they test the limits of what's possible within situations that otherwise threaten to degrade and to demean them (*American* 235). It follows, then, that ordinary gatekeepers conduct themselves prophetically when they identify and represent the agency and expertise of others.

3. *It may be wise for a rhetorician, as an instrument of social change, to seek not a sea-change in public policy but a better understanding of how ordinary people use "language and literacy to challenge and alter the circumstances of daily life" and to "facilitate actions" with those in need* (Cushman, "Rhetorician" 12, 14).

Why didn't the residents in Cushman's study resist gatekeepers more overtly? Wouldn't such resistance demonstrate agency more vigorously? Cushman disagrees. Community residents negotiated gatekeepers' linguistic cues subtly, rather than overtly, because they had too much to lose, both in a given encounter and in future encounters. An overt challenge would likely have made the gatekeeper click the latch shut, and as Barton and Hamilton remind us, social services participate in a larger network of public institutions. Once the word gets out to other caseworkers that a resident has behaved inappropriately, a resident could be "blackballed" from passing through the gates of other social service agencies (Cushman, *Struggle* 142). The complexity of this network means that linguistic agency can't be adequately measured in terms of its outcomes. For one thing, linguistic agency is a balancing act, a matter of selecting linguistic tools that keep one's cultural values intact (if out of view) while meeting the gatekeeper's expectations for proper behavior, for what a teen named Rachel called "'pol-White'" discourse (192). Yet even for the savviest negotiators in Cushman's study, gatekeeping encounters "rarely went as planned" (89). Accounts of Salliemae's and other gatekeeping encounters remind us that "multiple economic and social forces push hard on poor people" (187). But, linguistic agency isn't only about the resources on the other side of the gate. Even more, it acknowledges—without romanticizing—"the process of struggle" and "the sophistication of the tools" that community residents employ within the gatekeeping encounter itself (x).

7 The Community-Organizing Effort and the Community Think Tank: Local Publics Forged in Partnership with Formal Institutions

Both images featured in this chapter—the community-organizing effort and the community think tank—strive to correct the "checkered history" of relationships between "the town and gown" (Flower, "Partners" 95). The Open Doors Collaborative described in Goldblatt's "Alinsky's Reveille" is a single instance of community organizing that unfolded over an eighteen-month period. Invoking the discourse of Alinsky, partners "talk[ed] through conflict and negotiate[d . . .] tensions" in order to reach consensus regarding future joint action (Goldblatt, "Alinsky's Reveille" 289). In contrast, the community think tank described in Flower's "Intercultural Knowledge Building" refers to a general practice demonstrated through a series of documented community problem-solving dialogues. For the community think tank, the point of deliberation is not consensus among group members but the transformed understanding of individual participants made possible through the structured process of collaborative inquiry (Flower, "Intercultural Knowledge" 245). Despite these differences, both Open Doors and the community think tank are designed to foster the key feature missing from typical university-community relationships: mutuality—the give and take that positions all participants as both active contributors and learners. Both Open Doors and the community think tank promote mutuality by positioning university partners as problem solvers deliberating not *about*, nor *for*, but *with* community members.[1]

A Community-Organizing Effort: The Local Public in Goldblatt's "Alinsky's Reveille: A Community-Organizing Model for Neighborhood-Based Literacy Projects"

In Goldblatt's "Alinsky's Reveille," the local public is a community-organizing effort where partners transform problems into issues to act upon. A model practitioner, Goldblatt brought Alinsky's practical theory of action to bear on his own efforts in early 2002 to build connections across "the community-university divide" ("Alinsky's Reveille" 289). Along with Goldblatt, partners included five community leaders who directed adult education programs in North Philadelphia and university professor, Stephen Parks. Deciding upon a two-part strategy for improving literacy instruction, partners drafted a vision statement for the Open Doors Collaborative, a set of literacy programs supporting the goals and interests of adult learners in North Philly.

Distinctive Features: Complexity and Pleasure

For all of its complexity, Goldblatt commends community organizing as infinitely worthwhile—certainly because the process promises well-designed literacy projects, but also for the sheer pleasure of working together in this way.

Complexity. What's complex about getting together over hamburgers to "hang around and get to know the people and resources in an area" (Goldblatt, "Alinsky's Reveille" 278)? First, community organizing requires a cultural literacy that makes memorizing the lineage of Greek gods and goddesses look like child's play. You have to keep track of people at the table—their connections to other people and projects across time. People represent their own organizations' interests as well as the needs of others, so you also have to pay attention to the constituencies they represent, the organizations they work for, and those organizations' sponsors. Furthermore, even though they agree to work as partners, people in this new configuration are not entirely clear on the group's intent. The complexity of the composing process grows exponentially when people representing different needs and interests attempt to articulate and to actualize a shared, but initially ill-defined, goal. An effective community organizer knows how to close down this problem space. Yet the community-organizing effort's timetable and method differ from more publicized corporate and academic models. To violate this community ethic is to jeopardize the effort's success.

Pleasure. Engaging with others in a mutually respectful community-organizing effort is damned enjoyable, providing both an excuse for introducing friends and an opportunity for working with people you like but otherwise would not have known. A community-organizing effort also clears the space for partners in the embrace of friendship to ponder existential issues like "the effect that personal traumas have on one's vocational choices" for which mainstream culture has little patience (Goldblatt, "Alinsky's Reveille" 285).

The Community-Organizing Effort in Context: Location and Legacy

As a local public, the community-organizing effort grounds its concern for location in the legacy of Alinsky.

Location. Goldblatt and Parks traveled to the largely Latino neighborhoods of North Philly to hold Open Doors's meetings—first to a local lunch counter, later and more regularly to a North Philly rowhouse, and at least once to a "[community] center near the Fifth Street hub of the Puerto Rican neighborhood" (Goldblatt, "Alinsky's Reveille" 289). Located in North Philly neighborhoods, the meetings were "true[r]" than they would have been if held on Temple University's campus. More attuned to the needs of the community residents who would use Open Doors initiatives (289), these meetings could enact a "theory of action devised for neighborhoods rather than for higher education" (276). Goldblatt and Parks traveled—yes, literally, but also figuratively—to gain distance from their professional roles and to meet community leaders "on their own ground" (292).

In community-organizing discourse, location also stages the challenges through which community leaders earn the credentials that get them seats at the community-organizing table. Every location is a unique interplay of complex political, economic, and social (often ethnic) pressures, so neighborhoods provide a proving ground for community leaders. The reputations of Goldblatt's partners preceded them, Manuel having "worked in an organizing campaign for people living with the HIV in South Chicago" ("Alinsky's Reveille" 285) and Johnny being "one of the best-known figures in the community arts and cultural organizations of Philadelphia" (286). Proficient in Spanish and a former high school teacher in the neighborhood, Goldblatt had social currency of his own to trade.

Legacy. Goldblatt draws upon Alinsky's community-organizing campaigns to think about how universities can best support literacy education in the larger community.[2] Alinsky took issue with "privilege and power," especially the paternalistic attitudes and exploitative practices of big business and government that prioritize profit at the cost of everyday people's dignity and quality of life (P. Murphy and Cunningham 16). A famous obstructionist, Alinsky cultivated a reputation for in-your-face confrontation, including "militant tactics, including outrageous graffiti, picketing and packing public hearings" (19). These tactics were designed to make public authorities confront their abnegation of civil contracts for quality housing, for effective schools and safe neighborhoods, and for economic developments that would protect local interests over those of large corporate entities. Alinsky-led demonstrations, boycotts, strikes, and alliances were also the scourge of those responsible for managing distressed neighborhoods in trying times.

From Alinsky's legacy, Goldblatt took the principle that community groups gain power by organizing. Observing that universities have an especially urgent and long-neglected responsibility to participate as genuine partners in their communities, Goldblatt added that compositionists may facilitate the process through which partners arrive at consensus.

Tenor of the Discourse: Bite Tempered by Sweetness

How do you signal your identity as a radical agitator of Alinsky's ilk? Foremost by the unflinching honesty with which you name the injustices inherent in the paradoxes of the status quo—a stance that requires incisive insight and a stinging sense of humor, the radical's bite. Alinsky's "politics are consistently blunt and confrontational" (Goldblatt, "Alinsky's Reveille" 282), for "organizers [. . .] show courage and candor in the face of corporate threats" (280). Open Doors exercised the radical's bite by "making fun of foundations" (292). Driving the joke was the partners' desire to expose the ironies and inconsistencies in corporate and government funding practices that keep initiatives from doing as much good as they otherwise could. Goldblatt also exercised the radical's bite when accusing academic culture of mean-spirited posturing. In sum, bite signals Alinsky's deep suspicion of both top-down directives and the idea that corporate culture would ever willingly change the practices and policies that secure its privilege.

The community organizer's bite is tempered by sweetness, the radical's love for "ordinary people" and a commitment to making their "lives better" (Goldblatt, "Alinsky's Reveille" 276, 281). This sweetness was true of Alinsky who "cared a great deal about how ordinary people learn to act for their own good and the good of their neighbors" (276). It also characterizes Goldblatt's efforts to nurture a partnership that he sees could do such good. Likewise, the Open Doors Collaborative was grounded in a deep faith in everyday people and the dignity of their lives.

Consensus-Building Literacies

Community organizing provides an "identity kit" for the non-interventionist agitator, writing program administrators (WPAs) who want to be part of a "collective view of education" that makes literacy instruction more relevant not only to individual college students, but also to learners at adult-education centers where the stakes are higher and literacy instruction can make a bigger difference (Goldblatt, "Alinsky's Reveille" 293). The identity kit flags the political acumen of community-organizing discourse. It operates as a political argument, conceding that conscientious educators are right to worry about unintentionally reinforcing the power and prestige of the university but that this concern doesn't excuse inaction. Yet the identity kit is also an antidote to extremism, providing an alternative to the "radical fantas[y]" that would compel readers "to don leather jackets and give up tenure to work in storefront literacy centers" (Goldblatt, "Alinsky's Reveille" 282). A condensed version of the kit's instructions would read something like this:

A Guide for the Non-Interventionist Agitator

The non-interventionist agitator adopts an activist stance that lets you draw upon your unique assets as a WPA without assuming you have all the answers. The instructions stipulate qualifications in two senses of the word. As you'd expect, the list sets the requirements for a productive non-interventionist agitator. In addition, each item also sets conditions that you must respect to preserve the integrity of the organizing effort, making the non-interventionist agitator account-able to the ever relevant question: "who is serving whom?" (Goldblatt, "Alinsky's Reveille" 292).

- *Connect leaders* in the community, but recognize those you bring to the table may have connections of their own to offer.
- *Be candid* about your own interest in the partnership, but position your interest in terms of the neighborhood's needs.
- *Let those familiar* with the neighborhood *guide your assessment* of its needs, but by all means, contribute your own insights when they stand to enhance the quality of the conversation.
- *Invest time and energy* in the group's process without having to be in charge.
- *Leverage resources* responsibly. Take a look at the resources available to you because of your position in the university. Perhaps you could sponsor "assistantships, internships, and volunteer positions to aid small nonprofit organizations with few resources of their own" (293). Or you might be able to help by offering persuasive language for a grant proposal. However you decide to leverage university resources, do so "with [. . .] a clear purpose" and "a commitment to build relationships across institutions" (293). To do otherwise is nothing more than "cynical exploitation" (293).
- *Shepherd documents* through the group's composing process. As a writing teacher, you are familiar with the complexity of writing. And the process is bound to be complex when people with "different personal styles and organizational cultures" write together (290). So do all you can to take good notes during meetings—attending to "what people want [. . .] to work toward" (288). Texts don't have to be long to be helpful. In fact, shaping notes into "a one-page statement of [the partners'] purpose and goals" can give the group clarity and focus (288). Use your university's computer capabilities to facilitate the group's composing process, for example, by setting up a listserv to distribute documents among your partners.

This identity kit is an alternative to stock roles from the standard university repertoire: researcher, expert, and committee chair.

In addition to the above identity kit for the WPA-activist, community organizing also identifies meeting literacies required of all partners:

- *Talk:* Conversation is the main vehicle through which community-organizing efforts accomplish their goals. Open Doors relied on talk to elicit the conflicts and to sustain the friendships that permitted the group to conduct its most important work.
- *Listen:* Effective partners listen to others' perspectives. In this vein, Goldblatt listened carefully for the partners' interests in order to represent them in the group's drafts he crafted and circulated.
- *Make time:* Managing time is a literate practice, and community organizing depends on the good will of partners to make time to meet despite the numerous additional pressures pressing down on them.
- *Name and respond to conflicts:* To design a literacy collaborative that will work for all involved, partners should be forthright about the needs of their own organizations and the neighborhoods they served. Conflict spurs creative solutions.
- *Read and respond to text:* By assessing the adequacy of initial drafts and making the necessary revisions, partners reach consensus. The final document was one of the most valuable outcomes of the Open Doors Collaborative, "giving concrete expressions to the problems and possible solutions [. . . that] could apply to neighborhood literacy centers" (290).
- *Share expertise:* Partners' perspectives on the needs of their neighborhoods constitute valuable expertise. In addition, partners have experience running a range of projects and organizations, as well as securing funds from various sources—knowledge that serves their own organizations and can strengthen a joint project such as Open Doors.

Goldblatt capitalizes on the familiarity of talk, text, and time to commend the community-organizing effort to other compositionists.

Rhetorical Invention: Transforming Problems into Issues for Action

For the community-organizing effort, rhetorical invention is an indirect and protracted process of securing consensus, a by-product of three processes: forming relationships, building capacity, and communicating across institutional boundaries.

Forming Relationships. In stark contrast to Habermas's version of the public sphere, where citizens bracketed their personal interests and differences in order to deliberate for the common good, for the community-organizing effort self-interests pose "a potent weapon in the development of co-operation and identification of the group welfare" (Alinsky qtd. in Goldblatt 282).[3] Forming relationships means cultivating group trust so that conflict can spur creative solutions. Often, what is in conflict is whether the plan on the table adequately responds to the needs of the various neighborhoods that the partners represent. When action is the end goal, conflict means making hard choices. For instance, at one point, Open Doors's partners decided against submitting a grant proposal, despite the group's investment in it. Though difficult and possibly quite costly, the decision bore respect for the partners' conflicting positions on how to move their work forward.

Building Capacity. Open Doors built capacity by asking adults from the partners' community organizations to test and to refine project ideas—a process similar to the participatory institutional design that Grabill commends in *Community Literacy Programs and the Politics of Change.* Community organizing builds capacity in two ways. First, the process builds the leadership capacity of the individual learners who critique a plan's design and offer feedback to the program directors responsible for its implementation. Second, the process ensures that a literacy project's design is aligned with participants' own needs and interests. Quite simply, literacy projects attuned to participants' needs and goals are more likely to build the capacity of learners seeking their services (Grabill, *Community* 125). For instance, Goldblatt and his partners consulted a woman named Isabel to better understand the obstacles that formal education poses for adult non-native English speakers in North Philly. They designed Open Doors to serve the interests of adult learners like her. In addition, they asked another woman named Lourdes to test the idea of the community educator, a role that introduced her to Goldblatt's students at Temple University.

Communicating Across Institutional Boundaries. Communicating across institutional boundaries means putting the university in its place and keeping it there—but making sure it is a player, all the while. Goldblatt and his colleague entered the Open Doors Collaborative as leaders eager to engage with others in the community without having to call the shots. Communicating across institutional boundaries enacts "a new model" for neighborhood-based literacy projects, "one that comes from neighborhoods and draws on the university without being controlled by its demands" ("Alinsky's Reveille" 284). The promise of communicating across borders is the power of institutional leverage: the ability to do more together than alone.

Implications

1. *Gatekeeping isn't the only discourse available to social workers. Community organizing redeems the discourse of the public worker by orienting it toward social justice.*

Unlike Quayville's gatekeepers whom Cushman documented perpetuating social injustices by degrading those who sought social services, the public servants in Goldblatt's study were already committed to social justice. Although Open Doors's community leaders oversaw the very kinds of literacy centers and community groups whose leadership Cushman critiques in *The Struggle and the Tools,* never does Goldblatt question their ability to translate their "undying good humor" and "fierce commitment to social justice" into meaningful social action ("Alinsky's Reveille" 286). Instead, Goldblatt's respect for his community partners resonates with Joseph Harris's insight "that non-profits [. . .] help maintain some of the last remaining public spaces in our culture that are not directly sponsored by government or corporations" (16).

Goldblatt shows that not all social workers rely on the reductive schemas that plague gatekeeping encounters. Institutional constraints like those that confined Quayville's public workers also put pressure on community leaders in North Philly. Yet even before Goldblatt caught up with them, Manuel had made time to talk to Johnny about a liberatory vision for literacy education. Committed to building leadership capacity, they overtly rejected the idea of residents as needy recipients of human services. Rather than critiquing community leaders' motivations or efficacy, Goldblatt took his cues from them. In fact, their standards set the bar for his engagement.[4]

Goldblatt reminds educators to be humble and judicious in their assessments of the social workers whom they meet while forging university-community connections. In fact, we get the sense that what makes this deeper level of community organizing so enjoyable is the chance to experience first hand the synergy that phrases such as *distributed expertise, multiple intelligences,* and *community intellectualism* attempt to capture. In relation to Open Doors, *distributed expertise* captures nicely the different types of knowledge and kinds of practices that the partners brought to the table—all of it necessary, none of it sufficient (cf. Engeström *Interactive Expertise*). In educational contexts, *multiple intelligences* is Howard Gardner's phrase for the full spectrum of human competences; in relation to Open Doors, the phrase is a fitting description of the humor, compassion, understanding, and analysis that energized the group. In relation to Open Doors, *community intellectualism* underscores hooks and West's point that some of the most dynamic, thoughtful, informed, and interesting people of our day have made the welfare of their neighborhoods the focus of their lifework.

2. *Local public discourse gives rise to various kinds of conflicts. While conflict may destabilize a group's equilibrium, not all types of conflict are destructive, and under the right leadership some prompt discovery and change.*

Personality conflicts can destabilize a local public in destructive ways. You'll recall from chapter 5 that Heller in *Until We are Strong Together* depicts conflict as something to be absorbed—diminished or minimized. In contrast, for a community-organizing effort, conflict is a resource that partners negotiate to reach a consensus that is responsive to the diverse interests they represent. Likewise, conflict-driven consensus was central to Open Doors's collaborative process, work that led "to stronger final projects than anything that any of the partners could have devised in our offices alone" (Goldblatt, "Alinsky's Reveille" 284).

3. *As a local public, a community-organizing effort has merit in its own right—not on the basis of the group's longevity or the funding it secures to implement its plans—but because it provides an opportunity for people to work together toward a shared purpose.*

Open Doors does not offer a model for sustaining local public life. The partnership "broke up" after meeting for a year and a half (Goldblatt, "Alinsky's Reveille" 290). Within that time, it was not able to fund its two-part strategy for literacy education. Yet, measuring the success of Open Doors on the basis of its ability to secure funding is a lot like measuring a community resident's agency on whether she enrolled in college as a consequence of her admissions interview or secured an apartment as a result of the specific decisions she made completing a housing application—a judgment Cushman counters in *The Struggle and the Tools*. Assessing local publics like Open Doors calls for a more nuanced understanding of the rhetoric of public work.

Valuing local publics as potential sites of "actually existing democracy" is a good first step. As a local public, a community-organizing effort has merit because it engages people across institutions in a democratic process of discovery and change. Most relevant is not how long the partnership lasts or the resources it secures—though partners may certainly welcome longevity and funding. For instance, Goldblatt regards Open Doors "not as a failure but a long-term investment in helping neighborhood leaders identify problems related to literacy and work toward local solutions [. . .]" ("Alinsky's Reveille" 291). To accept this argument is to put democratic values before short-term accountability, people and process before products and results (284).

Scholarship in the area of institutional writing assessment can push our appraisal of Open Doors still further by posing additional questions:

- What did the members of the group *learn* that affected their future practice, including Goldblatt's teaching?
- Who *benefited* and how? (cf. Faber 58)

Such questions don't devalue the democratic potential of a local public, but they do prompt us to identify who benefits from the collaborative and in what ways. These are evaluative questions similar to those that Charles Bazerman poses in a hypertext using activity theory to consider "the vexed problem" of assessing writing (428). Comparing Open Doors to institutional writing assessment suggests the following starting points:

- The Open Doors partners were expert learners engaged in the activity of writing. As such, it makes sense that they would disband when they had finished learning what it was that brought them together—in this case, a vision for a literacy initiative that would serve their diverse interests.

- Because of the multiple community organizations involved, the Open Doors Collaborative was the nexus of multiple institutional interests, making assessment in some ways even more complicated than it is in university settings where fewer institutions may stake a claim in assessment results.
- Funding is one among many legitimate measures of community-university effectiveness. Like high-stakes testing, it looms large given the current political landscape, but funding is more accurately understood as one among many ways that a partnership circulates resources.

In keeping with Bazerman's argument about writing assessment, Goldblatt shows that writing makes activity "visible" so it can be "counted" (Bazerman 428). By channeling so much of his energy toward writing, Goldblatt demonstrates the evidentiary function that writing plays when creating a community-university partnership. He also demonstrates how a rhetor in residence can help a group both to read a complex rhetorical situation and to manage often complicated power dynamics. This view of assessment does not eliminate the need for outcomes or resolve the difficulty of respecting process while producing effective results. But it does challenge us, as rhetoricians, to hone our abilities to track how texts and practices do in fact circulate and to talk convincingly about processes of circulation with other stakeholders—including funding officers.

4. *Local publics pose options—not prescriptions—for democratic practice.*

Democracy is never a done deal, nor are local publics necessarily democratic entities. Local publics are like formal publics in this regard. As Iris Young observed: "Democracy is not an all-or-nothing affair, but a matter of degree; societies can vary in both the extent and the intensity of their commitment to democratic practice" (*Inclusion* 5).[5] But there's more to democracy than its ephemeral nature. There are also alternative ways to enact it, and images of local public life call attention to some of these options. The community-organizing effort commends two options for enacting democratic practices: "working from the bottom up" and using three processes (building capacity, forming relationships, and communicating across institutional boundaries) to forge consensus (Goldblatt, "Alinsky's Reveille" 280, 284). But even such a commitment poses further alternatives. Consider, for instance, the commitment to work from the bottom up. For the community-organizing effort, working from the bottom up means forging part-nerships with community leaders who know intimately the needs of neighborhood residents whose interests they represent. In the next im-age, this principle poses another option: to drawing everyday people (not only community leaders representing their interests) into joint inquiry with other partners in the community.

THE COMMUNITY THINK TANK: THE LOCAL PUBLIC SPHERE IN FLOWER'S "INTERCULTURAL KNOWLEDGE BUILDING: THE LITERATE ACTION OF A COMMUNITY THINK TANK"

In Flower's "Intercultural Knowledge Building," the local public is the community think tank that brings together a diverse mix of people to deliberate pressing social issues so that—having returned to their own spheres of influence—they may create options that are responsive to the life experiences and social circumstances of others. From 1999 to 2001, approximately fifty people participated in one or another of the think tank's roundtable sessions, typically held at the Community House, home of the CLC. The community think tank offers an in-quiry-based, deliberative process that participants use to frame open questions as a community, to elicit multiple perspectives, and to put those perspectives into generative dialogue and text.

Distinctive Features: Diversity, Conflict, and Tools

The community think tank is diverse and conflicted—demanding features for both the activist rhetorician designing a think tank and the people participating in its sessions. The think tank brings together for a single afternoon a diverse group of people who may be mak-ing one another's acquaintance for the first time. Consequently, rather than capitalizing on the pleasure that partners derive from working together over time, the think tank invests in tools that let a diverse group of people work together as "an intercultural body of problem solvers" (Flower, "Intercultural Knowledge" 244).

Diversity. Diversity refers not only to ethnic and economic differences among the fifteen to twenty-five people participating in a given think-tank roundtable session, but also to the diversity of people's roles and to the diversity of domains they represent. In contrast to an elite think tank whose policy analysts' credentials are their degrees from Harvard or Yale and their former experiences at the White House or Brookings Institution (Stone 2), the community think tank creates new knowledge by tapping the diverse experiences that participants have had with the problem at hand—whether as "urban employees and community workers [. . . or] business managers, social agency staff [or] policy makers" (Flower, "Intercultural Knowledge" 240). The think tank suggests everyone's perspective is valuable, that "the contribution of the inner city youth worker [. . . is] as critical as the perspective of a CEO" (245). In the crucible of collaborative inquiry, diversity has the rhetorical power to elicit, elaborate, qualify, complicate, and complement other ways of knowing the problem—and, in the process, to contribute to a more realistically complex understanding of the shared problem, as well as to an expanded set of options for wise, responsive action.

Conflict. Conflict is "buil[t] into the very structure" of the community think tank's design (Flower, "Intercultural Knowledge" 250). First, the issues of race, class, and economics that it raises are controversial and conflicted ones. For instance, a think tank on urban employment issues brought "open recognition of systemic racial, social and economic problems into the practical discussion of management and performance" (250). In addition, the community think tank "enfranchises" alternative interpretations of the problem at hand, recognizing that while problem representations are "interconnected" they are not readily reconciled (248). Even the discourse expectations people bring to the experience are in conflict. It's not just the "conflict and tension" between competing discourses (Gee 8). In addition, these discourses carry histories of "mutual incomprehensibility" (Flower, "Intercultural Knowledge" 250) and "suspicion of motives" (251). The think tank's response—asking everyone to suspend familiar discourses and stock responses to construct an alternative discourse for intercultural inquiry—pushes people from their comfort zones even as it dispels some competition among their default discourses. In that the community think tank "reorganizes normal patterns of communication and authority," it also poses an unknown that's likely to make some people initially uncomfortable—another source of potential conflict (245).

Tools. Conflict has the potential to "derail[. . .] learning, degrad[e] performance, and thwart[. . .] communication" (Flower, "Intercultural Knowledge" 254). This ever-present threat makes the community think tank's third distinctive feature a necessity: its tools. Without tools that participants use to build an alternative discourse for collaborating together, the odds are stacked against the community think tank engaging people in civil dialogue, let alone in the demanding process of constructing "more workable policies and operational action plans" (240). As interventions, tools shape its practice of inquiry. The community think tank's most powerful tool is performance. For example, at the beginning of story-behind-the-story sessions reported in "Intercultural Knowledge Building," college students read the scripts they had composed from critical incident interviews, described below. Likewise, a union president played the role of the bewildered new hire, and a human resource manager dramatically enacted the buddy system gone awry. Performances such as these harness the power of dramatization to focus attention on a real problem. Additionally, tools include the documents that arrive in participants' mailboxes prior to a think-tank session, the problem-solving strategies that the table leaders describe and model, and the table tents and crib sheets that nudge participants to assume the roles of collaborative problem solvers. Tools let a diverse group of people "spend[. . .] its energy imagining genuine, workable options" (254) rather than swapping rehearsed stories or falling into the "discourse of complaint and blame" (250).

The Community Think Tank in Context: Location and Legacy

As a local public, the community think tank is located in the history of its methods and Flower's social cognitive theory of literate action.

Location. Location matters to the community think tank in that it addresses a wide range of decidedly urban issues. In addition, its design can be adapted and exported to a range of contexts.[6] Elsewhere, Flower has treated the politics of location in relation to "community languages, such as black English vernacular" ("Partners" 97); "multiple forms of expertise" (Peck, Flower and Higgins 210), and "relationships of power and distrust" ("Talking Across Difference" 39). In

"Intercultural Knowledge Building," the location that matters most is the location of the think tank's method within the institutional history of the CLC. Over the course of this history, the community think tank's central practice was developed, namely the community problem-solving dialogue.[7] As Flower explains, from the CLC's "distinctive mix of street-wise and research-based literate action" emerged its central method: "a strategy for structured, intercultural dialogue" ("Intercultural Knowledge" 245). Flower and her think-tank team then turned the community problem-solving dialogue "to a new purpose, bringing business, policy, and neighborhood 'experts' together into a more sustained and interactive dialogue on timely urban problems" (245).

Legacy. To make a case for intercultural inquiry as an intellectually demanding and decidedly social act of public engagement, the community think tank brings together three intellectual traditions: Deweyan pragmatism, the rhetorical tradition of public deliberation, and social cognitive rhetoric. Together, these traditions inform intercultural inquiry as a public practice.

> *Deweyan pragmatism.* Many of the decisions that everyday people make on a daily basis—including the conditions that frame these decisions and the consequences that follow from them—are sites of legitimate public concern. In terms of the community think tank's workforce-workplace-worklife issues, this goes for the human resource manager who implements an on-the-job training program, a new hire choosing whether to ask for help or go it alone, co-workers on the floor responding to the new hire, and the policy makers legislating regional welfare-to-work requirements. According to Dewey, such decision points are sites of knowing where one puts one's best or favored hypotheses about how the world works to the test of experience, "a process of undergoing" (Dewey, "Need" 25). These "undergoings" provide data that people then use to refine their understandings of situations. Orienting themselves in the midst of problems, people use their "critical intelligence" to expand their opportunities by better gauging the conditions and consequences of their choices (*Characters* 378–431). The ability to engage problems in the world and to use data to refine one's understandings of those

problems—that's what Dewey called "an experimental way of being" ("Quest" 132).[8]

Public deliberation. The think tank enters the debate over public deliberation around the question: "who is at the table and what discourse is sitting at the head?" (Flower, "Intercultural Knowledge" 251). To answer this question, Habermas harkened back to Enlightenment-era Europe and invoked a model of disinterested rational argument. In the "coffee houses, the salons and the cafes of middle class society," educated, propertied men debated issues of "common interest" (Flower, "Intercultural Knowledge" 252). As Donald Abelson and Evert Lindquist describe, the contemporary prestige think tank operates largely according to this model, as evidenced by its selective invitation list, its prestige discourse (argument) and the singular voice that authorizes its publications. There are, however, problems with this model. The citizens deliberating in Habermas's public sphere were not so disinterested after all, for the "common interest" of a sheltered, homogeneous elite "excludes the concerns of women, the working class, and disenfranchised minorities" (Flower, "Intercultural Knowledge" 252). And, as discussed in chapter 3, the model doesn't reflect how "democracy actually works" (Flower "Intercultural Knowledge" 252).

In contrast, the community think tank offers an "alternative model of public discourse" concerned not with "theorizing an ideal" but letting the discourse of local vernacular publics "do[. . .] its work" (Flower, "Intercultural Knowledge" 252). To participate in the "untidy communicative practices" of everyday public life (Hauser, *Vernacular* 55), there's no requirement that participants should bracket their differences. "There are instead people with diverse interests—and emotions and commitments—who are drawn together around an issue" (Flower, "Intercultural Knowledge" 252). Thus, it is the rhetorical exigency of a shared problem that draws stakeholders together as a public. Borrowing Hauser's lens to locate a public for a workplace problem, Flower writes: "Melissa [a new hire], the manager who hires her, the co-workers who support and suffer her actions, and the legislator who mandates the work-to-welfare program are *all drawn together into a public*" (252, emphasis added).

The community think tank operates within a counter tradition of public discourse, one that dates back to fifth century sophists who knew argumentation wasn't the only rhetorical game in town. Sophistic rhetoric, like the pragmatism governing the community think tank's design, "seek[s] the basis for wise judgments and prudent actions" over internally consistent arguments, explanatory accounts, or novel insights (Flower, "Intercultural Knowledge" 280). Thus, claims and evidence are two in a wide "array of knowledge-making moves," including narrative, cultural value judgments, and personal priorities that "puts knowledge building in the hands of ordinary people" (271). Efforts to evaluate the think tank would look for ways that the knowledge it produces actually changes everyday practice, or when it—in Engeström's words—"transform[s . . .] social structures from below" (qtd. in Flower, "Intercultural Knowledge" 271).[9]

Given Pittsburgh's "intercultural context, with its deep-rooted cultural conflicts and history of social injustice" (Flower, "Intercultural Knowledge" 271), Flower finds Engeström's criterion for transformational knowledge compelling, but also "rather vague" (271). To account for change in everyday practice and for the contribution that intercultural inquiry makes to this process, Flower turns to social cognitive rhetoric.

Social cognitive rhetoric. For Flower, change in everyday practice is evidence of a social cognitive phenomenon, at once intellectually demanding and socially situated. People change their practices as a result of having "restructured" their "understanding" of the related problem (Flower, "Intercultural Knowledge" 243). People build mental representations of a problem, and these flexible, mutable multi-modal mental networks can direct people's decision making and actions (cf. Flower, *Construction* 36–84). Mental representations are participants' working theories of a problem—dynamic accounts of not only what causes the problem and the conditions that create it, but also who the players are and how to respond to it (cf. Flower, *Construction* 260–62). The community think tank creates significant public knowledge when it informs—even transforms—the working theories that participants use to represent shared cultural problems as options for action.

Tenor of the Discourse: Prophetic—Principled and Inventive

West's prophetic pragmatism orients the community think tank in its distinctive register. Prophetic pragmatism calls readers "to identify the causes of injustice and social misery and organize morally activated collaborative action against them" (Flower, "Intercultural Knowledge" 257). In West, Flower finds expression of a distinctive temperament: the problem-posing stance and democratic faith that characterizes the black freedom struggle.[10] For Flower, the question is, *what are the actual discursive moves that enact such temper, such faith?* She contends people enact such democratic faith when they strike the strong rival-hypothesis stance.

Remember that imaginary recording device that tapped the hidden transcripts of Quayville's gatekeeping encounters in chapter 6? Its value was its capacity to record conflicting perspectives, whereby upholding the democratic (if often unrealized) potential of gatekeeping encounters to negotiate alternative perspectives. A similar device would be helpful here, one also attuned to competing—even conflicting—perspectives. But this device wouldn't be attuned to dueling dualities. In fact, the community think tank is designed to circumvent the tendencies of default discourses to pick a fight, to trump the opposition, or—for that matter—to smooth over genuine differences. Rather, the device would record two levels of knowledge building. It would record the *external sounds* of social engagement among think-tank participants—the audible turn taking that tape recorders actually did record. (There was one at each table.) It would also record the *internal sounds* of knowledge construction inside and across the minds of the individual think-tank participants. This internal meaning making "matters most" to intercultural inquiry, for this is "the understanding [. . . participants] left with or retained the next morning" and would recall and quite possibly act upon in the future (Flower, "Intercultural Knowledge" 265). Internal knowledge construction is a lively—even noisy—process, for the "voices" operating in individuals' networks of meaning are not tidily bounded but rather overlap, inform, and restructure one another in acts of negotiation (263–65).

Design and Inquiry-Driven Literacies

To construct new knowledge, the community think tank depends upon both *design literacies* that sequence and scaffold the roundtable sessions and *inquiry-driven literacies* that participants use to enact their provisional identities as "an intercultural body of problem solvers" (244).

Design Literacies. Design literacies craft and orchestrate the processes, events, and documents required to construct a community think tank and to document the knowledge it creates. For the sake of comparison with the knowledge activist's identity kit, I use the second person:

- *Research the problem:* Do the groundwork for participants' deliberation by conducting critical incident interviews with those who have first-hand knowledge of the problem at hand. Use these interviews to augment the conventional literature review of academic analysis. Listen for and uncover "competing representations of the problem" (Flower, "Intercultural Knowledge" 254). Based on this analysis of "live issues" and "locally grounded data" (255), craft a prototypical problem scenario and a set of decision points to serve as discussion starters for upcoming roundtable sessions.

- *Design materials to scaffold inquiry.* Craft a briefing book to feature the problem scenario and decision points discovered earlier, including "strong 'rival readings' of its problematic events" (Flower, "Intercultural Knowledge" 255). Use white space, lines, columns, and bullets as visual cues to invite participants' written responses and to guide their interpretations, comparisons, and discussion. Design additional materials to scaffold inquiry during roundtable sessions, including "a crib sheet on dialogue strategies" and the script for the table leader to read to introduce rival-hypothesis thinking and the goals of intercultural inquiry (259).

- *Sequence intercultural inquiry:* Orchestrate a series of sessions that invite "a diverse body of people" to engage with one another at different points in the inquiry process. After coordinating critical incident interviews, plan, prepare, and hold Story Behind the Story sessions to hear how these different stakeholders interpret "'what is happening' in the scenario," followed by Decision Point sessions that "shift the focus to choices, decisions, and action" (255). Finally, support participants to hold their own *Local Action Think Tanks* back in their home organizations as the union president did when he held an inquiry into "the organization's flawed promotion process" (279).

- *Document knowledge building:* Use notes and tape recorders to keep track of participants' insights during Story Behind the Story sessions; then formalize that knowledge in a document called *Findings.* Design the document to remind participants of what they discussed—so that "it clarifies, consolidates, and invites reflection" (266). As you design this text, also keep another group of readers in mind: participants' "colleagues, Local Action sites, Internet readers" (266). An inventive "mix of narrative, argument, evidence, testimony, and practical plans" provides a culturally appropriate way to talk to such readers about the issue at hand while inviting readers to negotiate and integrate rival perspectives from the text for themselves (255). Finally, circulate the *Findings* to other readers and organizations.

At their best, design literacies spur individuals to rethink how they understand a problem and coordinate this process for an entire group. Design literacies also pull other readers into the process of negotiated meaning making by dramatizing "critical features" of the problem at hand, "conditions under which [an option] might work out—or unravel[, . . .] possible outcomes and predictable problems" (272).

Participants' Inquiry-driven Literacies. The strong rival-hypothesis stance is a complex and demanding intellectual practice that requires participants to be able to elicit the local knowledge that participants use to interpret the problem at hand, to use difference to expand understanding, and to explore options for action.[11] These rhetorical capacities create the alternative discourse that the community think tank uses to produce its knowledge. Specific strategies for developing these capacities include:

- *Critical Incidents.* Capitalizing on narrative as a resource for interpreting complex problems, these paradigmatic problem scenarios elicit carefully contextualized accounts of how people actually experience phenomena such as workforce development and urban health care. Participants' richly situated interpretations of these incidents allow for a dynamic interchange.

Composed in text, critical incidents translate lived experiences into tangible resources for sustained joint inquiry.

- *Story Behind the Story.* The story-behind-the-story strategy supports narrative-based problem analysis by asking participants to narrate the "movies of the mind" they may call upon to interpret a complex situation. The strategy reveals a logic invaluable to deliberative inquiry: the hidden logic of often unspoken motives, values, and assumptions that people use to interpret complex situations. Once articulated and shared, hidden logic permits other stakeholders to grasp the interpretative power of cultural knowledge other than their own (Flower, "Talking Across Difference" 40).

- *Rivaling.* Rivaling asks participants to imagine alternative interpretations of a question, conflict, or problem. Rivaling seeks not some quick around-the-table inventory of positions, but rather a range of responses to an issue and the reasons behind them. Rivaling often takes the form of talking back to characters to imagine alternative arguments. In putting difference into dialogue, rivaling does not suggest that one appraisal would ultimately prevail over the others but rather that participants, as decision makers, need to develop working theories of the problem that are robust enough to acknowledge these rival concerns. Rivaling also asks participants to seek out differences and gaps in their interpretation and experience in order to critically assess and expand their own knowledge of a problem. It means acknowledging counter claims that qualify and or set conditions on one's favored interpretation.

- *Options and Outcomes.* The community think tank provides scaffolding that helps participants generate specific options that emerge from their carefully situated analysis. To draw people into this deliberative process and to focus Decision Point sessions on choices and their consequences, the think tank teaches the options-and-outcomes strategy. First, this strategy asks participants to generate multiple "real" options—a move designed to counter the common tendency in decision-making to consider only one option and then decide "yes" or "no." Then, because the responses to complex problems often involve trade-offs (that is, there isn't one "good" option), the strategy asks participants to project and to compare possible outcomes, weighing values and the probability of an outcome (Flower, "Intercultural Knowledge" 259). This strategy lets decision makers hear what their decisions might mean in the lives of people affected by them. The test of the decision that a manager or teacher makes rests in its consequences—yet employees or students are often far more able to project accurately those consequences than those in power (260–61).

Interventions like these do not imply that the people who use them are somehow cognitively or culturally deficient. Rather, such scaffolding honors the demanding work of transforming lived experience into new knowledge that serves the aims of problem analysis, collaboration, and argument. These strategies are tools of rhetorical invention, but in the context of intercultural deliberation, they help participants figure out not just what to say but to invent with others the very discourse in which to say it.

Rhetorical Invention: The Construction of Negotiated Meaning

The heartbeat of the community think tank's rhetorical activity is the constructive process of negotiation through which the rhetor transforms conventional practices (such as a training program for new hires) into inventive and purposeful literate action. Here, *negotiation* and *conflict* are theoretical terms whose features have been named, identified, and made operational for the purpose of rhetorical analysis and theory building (cf. Flower, *Construction* 55). Negotiating conflict is the rhetorical work demanded of rhetors who deliberate over interpretations of a shared problem. According to negotiation theory, *conflicts* shape meaning making in the form of "multiple 'voices' or forms of knowledge" (Flower, "Intercultural Knowledge" 243). These voices include "the *live* voices" of those at the think tank roundtable and also "the *internal* voices of personal intention, knowledge and emotion, and the *internalized* dictates of convention, language, and ideology" (243). Conflicting voices, for instance, shaped how the African American union president represented the problem of on-the-job training that he deliberated with the human resource manager and policy analyst at his table (243). The conflicts that matter—those that have the potential to shape problem representations—are the ones that people actually attend to as "live options" (243).

Of course, there's no guarantee that the restructured understandings will change the daily choices people make. But as an observation-based account of literate action, negotiation theory offers a plausible explanation of how socially situated individuals make difficult decisions in the face of multiple, internalized, competing public voices. Flower's theory of negotiated meaning posits that participants restructure their understandings when they actively engage competing voices and forms of knowledge. Negotiation lets people build more robust representations of the problem and consequently draw on these revised, enhanced understandings should similar situations arise for them in the future. Through such acts of negotiated meaning making, people challenge the limiting effects of what Pierre Bourdieu has called "habitus"—the socially conditioned attitudes and behaviors that otherwise circumscribe so much of our daily lives (53).

Of all the local publics reviewed in this book, the community think tank takes the most explicit approach to rhetorical invention. Through the table leaders' scripts and the crib sheets on the tables, and the strategies table leaders explicitly teach, the think tank offers adaptive heuristics to help participants tread unfamiliar intercultural waters.

Implications

1. *The Open Doors collaborative and the community think tank represent different appraisals about the best that the field of rhetoric and composition has to offer community partnerships and how to translate that potential into action.*

Goldblatt and Flower agree that mutual and respectful relationships build healthy and sustaining community-university partnerships. In commending the identity of the knowledge activist (Goldblatt) and the intercultural dialogue designer (Flower) to rhet/comp scholars, both commend principled and responsive social identities for fostering such partnerships. Both also demonstrate commitments that outlast the lifespan of a given project.

However, Goldblatt and Flower assess differently the most valuable good that rhet/comp has to offer community partners. For the knowledge activist, the most valuable commodity is the WPA's knowledge of the writing process—a "logic [. . .] resonant [. . .] with [Alinsky's] principles of community organizing" (Goldblatt, "Alinsky's Reveille" 284). The knowledge activist is an expert writer and facilitator of the writing process; thus, he or she also knows how to gauge the group-writing process—when to back off a plan to pursue funding, for instance, in order to cultivate the group's cohesion.

The community think tank designer's expertise is also methodological and requires a good share of writing. But rather than producing a jointly authored text for a small team, the designer prioritizes engaging a larger group of participants in the process of intercultural inquiry and documenting the knowledge they build for these and future readers. For the community think tank designer, the most valuable good that a practicing rhetorician contributes to a community-university partnership is her knowledge of collaborative inquiry, the "ability to elicit and document the intercultural knowledge building of this diverse group" (Flower, "Intercultural Knowledge" 245). Just as the knowledge activist's stance requires choices and trade-offs, so, too, do these design literacies (248), but the goal for the latter is to put difference into generative dialogue, rather than to preserve working friendships in order to reach consensus.

2. *These same judgments (what rhet/comp has to offer community partnerships and how to enact this offer) affect whether we deliberate most with established community leaders or community residents themselves. In a discipline that values writing and deliberating with the community, forums that engage community residents themselves constitute valuable sites of democratic practice.*

For Open Doors, partners' credentials as leaders earn them a seat at the community-organizing table. Credentials refer not to a paper transcript or diploma but to demonstrable leadership skills and know-how that people like Manuel and Johnny have tested and refined over the years by implementing "effective approaches to actual problems" under pressure in distressed communities (Goldblatt, "Alinsky's Reveille" 289).

In contrast, it's everyday people more like Lourdes and Isabel (the ESL learners who tested Open Doors's project design) whom the community think tank invites to the table as experts.[12] Yes, the community think tank included business people, academics, policy analysts, and community leaders at its sessions. But to build relevant new knowledge on workforce-development issues, the experts that the think tank needed most were "people who had 'been there,' on welfare, on the street, or [. . .] 'churning' from one low-paid job to another" (Flower, "Intercultural Knowledge" 250).[13]

The choice between deliberating with established community leaders or ordinary community residents is a significant one. Too often, civic deliberation doesn't involve those whom the deliberation most directly concerns, especially when that constituency is young (Fleming "Subjects") or poor, underemployed, and female (Higgins and Brush). In his study of a campaign to revitalize Cabrini Green in downtown Chicago, David Fleming found public discussions characterized residents of the urban housing project according to predictable *topoi* emphasizing "social disorder": pregnant or truant youth, unfit parents, alcoholic adults ("Subjects" 227). It's not that residents of Cabrini Green weren't aware of these representations or that they fell entirely victim to them, but that the discourses in which residents represented themselves were "marginal in the overall discussion" (238). Furthermore, these representations cast residence as "consumers of government services'" rather than "as citizens in a political sense, individuals empowered to participate fully in the collective self-determination of their city" (238). As Iris Young and Gerard Hauser warn, in a democracy, forums in which diverse mixes of everyday people deliberate over shared social problems are as necessary as they are problem ridden. The community think tank is a counterexample of the trend Fleming observes. As activist rhetoricians, we do well to help design and structure forums where everyday citizens deliberate with one another over pressing social issues.

3. *Creating a local public depends on the way institutions (community centers, public schools, universities, city offices) are drawn into the process of public making, offering needed space, money, people, and validation. However, sponsorship can also change the sponsor.*

Organic images of local publics—the garden and womb—stress sponsors who provide material resources to create welcoming spaces for participants. The community think tank extends this idea of sponsorship by providing a forum and a sequence of events that upset people's expectations and draw them into a new kind of discourse. It also provides evidence that sponsorship can change the sponsor.

When graduate students at CMU's school of public policy enlisted the community think tank model to hold a conference on imminent changes in welfare policy, their project replaced the traditional meeting of black and white civic leaders with a ballroom full of people—including a large contingent of women on welfare—who were engaged in direct deliberation on better options with researchers, policy makers, government officials, and social workers (cf. Flower, "Intercultural Knowledge" 252–53). It produced a substantive report and—contrary to a dean's preconception of "community" events—a substantive discussion (cf. Higgins, Long, and Flower 19).

The community think tank offers deliberative intercultural inquiry as a performative rhetoric that needs to be structured and modeled if we, as activist rhetoricians, hope to create viable alternatives to the more prevalent interest-group discourse and false consensus.

4. A local public doesn't have to reconcile conflict—to absorb difference—to constitute a viable forum. In fact, when a local public encodes difference in the texts it circulates, the dynamism among conflicting perspectives can pull new readers into the problem space and get them to negotiate conflicting voices for themselves, possibly extending their understanding of the problem at hand.

The community think tank sets out to elicit and to document difference—and to challenge participants to manage and to accommodate differences for themselves. Furthermore, the think tank's *Findings* compile conflicting perspectives, following a decision point and several options with blocks of text capturing the rival commentary of an employee, a federal policy analyst, a human resource manager, and an educator. Although these pages of working theory don't conform to the conventions of rationalist argument, the knowledge presented here has a "complexity and coherence" of its own as a contingent plan for action (Flower, "Intercultural Knowledge" 268).

The role of conflict in community life is often misunderstood. For instance, Patricia Roberts-Miller argues that theories informing compositionists' understandings of discourse communities prioritize *agreement-expression* over *disagreement-deliberation,* leading educators to interpret conflict and dissension as bad because they threaten a cohort's unity and cohesion. This misunderstanding comes at a high cost: "To the extent that a theory (or pedagogy) assumes that a good community has minimal conflict it is almost certain to founder on the problems of inclusion and difference" (545). For the think tank, community is symbolic, forged in the act of deliberation and among an inherently diverse group of people. Moreover, conflict—in tandem with the necessary scaffolding—transforms understanding and changes everyday practices. Local publics like the community think tank test the field's emerging theories about conflict, deliberative local publics, and the texts they circulate. Unlike Open Doors's vision statement, the think tank's *Findings* is not a decision document or policy statement. Rather, it asks people who are decision makers both in their own lives and on the job to take their experience with collaborative inquiry and the options proposed in the *Findings* back into arenas where they have choices to make. Ultimately, rather than offering a solution, the think tank and the findings it produces pose the question, *How can you create options in your own spheres of influence that are responsive to the life experiences and social circumstances of others?*

5. *Local knowledge is a resource with a market value that some entrepreneurial local publics mine to sustain themselves.*

The community think tank further capitalizes on local knowledge, arguing that the ability of intercultural inquiry to elicit and to document local knowledge makes it "a significant, but significantly underused tool for addressing the really pressing problems" (Flower, "Intercultural Knowledge" 245). Flower used this argument to secure the think tank's initial funding. Flower's success in securing monetary support is one example of local knowledge's market value; the youth organizations featured in Art*Show* is another (Flower and Heath). The organizations portrayed in Art*Show* market teens' dramatic productions to "juvenile detention centers, parent support groups, drug and alcohol rehabilitation programs, schools, and the city's convention planning center" to purchase as programs for their clientele (Flower and Heath 48).[14] Sure, other expert consultants offer programs covering similar content—on the dangers of drug use or other "hot topics" at a given time. Art*Show*'s competitive advantage, however, is the teenaged actors' and producers' local knowledge—in this case, situated rhetorical knowledge for crafting technical information in accurate and compelling ways and for leading teen-based discussions on this information. Underwriting "the energy, imagination and knowledge of local youth" makes sense, write Flower and Heath (48). "[S]uch pay amounts to a community organization investment, for the fees go back into the nonprofit organization to enable them to sustain their work over several years without being donor dependent" (Flower and Heath 49).[15]

6. *Future theory-building efforts in community-literacy studies will need to articulate the rhetorics of sustainability that currently circulate quite tacitly within the literature. In the process, such rhetorics will set competing commitments to outcomes, institutional relationships, and social action in relation to one another.*

Competing images of local public life pose a quandary for activist rhetoricians who want to contribute to the future of local democracy. One familiar frame would cast the problem in terms of *sustainability*. Yet even framing the topic this way privileges an institutional interpretation of the activity when, in fact, a whole set of nested alternatives are available. Consider, for instance, some of the alternatives featured in this book: Do community-university partners do best to prioritize an ever-growing network of *relationships* in the faith that they will mobilize in response to exigencies that arise in the future? Is it these relationships that we should be trying to nurture (cf. Goldblatt "Alinsky's Reveille"; Mathieu *Tactics*)? Or should we, instead, focus on circulating broader, more inclusive attitudes toward literacies—what literacy means and how it is practiced? Is it this *conversation* about literacy on which we should set our sights (cf. Comstock)? Or should partners focus on pooling rhetorical expertise to support community-based agencies that, in turn, sponsor local publics? That is, is the problem of sustainability primarily an *institutional* concern for material resources, institutional interests, and social capital (cf. Cushman, "Sustainability"; Grabill *Community Literacy*)? If this is the case, we would do well to prioritize processes of research, methods, and outcomes. Or is the top priority *rhetorical engagement* on pressing social issues? If this is the case, what kinds of rhetorical interventions are up to the challenge of helping everyday people bridge the cultural differences that otherwise threaten to keep us apart (Faber; Flower "Knowledge Building"; Flower and Heath)?

This is not the first time members of the field have ventured into the complicated terrain of competing options that must be negotiated. For instance, doing so resembles negotiating the competing goals for empowerment—focused on "political, rhetorical, and intercultural outcomes"—that are central to *Latino/a Discourses: On Language, Identity and Literacy Education*. In the *tertulia* concluding the collection of essays, Flower warns, "[I]t rarely helps to think we can focus on just one [form of power], and the other forms of power will tag along" (131). Likewise, chapter 9 in this volume examines strong conflicts and contradictions among classroom practices associated with public writing. In sum, effective writing partnerships are rarely a matter of ecumenical melding of available options for writing *in, for,* or *with* the community as suggested in Joseph Harris's review of *Writing Partnerships.* Rather, goals for local public life reflect distinct working theories. So even when we attempt to honor a rich set of values and priorities, the different conceptions of local public life and what it is good for can not be readily reconciled.

There is another wrinkle. The material realities of local publics place us in terrain that we aren't necessarily accustomed to traversing as educators. That is, whether or not I wrestle with problems of textbook prices, tuition, student retention, state legislation, or overhead costs, students will likely show up in my sufficiently equipped classroom each September with books in tow. Because of a whole host of arrangements that transpire without much involvement on my part, it can feel as though *classrooms happen.* The same can not be said of the local publics featured in this chapter. For all their symbolic and rhetorical richness, these local publics also depend upon material conditions that activist rhetoricians help supply.

Furthermore, the decision to privilege a given goal for local public life—say, rhetorical engagement—often depends on having met institutional and relational goals which entails either attending to these goals behind the theory-building scene or having others within the writing partnership willing and equipped to nurture relationships, to secure funding streams, and to forge institutional partnerships. (It is this capacity for parallel processing, I believe, that made Wayne Peck, Linda Flower, Lorraine Higgins, and Joyce Baskins such a powerhouse in the late 1980s when they established the CLC.)

These nests of competing goals are evident in how Goldblatt and Flower approach the task of theory building. What Goldblatt foregrounds, Flower treats as background information. That is, while "Alinsky's Reveille" documents community leaders' efforts to organize themselves before carefully and deliberately pursuing options for funding, "Intercultural Knowledge Building" makes quick mention of Flower's move to secure financial support by responding to the concerns a funding officer raised about the workforce development issues facing Pittsburgh. As director of CMU's Center for University Outreach, Flower was responsible for securing funding for the Center's initiatives; however, the intellectual, rhetorical work it took to align the necessary resources stays in the background. Instead, Flower builds theory from the activity that happened next when "diversity [. . .] s[at] down at the table" to deliberate over a shared problem ("Intercultural Knowledge" 239).

And yet, it is clear from "Intercultural Knowledge Building" that this rhetoric of engagement, the activity of building intercultural knowledge, and the theoretical value of intercultural inquiry could not exist without the enabling community relations Goldblatt elaborates. In sum, the meaning and significance of Goldblatt's community-organizing effort are ultimately inseparable from the kinds of outcomes the effort generates and its contribution to the academic discourse he works to affect.

But ultimately, for all the responsibility we have to this teleological challenge, it is, ultimately, not ours alone to solve. Instead, taking wise action will depend upon the intelligences and expertise distributed among community intellectuals, as well.

8 The Shadow System: A Local Public that Defies Formal Institutions

In Cintron's *Angels' Town: Chero Ways, Gang Life and Rhetorics of the Everyday,* the local public is a shadow system where everyday people demand respect under conditions that yield little of it. The image of the shadow system organizes Cintron's analysis from the late 1980s to mid-1990s of Angelstown, Cintron's name for an industrial city just west of Chicago. Though the shadow system operated throughout the city's street life, it was particularly intense when street gangs such as the Almighty Latin Kings Nation (or Kings) went public with their demand for respect. This intensity set in relief the contours that distinguish the shadow system as a distinctive local public.

DISTINCTIVE FEATURES: MIMICS AND SHELTERS DIFFERENCE

In mimicking the mainstream culture, or system world, the shadow system protects the difference between itself and the system world, and claims this difference as its identity.

Mimics. The shadow system mocks the system world of the dominant culture. Cintron explains: "[. . . T]he system world is the 'substance' that casts the shadow, a shadow that has the shape but is not equivalent to the system itself" (*Angels' Town* 176). The shadow system flaunts its parody of the system world.

Shelters Difference. The shadow system protects its parody of mainstream culture as its identity, "sheltering and nourishing its guerrilla life against a[n exclusionary] public sphere" (Cintron, *Angels' Town* 176).

The Shadow System in Context: Location
and Cultural Imaginary

Shadow systems emerge where a cultural imaginary is at play, characterized by topoi, fissures, and ruptures.

Location. Location instantiates the cultural imaginary, whereby giving ideology its "muscl[e]" (Cintron, *Angels' Town* 160). The cultural imaginary is the ideological landscape that links cultural forms and the political unconscious to specific material conditions. Above all, the cultural imaginary of Angelstown humiliated those without capital—even as it worked to ensure that their access to capital wouldn't significantly change. To individuals, lack of capital meant "raggedness" (223)—a condition that is itself humiliating in a materialistic culture with a fetish for "the neat and clean" and the "classy and noble" (172–73). To the Latinos of Angelstown, lack of capital meant being shunted to Ward 2, an area of town with one of the lowest property values—a political jurisdiction with limited voice in the local government, little access to the city's resources, and home to several rival street gangs.

Topoi. Topoi are the commonplaces through which ideology structures the interpretative landscape of a given location, creating "a very tight knot of emotion, reality, and ideological interpretation" (Cintron, *Angels' Town* 152). Topoi exist in the culture at large and thus precede any shadow system. They are the fund of cultural meanings from which a shadow system manufactures its own subterranean and esoteric meanings. The rhetorical power of a single topos is its capacity to invoke simultaneously both itself and its opposite. The topoi that dominated the cultural imaginary of both Angelstown's system world and the Kings's shadow system include:

- neat and clean vs. dirt, death and decay
- tame vs. wild
- nation (stability and power) vs. individual (aloneness and fear of chaos)
- inscription vs. erasure
- respect vs. disrespect
- rationality and order vs. madness and disorder

Topoi from the system world provide the basis on which the shadow system constructs its power. Gangs' names such as the Insane Deuce Nation, The Insane Gangster Satan's Disciples Nation, and The Maniac Latin Disciplines Nation played/preyed upon the system world's claims on rationality and the flipside, its terror of the unpredictable, the disorderly, the irrational.

Topoi exert their ideological force by creating a "common sense" interpretation of the way things are. Topoi operating in the Kings's shadow system reinforced a logic of violence, an interpretative scheme based on the topos of disorder and, by extension, the assumption that "life is tough; most people are not to be trusted; always be wary; and defend yourself or get beaten up" (Cintron, *Angels' Town* 154). This is the same logic—based on the same topoi—that the system world of Angelstown (the police, city council and newspaper editorial staff) used to justify the moral high ground from which they judged and punished gang members, as much for the ideological threat they embodied as for the criminal activities they perpetrated. As they operate within the logic of violence, topoi dispel ambiguity and provide a "guiding ethos, in short, a sensible way (in some cases, a guaranteed way) to handle particular problems" (152).

Fissures. Exposing the artifice of the dominant culture, a fissure is a fault line that breaks open when mainstream topoi "fail to inspire" members in the margins of the system world (Cintron, *Angels' Town* 179). For instance, as an "overarching nation," the United States (and the local government for that matter), failed to inspire dedication and sacrifice from the disenfranchised in Angelstown, despite its claims on law and order. In that Angelstown's system world humiliated the Kings, its inability to inspire disenfranchised residents exposed "the chaos that [the nation state's] veneer of continuity, cohesion, stability and power were meant to seal" (179).

Ruptures. Erupting in the cracks of the system world, these ruptures redeem the shadow system; these acts demand respect by defying the system world that humiliates the shadow system. Operating within a logic of violence, ruptures in Angelstown's shadow system redeemed the shadow system by conquering space, appropriating symbols, and demanding respect. For example, a gang ruptured the system world by holding a picnic in the city park for two thousand of its members. "From the perspective of the lifeworld of the gang members, the [picnic] scene was 'righteous' insofar as it asserted a defiant and just empowerment of their nation over and against the system world's more bankrupt authority" (Cintron, *Angels' Town* 180).

TENOR THE DISCOURSE: THREATENING AND HYPERBOLIC

The shadow system exploits the capacity of its discourse to sound different to different audiences. Its exaggerated bravado sounds "unpredictable, menacing and violent" to members of system world who populate "the public sphere," as well as to rival gangs (Cintron, *Angels' Town* 181). The same discourse is the sound of "solidarity and status" to fellow gang members (181).

TACTICAL LITERACIES

Through "artful dodges" a shadow system asserts its presence—both to rival shadow systems and to the outside system world (Cintron, *Angels' Town* 176). The term *tactic* comes from de Certeau's analysis of power: "a tactic is mobile; it makes use of the cracks that appear within the 'surveillance of the proprietary powers. It poaches in them. . . . It can be where it is least expected. It is a guileful ruse . . . an art of the weak'" (qtd. in Cintron 175).[1] The Kings relied on the following tactics:

- *Graffiti:* highly stylized, unlicensed writing through which gangs proclaim *heart*; "a potent street term that conveyed one's courage and love, indeed, one's identity with a particular street gang" (*Angels' Town* 177).
- *Throwing (hand) signs:* the use of hand gestures to assert the presence of one's gang and, conversely, to disrespect rival gangs. For instance, the Kings threw the sign of the crown (holding down the right finger with one's thumb) to assert the gang's central symbol: the crown, proclaiming the "rulership" of the Kings (173).
- *Referencing:* appropriating available cultural material—from colors, clothes, jewelry, tattoos—to signal one's allegiance to a gang, reinforcing its presence and dominance in a given territory.

Of these tactics, graffiti best exploits the capacity to function both as a *tactic of action* and a *tactic of language*. As a tactic of action, graffiti is a transgressive act that seizes property through force and bravado. As a tactic of language, the graffiti asserts discourse into the larger "public sphere" that otherwise would stay contained within the shadow system (175). For instance, the topos of nationhood permeated the letters, speeches, and plans that leaders of the Kings circulated among its members. The Kings's graffiti captured and condensed these "subaltern narratives" of nationhood (themselves manufactured from system world's topoi) and then broadcasted them to the larger public, as in a stretch of graffiti that included an elaborately painted crown and the letters *L* and *K* for Latin Kings (171). To borrow from Warner, tactics exploit the world-making capacity of style.

RHETORICAL INVENTION: CULTURAL APPROPRIATION

Appropriation takes a symbol from the system world and ascribes to it a new meaning that reinforces the internal integrity of the shadow. The shadow system depends on the system world's "cultural material" as its "fund" of meaning (Cintron, *Angels' Town* 167). For instance, the grammar through which the Kings' graffiti disrespected rival gangs was predicated on mainstream "negative morphemes" such as "'non,' 'un,' or 'not'" (169). The act of appropriating a cultural symbol from the system world also renders the symbol incomprehensible to the system world. Consider, for instance, Angelstown's gangs' appropriation of athletic clothing, a Pittsburgh Pirates baseball hat, or a sport jacket from the Iowa Hawkeyes or from the L.A. Kings. Once the clothing had been appropriated from the system world, the emblems and colors no longer referred to corporate sports teams but to street gangs. For instance, five holes left open on a basketball shoe symbolized "five," the ruling number among Kings whose symbolic crown has five points. Cintron observes: "The referencing could be enormously elaborate, the only limit being the inventiveness and willingness of the King" (166). To signal their gang affiliation, members of the Kings appropriated anything from the initials of a sports team to the colors of a jacket or insignia.

IMPLICATIONS

1. *To understand a defiant local public is to understand the potential complexity of its relationships to other publics.*

As a shadow system, the Kings appropriated the system world's symbols as much to insult, impress, and dominate rival gangs as to defy the system world. Cintron observes that young gang members asserted their nationalistic affiliations to a gang not on the basis of politically motivated resistance to the overarching nation state (that education often came later, in prison) but rather in relation to "the increasingly organizational status of rival gang nations" (*Angels' Town* 179). So the tensions among their own and other subaltern publics may be more salient to a shadow system's members than their oppositional relationship to the dominant culture.

This insight is important to community-literacy studies. The term *counterpublic* holds great sway in contemporary discussions of public life (Squires 457–63; Warner 65–124). The term signals the way some local publics shelter oppositional identities and circulate discourses about those identities and interests to other publics (Coogan "Counterpublics"; Flower "Intercultural Knowledge"; Higgins, Long, and Flower). However, Cintron emphasizes that to understand shadow systems in terms of the literature on counterpublics, it's important to attend to the possibly complex (rather than simply dichotomous) relationships among multiple publics, both subaltern and dominant (cf. Squires).

2. *To exclude participants from local public discourse is to limit inquiry into pressing social issues.*

In that gangs commit egregious acts of murder, one could reasonably argue that gang life violates the very premise of civil society, thereby disqualifying gang members from legitimate civil discourse. Cintron himself anticipates and responds to this objection, and he offers three reasons to include street gangs in public discourse:

- To exclude gang members from public discourse is to "demonize" them (*Angels' Town* 224), to cast them as so "barbarous and verminlike, so completely outside the fold of the human community that they deserve to be removed" (166).

- To exclude gang members from public discourse is to reinforce Habermas's ideal public sphere that certifies only an elite to speak. Such a restrictive ideal is not only exclusionary, but it also limits the quality of discourse that a public can generate. Cintron puts it this way: "Within a restricted public sphere, not even contesting parties represent the entire realm of contestation that cycles throughout a society. The breadth and depth of contestation does not become aired partly because not all the varied voices have been certified [. . .]" (175).
- To exclude gang members from public discourse is to ignore the ways in which the larger political and economic forces create the conditions that give rise to gangs and their tactics. In part, exclusion from a public sphere forces marginalized people to develop their own "guerrilla life" and "tactics" in the first place (176). Cintron frames this issue as a question: "How expansive can any participatory democracy be when, lying at the furthest limits of its embrace, there exists criminality that is, at least, partially determined by the same socioeconomic and power differences that give rise to subaltern counterpublics?" (186).

Such arguments were enacted at Pittsburgh's CLC in the 1990s. Among the many things that Mark, Pierre, and other young men at the CLC taught me is that—at least for young men in Pittsburgh at the time—gang membership was not necessarily clear cut. As teenagers, Mark "flirt[ed] with the possibility of joining a gang" (Peck, Flower, and Higgins 199), and Pierre knew first hand how a group of friends could turn to and into a gang "for power and control" (217). Yet because of the situated knowledge and rhetorical prowess that these young men brought to community problem-solving dialogues, their commentaries lifted local public deliberation on issues of risk and respect to a degree other contributors couldn't rival—particularly regarding schools' suspension policies, the police department's racial profiling practices, and the city's curfew policy.

Cintron's interpretative scheme of a shadow system is interesting in its own right. It also helps to illuminate implications that follow from other defiant local publics, such as those included in table 6:

Table 6. A comparison of three defiant local publics.

1. The Guiding Metaphor and Its Features		2. Context and Prominent *topoi*	3. Tenor of the Discourse	4. Literacies	5. Rhetorical Invention
Cintron's shadow system	mimics, shelters difference	a predominantly Latino neighborhood: *respect vs. disrespect*	transgressive / hyperbolic	tactical literacies: e.g., graffiti, throwing signs	cultural appropriation
Gilmore's theater	public, prominent	a public school's playground: *cultured vs. "street"*	nasty / proud	doing steps: e.g., a mock instructional routine	organized competition
Pezzullo's theater	risky, mobile	doorsteps of corporate offices: *detection vs. prevention*	offensive / persuasive	cultural performances: e.g., exposing mastectomy scar	a "circular pattern between the [. . .] social and the stage"

- the local public in Gilmore's 1991 study of literacy achievement in an inner-city public school, where on the playground girls confronted teachers' unsound judgments about them as learners; and
- the local public in Pezzullo's 2003 study of the Toxic Link Coalition (TLC). Parading throughout San Francisco's financial district, the TLC's toxic tour exposed corporations responsible for producing and profiting from cancer-causing chemicals and toxins.

Gilmore's Public Performance. The local public in Gilmore's "'Gimme Room': School Resistance, Attitude, and Access to Literacy" is a discursive site of "public and prominent [. . .] performance" (67). The performances were public in that they transformed a public-school playground into a public space where girls confronted "the school's undermining doubt in their ability" (69) and pleaded for their "right [. . .] as individuals [. . .] to instructional circumstances where pride and ownership are the central features of learning" (69–70). Their exuberance performances pervaded recess, "turn[ing] passersby into audiences" (59).

Teachers and administrators heard the tenor of girls' discourse as "'[n]asty,'" associated with "black 'street'" culture, so they banned the discourse from the playground (Gilmore 65). To the girls, the discourse sounded something closer to collective pride: "[N]ot merely defiant; [. . .] not merely black[, . . . but also] face-saving, a way of maintaining dignity through collective autonomy" (69).

What literate practice could cause such controversy? The girls called it "doing steps," playsongs incorporating rhythmic chants with choreographed movement. The most controversial was "Mississippi," a "mock [. . .] instructional routine" in which a chorus of girls performed the role of "an aggressive and suspicious teacher" who challenges a student to spell the difficult word, *Mississippi* (Gilmore 69). One of the girls would then assume the role of student, "tak[ing] on the dare" with a "swagger" indicating "that the performance is fully within the range of her competencies" (69). What really got the teachers was the sexual undercurrent in the girls' movements. Shaping their bodies into the letters required to spell Mississippi, when steppers came to the letter S, they moved in ways that teachers said looked "'suggestive [. . .] like an orgasm'" (65). The "taboo breaking and sexual innuendo" that Gilmore characterizes as "consistent with tradition in children's folklore" (59) teachers read as evidence of the girls' "sexual experience" (71). On the basis of the "bad attitude" the discourse embodied, girls who "did steps" were banned from the Academic Plus Program. Consequently, "a bright child who might be achieving academically, but whose behavior is characteristic of a 'bad attitude,' would not be admitted" (58).

3. *The gutsy willfulness to lift the veil on the system world's hidden hypocrisies is part of what makes the rhetorical force of a counterpublic so compelling.*

We don't have to venture into gang territory to find fault lines. A fissure is evident, too, in Gilmore's "'Gimme Room.'" As a microcosm for the system world, the school upheld such topoi as:

- white vs. black
- cultured vs. street
- control vs. unruly
- polite vs. bad.

The fault line ruptured when these topoi ceased to inspire girls to suspend their "black street vernacular" in order to learn in school (Gilmore 70). For instance, the teachers' descriptions of stepping exposed the *control*-vs.-*unruly* topoi that infiltrated the school grounds. In those situations when teachers didn't read the performances as sexual, they said the found the steps incomprehensible, "'like nothing I've ever seen before'" and "'like an epileptic fit,'" another "disordered" and "unruly" force that mainstream practices are hard pressed to control (Gilmore 65). Cintron's observation about Angelstown is apt here, as well: "Locate the anxiety of a public sphere, and one will have located the limit for engaging in rational discourse[. . . . A] public sphere can not 'think' beyond what terrifies it" (*Angels' Town* 194). In exposing a fissure in the *control vs. unruly* topoi, the girls exposed one of mainstream culture's worst fears: that not just teachers but society at large will lose control of "threat[ening]" and "aggress[ive]" African American youth (Gilmore 71).

Seizing this fissure, the steppers' shadow system exposed the hypocrisy that mistook decorum for intellectual aptitude and suitability for the Academic Plus Program. In the quote that follows, Cintron is talking about Angelstown's civic response to newspaper coverage of a street-side funeral for gang members, but he could just as well be describing teachers' responses to the girls' steps: "In gobbling up the images, the mainstream felt that it had the evidence that proved the legitimacy of its views" (167). The irony, of course, is that the alleged legitimacy of the teachers' judgment is itself based the logic of violence "in so far as the mainstream positioned itself atop a moral high ground from which to judge and punish" (Cintron, *Angels' Town* 167). Atop this moral high ground, the teachers in Gilmore's study judged and punished students by excluding them from academic enrichment. "Though a good attitude was seen as a means to an end (i.e., literacy achievement), the focus was so intense and exclusive that instructional interaction simply got stuck there" (Gilmore 69). By choosing to do steps on the school playground, the steppers exposed the hypocrisy in their teachers' judgments about them.

4. *As rhetoricians we do well to think carefully about the legacies of vernacular literacies, their consequences, and the possibility of also designing and supporting inventive literacies suited to border crossing.*

Incomprehensibility is the measure of effective appropriation. Steppers successfully appropriated the instructional routine they mocked. Not only were "the words and meaning [of the girls' stepping routines] virtually intelligible" to the teachers, but stepping also hid evidence of the very linguistic competencies the teachers said the students lacked (Gilmore 66). The irony, of course, is that in achieving this feat of appropriation, the children lost out, severed from the resources of a challenging if contrived academic enrichment program.

On the one hand, a reader might anticipate that Gilmore would defend stepping as a practice that kept children in touch with their ethnic heritage, for stepping and other playsongs have a rich tradition in African-America culture (Logan; Richardson; Smitherman). But a mother who read the draft of Gilmore's study rejected this interpretation. Sure, it was racist to associate "polite" with "white" and "black vernacular culture" with "bad" (71). But she emphasized that stepping, its counterpart stylized sulking, and for that matter Gilmore's study itself cast children in reductive roles reminiscent of racist portrayals of African Americans in American history (71).

The mother's insight makes me wonder, *What options did the teachers and administrators at the girls' public elementary school have, besides prohibiting the girls from expressing resistance in the schoolyard?* Fast forward fifteen years, and consider an after-school-program that offers stepping as a formal group activity. To my mind, the program reveals a problematic aspect of appropriation: the system world can readily reappropriate cultural material to serve its own interests. Representing an urban neighborhood organization, a group of young steppers took a thirty-mile bus trip in the spring of 2006 to perform publicly at the college where I was then teaching. On the one hand, seeing so many kids exert so much of the same energy at the same time and in the same space was fun to watch. But performed on the stage of a college auditorium, stepping lost much of its rhetorical force. It was the pervasive groupthink that got me, kids chanting in unison a message that in light of Gilmore's essay could only sound ironic: "Take away all these wonderful teachers, and who will teach me?" and "Help me bloom into a beautiful flower" (*Fusion*). Possibly the community organization also sponsors programs where kids get to think and to speak for themselves. But promoted as the organization's flagship after-school program, only the steppers got to go public.[2]

My point isn't to criticize a specific program but rather to emphasize that as community educators we have options besides either banning or reappropriating a subaltern's tactics. Cintron allows himself a long paragraph to imagine some design literacies for creating a "public forum" in Angelstown that could have constituted a viable form of local social justice (*Angels' Town* 195). He sketches a forum where members of gangs and mainstream culture "document[. . .] the assumptions and beliefs of all parties so that they could be later deconstructed" (195). But for as much that Cintron ventures forth, he is also quick to add an important qualification. "In the Angelstown of 1990 and 1991 such an approach would have been outrageous" (196). Conceding that his "solution [. . .] lacks the necessary subtlety," he also defends it on the grounds that "rhetorical invention must begin somewhere" (196). By documenting the challenges and pitfalls inherent in this test case, Cintron identifies ways in which design literacies may serve as experiments in local social justice, inviting participants to think past us-them dichotomies and to expand literate repertoires "to cross publics" (Higgins and Brush 699).

Additional implications of the shadow system as a distinctive local public are evident in Pezzullo's study of a toxic tour that used obstructionist tactics to visit the doorsteps of corporations who produce or profit from carcinogenic chemicals.

Pezzullo's Risky Mobile Theater. The local public in Pezzullo's "'National Breast Cancer Awareness Month': The Rhetoric of Counterpublics and their Cultural Performances" is a "risky mobile theater" through which the TLC toured the financial district of San Francisco in October 3, 2001 (Pezzullo 355). The tour was mobile in that through its performances it "took TLC's grievances to the doorsteps of institutions that it believes are responsible for producing and enabling toxic pollution" (347). The tour called attention to companies that "pinkwash" breast cancer by sponsoring National Breast Cancer Awareness Month (NBCAM) in order to cast their companies as promoters of women's health, but obfuscate the fact that their companies profit from the sales of carcinogenic chemicals or the manufacture of cancer-causing toxins. Pezzullo points to AstraZenica, a company that not only sponsored NBCAM but also profited from the sales of pharmaceutical drugs that treat breast cancer (346). The TLC aimed at exposing such inconsistencies.

The toxic tour risked offending potentially sympathetic audience members. Not only did the tour defy pedestrians' and drivers' efforts to get to their destinations, but the tour also capitalized on and circulated ghoulish iconography, most prominent the pink breast-cancer-awareness ribbon inverted to represent a noose.

Though offensive, the tenor of the discourse also attempted persuasion. Striking a chord that was "difficult to ignore and perhaps even more difficult to forget," the discourse "shock[ed]" and "disgust[ed]" onlookers (Pezzullo 356). The same discourse also struck a "potentially persuasive" tenor (361) by rivaling the early-detection message of the NBCAM with an alternative: to "stop cancer where it starts" (354). Pezzullo explains: "By linking toxins and cancer, health and wealth, environmental justice and feminism, TLC has offered a potentially persuasive counterdiscourse to NBCAM's response to the U.S. breast cancer epidemic" (361). The toxic tour demonstrated "the limits of a dichotomous conceptualization of publics and counterpublics" (345). Pezzullo writes: "[W]hen public dialogues reflect a multi-faceted negotiation of power, it is particularly important to recognize the complexity of various public spheres without reducing conflicts to mere binaries" (349).

The tour featured "cultural performances" (Pezzullo 356). Some performances the TLC had planned, such as that of Queen and King of Cancer who had "painted their faces white with large black circles around their eyes and dark lipstick" to "heighten their deadly looks" (355). Peeling from the King's face was dead skin, "contributing to his aura of deterioration" (355). Other performances were more spontaneous. For instance, though not part of the scripted five-stop itinerary, a cancer-survivor named RavenLight drove up to the mobile theater and emerged from her car in order to "lend her body" to the protest (355). RavenLight "walked in front of the police line, unbuttoned her dress, pulled out her right arm, and exposed her mastectomy scar" (356). "As the tour crowd cheered," RavenLight and her companion, donning a gas mask, "began posing for photographs" (356). Witnessing the performance, the police did nothing. Had RavenLight exposed a breast, she could have been arrested for indecent exposure. However, in revealing the scar, she denied the police the grounds to arrest her.

5. *It may be that at its best, a shadow system opens up a discursive space that suspends the logic of violence and replaces it with an alternative that tolerates ambiguity.*

Cintron explains that the logic of violence in Angelstown turned on a notion of moral high ground that was itself anchored in the same exploitation of power. Angelstown's shadow system took this contradiction to its logical extreme. In stand-offs between the Kings and majoritarian society (and the Kings and its rival gangs), each group leapt to what it considered the moral high ground to justify annihilating the other. With its finger-pointing and blame-laying, the logic governing toxic tour in Pezzullo's study makes a similar claim to the moral high ground; likewise, this moral high ground destabilizes the group's rhetorical effect. To the extent that the leaders of the toxic tour wanted not only to expose hypocrisy but also to change practices, the TLC's allegations against corporations may have been "right," but its shame-blame game—with its strong moral underpinnings—would have likely undermined the activists' ethos within the system world rather than convince corporations to change their ways.

Ultimately, Pezzullo credits the toxic tour not with persuading corporations to change their practices or even persuading onlookers to join their contempt for corporate deception, but with opening up an alternative space for human connection. In sum, the rhetorical power of a shadow system may lie not in its capacity to invoke the logic of violence with which to intimidate others through threatening hyperbole, but rather in the capacity to create surprising moments that suspend this very logic—moments based on an alternative logic that is capable of tolerating ambiguity.[3]

Consider an encounter between a passerby and RavenLight. Here, RavenLight's act of defiance—obstructing law and order by turning an anti-obscenity law on its head—led serendipitously to a quiet moment of human connection. Pezzullo relays the encounter like this:

> Continuing on the tour, we walked up a steep San Francisco street and RavenLight turned to the side to look for oncoming traffic. A woman who looked to be under 30—perhaps only because she wore pigtails—stepped between RavenLight and me. When she saw RavenLight's chest, she gasped. We stopped. RavenLight glanced back in the woman's direction. The young woman then reached one hand out in the direction of RavenLight's exposed scar as she brought her other hand to her own chest, which was covered with a T-shirt that sank to her touch. Her eyes filled with tears and she said, "Sister—you are so brave." RavenLight smiled, and they hugged. (356)

In this moment, RavenLight's performance operated no longer within a logic of violence—invoking law and order by defying it—but something that could well fall under what Cintron has called "the logic of trust" (*Angels' Town* 146). "In that moment, [. . .] expos[ing] our physical, emotional, and political scars [. . .] all three of us, the woman in red who risked contact, the woman in pigtails who risked reaching out to communicate, and the observer who risked sharing that intimate exchange, felt present" (Pezzullo 356). For Cintron, the logic of trust depends not upon some gooey altruism but on an intellectually and emotionally rigorous way-of-being that engages ambiguity. Below, Cintron contrasts the logics of violence and trust, particularly the former's inability to entertain ambiguity:

> The logic of violence represented a kind of brute cause and effect relationship [. . .] and I grudgingly admired its mythic, destructive clarity [. . .]. In contrast, the logic of trust deflected the momentum and inevitability of the logic of violence by calling some its premises into question. In a sense, the logic

> of trust interrupted the relationship between cause
> and effect; it *destabilized* judgment and punishment
> and made both *less sure* [. . .]. (*Angels' Town* 151–52,
> emphasis added)

Like West's freedom fighter (*Race* 150) and Flower's rival-hypothesis stance, the logic of trust tolerates ambiguity. "[T]he logic of trust weakens [. . . violence's] scaffolding by *finding doubt* and heretofore *unimagined complexity*. It is not as swift, divisive, obvious, nor, of course, as divisive" (Cintron, *Angels' Town* 153, emphasis added). Cintron doubts that the people whom he observed in Angelstown would choose to suspend the logic of violence for the logic of trust. Rather than documenting it happening—even once—he capitalizes on the limits of public discourse (194–96). The promise of Pezzullo's study is the glimpse it provides of an alternative public discourse forged not in the certainty of defiant violence, but in the ambiguity of trust.

6. *Embodied rhetoric makes a place for the body politic, affect, and desire in local public discourse.*

While Cintron holds to the *rationality and order* vs. *madness and disorder* topoi for their explanatory power, Pezzullo's analysis of a defiant local public evokes then moves beyond these topoi. Tracking the *rationality and order* vs. *madness and disorder* topoi at play in Angelstown leads Cintron to two of his most significant insights: (1) a public can't think beyond the fear that terrorizes it, and (2) the topos of disorder is often evoked by "those who perceive that the management of society has failed them" (*Angels' Town* 184). These insights are relevant not only to Angelstown, but to the local publics in Gilmore's and Pezzullo's studies, as well. For instance, the steppers' apparent epileptic seizures and orgasms threatened the teachers' senses of rationality and control. Likewise, RavenLight threatened chaos by thwarting the police's claim on law and order. Yet Pezzullo's study not only relies upon the *rationality and order* vs. *madness and disorder* topoi but also moves beyond them.

Pezzullo positions the TLC's toxic tour in terms of one of the most radical arguments in contemporary public-spheres studies: that "the body, affect, and desire disrupt the normative discursive logics of publics" (Deem qtd. in Pezzullo 351).[4] Debunking the privileged status not only of rationality, but also reasonableness, in public discourse, toxic tour activists "challenged and changed the meanings of the world not through good reasons but through vulnerable bodies, not through rational arguments but through bodies at risk" (Deluca qtd. in Pezzullo 357).[5] By exposing her scar, RavenLight made members of her audience confront the fears that terrorize it—challenging some in the audience to relate to her more fully because of her performance.

7. Public rhetoricians can make significant social contributions by interpreting embodied rhetoric for others.

Looking for meaningful work as an activist rhetorician? Pezzullo describes a position available to qualified practitioners. To a system world accustomed to point-driven reasoning, the meaning of embodied rhetoric can be hard to grasp, difficult to retain, and, thus, tempting to dismiss. In the same way that Cintron decodes the logic of violence operating in Angelstown, Pezzullo interprets the significance of RavenLight's performance within the rhetoric of the toxic tour:

> Her [RavenLight's] body's performance [. . .] *suggests* that if we wish to transform politics, *we need to expose* our physical, emotional, and political scars. *We need to wonder* why we feel compelled to look and/or to look away. In terms of TLC's political campaign, *we need to consider* the costs of our production of toxins. *We need to examine* the reasons why a breast cannot be present in our body politic until it is absent. By extension, *we need to ask,* what is the place of women in our body politic? (emphasis added, 356)

Pezzullo calls for discourse ambassadors who can cross local publics to interpret body politics for audiences not yet literate in such rhetorics. Fluency with public literacies is likewise the goal of many college-level public-writing courses, the focus of the next chapter.

9 Pedagogical Practices

This chapter takes students as the primary focus of attention to ask: *How do college students go public? And, as educators trained in rhetorical theories and practices, how can we best support them?* This chapter gathers recent pedagogical scholarship from the field of rhetoric and composition, including scholarship in community literacy, service learning, community action, university outreach, and public writing. Each source—from A. Suresh Canagarajah's "Safe Houses in the Contact Zone" to Welch's "Living Room: Teaching Public Writing in a Post-Publicity Era"—addresses pedagogical issues. Each also stakes a unique position within this discussion. The scholars' positions account for the different versions of local public action that circulate in the field. Yet for all their differences, these pedagogies tend to cluster around many of the same literacies reviewed in current views, chapters 4 through 8. These clusters reflect the larger disciplinary efforts, for instance, to adapt familiar interpretative literacies to community settings; to celebrate tactical literacies of resistance and surprise; and, most recently, to theorize public performative literacies. table 7 summarizes these clusters of pedagogies, the version of public action each endorses, and the sequence in which these pedagogies are addressed in this chapter in relation to the order they appeared in current views.

As the reader would predict, the pedagogical practices discussed in this chapter do not rest in easy relation to one another. Strong conflicts and contradictions exist among them. Taken together, this collection of practices poses a number of quandaries for educators, including the following questions:

- Do we best support students by asking them to venture into the borderland of a classroom's safe house (cf. Canagarajah "Safe Houses") or to risk police arrest downtown (cf. Welch)? by forging a cross-institutional no-man's land (cf. Goldblatt

Table 7. How students use prominent literacies to go public.

Pedagogies / Public Action	I Interpretative	II Institutional	III Tactical	IV Inquiry-Driven	V Performative
Students take public action by . . .	. . . going somewhere new, building relationships, confronting and revising familiar stereotypes	. . . learning professional methods for recognizing the expertise and agency of others	. . . learning to circulate their own public writing that challenges the *status quo*	. . . deliberating pressing social issues with community partners; circulating documents that serve as catalysts for social change	. . . engaging as rhetors with others to gain the practical wisdom required to build inclusive communities for effective problem solving
Prominent literacies used to take public action	interpretative	institutional	tactical	inquiry-driven	performative and inquiry-driven
Chapter/s in current views featuring these literacies	Chapter 5	Chapter 6	Chapter 8	Chapter 7	Chapter 4 & 7

"Van Rides") or by providing access to public homeplaces (cf. Coogan "Counterpublics")?

- Do we best support students by trusting their spontaneous willingness to develop on their own terms and at their own pace (cf. Canagarajah "Safe Houses"; Coogan "Counterpublic"; Goldblatt "Van Rides") or by setting demanding rhetorical expectations and helping students manage the challenges entailed in meeting them (cf. Coogan "Service"; Flower "Intercultural Inquiry")? If we opt for the latter, at what point do the inherent conflicts in local public rhetoric frustrate students beyond the point of productive cognitive dissonance (cf. Deans 138)?
- Given time constraints, how do we best support students to circulate their public writing (cf. Wells): by providing websites where students can post their work (cf. Flower "Intercultural Inquiry")? by sponsoring venues for live public performances (cf. Fishman et al.; Flower and Heath)? by working behind the scenes to position research projects within the community (cf. Coogan "Service")? or by placing the responsibility for producing and circulating texts on students themselves (cf. Welch)?

Along with exposing difficult choices, this collection of practices has several attributes to offer.

First, these practices make innovation accessible. Clearly, the politics of forging mutually beneficial community-university partnerships are daunting, but such complications haven't stopped these scholars from radically reshaping students' rhetorical education and their own rhetorical scholarship. Rather, these very complexities and potential benefits motivate scholars to test their own rhetorical know-how and to forge innovative institutional relationships for local public action. Second, the practices capture educators' situated problem solving as they grapple with the challenges that inevitably arise when pedagogy "gets real." Third, the practices represent the synergy that circulates among a loosely organized group of educators who grapple with how to make good on the promises and challenges of contemporary rhetorical education. This cross-fertilization allows for the borrowing and blending of situated-public literacies, and it permits educators to exchange one set of literacies for another over the course of his or her own inquiry into community outreach and curricular design. These practices, then, represent not only synergy among the pedagogical studies reviewed here, but just as importantly, the categories (interpretative, institutional, tactical, inquiry-driven, and performative) provide a scheme for comparing other pedagogical discussions, as well.[1]

As Weisser acknowledges: "Involving students in 'public writing' is fraught with headaches of all sorts" (xi). In consolidating these best practices, I can't promise to alleviate such headaches. But by putting pedagogical practices in relation to one another, I hope to offer some options that might fuel readers' inventional processes as they design their own community-literacy courses. In pooling our collective experiences, my hope is that we might free ourselves from at least some of the day-to-day trouble shooting that community-literacy courses entail so that we may have time and energy to join students in grappling with some of the most interesting, difficult, and invigorating issues of our day.

OVERVIEW

In this chapter, I ask readers to repeatedly shift perspectives from that of *students* going public to *teachers* employing pedagogical practices to support students' public actions. Though this shift in perspective makes particular demands on readers, I believe it best captures the dynamics of rhetorical intervention. To encourage the reader to make these shifts in perspective with me, I employ a couple of simple text conventions.

The chapter is divided into five sections, each describing pedagogical practices that support different ways that students take public action. Each section lists in bullets several exemplary community-literacy courses.

The thrust of each section is how *students* use situated-public literacies to take public action. In each section, students' public actions are set in italics and enumerated—1, 2, 3—the same conventions that marked the implication section following each analysis in current views. A brief description of the public action then follows.

Instructional practices are listed after each public action, with the practices set in italics and followed by commentary synthesizing relevant pedagogical studies. These are instructional practices that *educators* have used to support students' public activity. To remind the reader that these instructional practices are not new public actions that students take but rather what teachers can do to support them, each pedagogical practice is introduced with an ellipse and completes the phrase, *What teachers can do to help. . . .*

Some of the earliest community-literacy pedagogies adapted the English department's stock in trade: interpretative literacies for engaging with texts. So it is with interpretative pedagogies that our discussion begins. Interpretative pedagogies commend reading and writing as acts of intense public involvement.

INTERPRETATIVE PEDAGOGIES

Interpretative pedagogies stress that students take public action when they venture somewhere new to build working relationships with others. In the process, they interrogate and reinterpret outmoded assumptions, for instance, about what constitutes literacy (Goldblatt "Van Rides") or what the people and neighborhoods are like beyond campus borders (Coogan "Counterpublics"). Interpretative pedagogies emphasize the interactive engagement between readers and writers (Brandt *Involvement*). Based on their experiences reading and writing with others, students develop and circulate new insights. In the process, they forge communicative links between the university and neighboring communities. Exemplars include the following:

- the Literacy Practicum at a Catholic university in Philadelphia (Goldblatt "Van Rides")
- a pre-college composition course designed to retain minority students at the University of Texas at Austin (Canagarajah "Safe Houses")
- Phase One of a community-based Interprofessional Research Project (IPRP) at the Illinois Institute of Technology (IIT) in Chicago (Coogan "Counterpublics").

1. *Students stir things up in their own minds by venturing somewhere new.*

The academy has structural blind spots that make some really poor ideas seem natural, commonsensical, just the way things are. Take the idea of "public housing" for instance, and, by extension, the people who live there. Assigned to work in a public housing development near his school, a student named Andy was surprised to find that residents were "'honorable and respectable'" and not at all "'mean or tough'"

(Coogan, "Counterpublics" 461) as he had assumed. To set culturally loaded terms like *public housing* in relief so they can be identified, interrogated, and revised, students need some critical distance—something best gained from a new vantage point and in relation to others who provide new perspectives.

What teachers can do to help:

. . . *Arrange for students to get off campus to work and to write with others.* Goldblatt worked with the Center for Peace and Justice Education at his university to offer a literacy practicum that placed students as tutors at either a prison or a community literacy center. In this way, Goldblatt and his students were positioned at the intersection of several institutions, a stance that permitted them to "explor[e] the ways that each institution shaped literacy experience" ("Van Rides" 81). Similarly, Coogan took advantage of the community-based IPRP at IIT which places teams of students in work sites to study "real-world" problems ("Service" 680). Coogan placed students with community leaders who were committed to building "public homeplaces" in Chicago's south side ("Counterpublics" 473). These leaders were willing to support students' moral development not on the basis of their race or gender but simply because students belong to "the human family" (473).

. . . *"Stay grounded" in the rhetorical practices of your community partners.* "Stay[ing] grounded" means using interpretative literacies to identify the rhetorical traditions operating in the communities with which one works (Coogan, "Counterpublics" 468). Coogan found that community leaders in Chicago's south side didn't often go public by "waging arguments in a public, citywide forum" (468), but rather by "convert[ing others] to the cause of community development" (465). Thus, Coogan needed to design research projects to coincide with community leaders' rhetorical expectations and to support "ideals of social change" and "forms of community involvement" that differed from conventional academic formulations of rational-critical public discourse (468).

Interpretative pedagogies strive to balance students' personal growth with the interests of the community, a balancing act that poses challenges to both students and educators. The next set of public actions and instructional practices strives to achieve this balance.

2. Students prioritize both new working relationships and deeper under-standings of loaded cultural issues.

Interpretative pedagogies value students' personal growth; however, critics caution that the focus on relationships "may encourage a detachment from social analysis of injustice and naïve identification with the other" (Coogan, "Counterpublic" 476). The concern here is that students will get so focused on building new relationships (or managing obstacles in the way) that they will not interrogate the larger structural forces that cause the injustices that outreach programs are designed to address.

Increasingly, advocates of interpretive literacies cast the challenge another way. They say the point is not to subordinate personal relationships in favor of social analysis but to support authentic, rigorous rhetorical engagement with others across difference. Moreover, there is no reason to expect that students' insights will match the ideological form and terms of academic cultural criticism. Students' insights are likely to be provisional, exploratory, and cast in terms of their own interpretive schemes. To explain, Coogan describes the personal narrative that a student named Cindy wrote after shadowing Tyrone, the leader of a public art project called the DreamCultivation Mural. After learning that Tyrone had dedicated a mural to a teenager from the community who had been killed in gun crossfire, Cindy wrote that she found the dedication moving and that it "'helped [her] put [her] life into perspective'" ("Counterpublics" 476). Although Cindy didn't sustain an extended social analysis in her response, it is evidence of rhetorical engagement, and Coogan values it accordingly: "When confronted with that work in its cultural context, [Cindy] cannot *not* react to it. Nor would the leaders that I have met through this project want her to bypass her emotional responses or privately held opinions. They would want her to confront them head-on" ("Counterpublics" 477).

Interpretative pedagogies attend to the pressing question in community outreach: *who benefits and how?* Instructional practices balance students' personal growth (where students are the immediate beneficiaries) with rhetorical work that serves community interests according to the terms that community partners themselves set.

What teachers can do to help:

. . . *Assign personal narrative and public writing.* To balance student growth and community interests, Coogan assigned his students both

personal narratives (like Cindy's reflection) and public writing. To determine the shape of the public-writing assignment, Coogan worked
with his community partners at Urban Matters in advance of the new
academic year. He found that Urban Matters trained community leaders; it offered programs and graduated community leaders whose activities in their own communities were one of the best indicators of the
program's impact. However, Urban Matters did not have the time to
follow up on these graduates to document their community-develop-
ment achievements and activities. In response to this need, Coogan
proposed that students research and write leadership portraits featuring Urban Matters alumni. Once written, Urban Matters could use
these portraits to seek greater visibility and continued funding.

   *. . . If you want students to build alternative interpretations of complex is-
sues, support alternative means of reflection.* For the Literacy Practicum,
Goldblatt assigned more conventional weekly readings, mailbag entries, journals, mid-term reports and essays ("Van Rides" 82). Just as
crucial were the conversations students had on the vans they took to
and from their tutoring sites. Such conversation "helped [students]
process the extreme diversity of the individual tutoring experiences [.
. .] and it fostered complex thinking" (83). Assessing the interpretive
insights that these van-ride conversations cultivated, Goldblatt writes:
"These young adults were facing ways of living they had never encountered before, and they needed each other to *find the familiar* and to
comprehend the strange in what they met" ("Van Rides" 83, emphasis
added). To make these institutional forces salient and distinctive to
students, Goldblatt and his students compiled institutional portraits
of the "priorities, regulations and social pressures" shaping literacy
within each locale (79).
   Reflection—especially structured reflection that prompts students
to turn some level of attention to sites of contested meaning making—
is discussed further as a feature of performative pedagogies.

3. *Students circulate their new insights.*

Finally, interpretative pedagogies emphasize that students share what
they have learned over the course of their off-campus experiences.
Sure, their insights are likely to be provisional. They may be posited as
questions or problem narratives rather than statements or full-blown
theories. But the goal is for students to unearth and to interrogate ill-

founded assumptions and to circulate more informed interpretations in their place, so it is imperative that they share what they have learned with others.

What teachers can do to help:

. . . *Assign students to circulate their new insights within larger publics.* This is what Canagarajah did within a composition course designed to introduce African-American pre-college students to academic discourses. Formulating ideas in the security of the "classroom's safe house" was one thing. But for students to go public with their ideas, they had to circulate them in "public sites of the contact zone" ("Safe Houses" 176). In the context of Canagarajah's classroom, students made the public turn by moving ideas from the safe house (e.g., informal, highly charged e-mail exchanges and classroom discussions) to the larger academic domain by incorporating these ideas into their formal academic essays.

Since Canagarajah's essay was published in 1997, some rhet/comp scholars have debated the extent to which academic classrooms constitute public spaces (cf. Trimbur, "Circulation" 194; Weisser 43); others have identified criteria that distinguish academic and public domains (cf. Barton and Hamilton 9–10). Instructional practices that help students circulate their writing outside the academy are addressed further in each of the pedagogies discussed below.

. . . *Acknowledge that intercultural, institutional border crossing is rhetorically significant in its own right.* Coogan stresses that the effort to leave campus and to take up learning with strangers in a new locale is itself rhetorically significant. It forges a "communicative link [. . .] between the counterpublic spheres of public housing and the larger public sphere that students represented" ("Counterpublics" 480). In connecting with others across institutional boundaries, students construct the kind of communicative link that in chapter 6 we saw Shirley forge in Springside as a liaison and border crosser. Assessing the outcome of this IPRP, Coogan explains: "The students did not just cross the street to receive this message. Their presence enabled the construction of the message, and hence, the construction of a new public sphere linking community leaders, public housing residents, and IIT students" ("Counterpublics" 480).

As interpretative pedagogies adapt familiar interpretative practices to community settings, the next set of pedagogies strive to invent new practices within familiar institutional settings.

INSTITUTIONAL PEDAGOGIES

Institutional pedagogies focus on students' futures—especially their careers as technical communicators and human service workers. As we saw in chapter 6, Cushman's *The Struggle and the Tools* testifies to the agency and local knowledge of community residents. Cushman's study shows that community residents' knowledge isn't necessarily cut off from formal public knowledge. Residents may be fluent in many public institutions' forms, regulations, and procedures. They may also have something to say about institutional discourse that isn't usually part of collective social knowledge; moreover, they know something about the gaps between the professed intent of specific public policies, on the one hand, and how they play out in lived experience, on the other. In many institutional settings, this situated knowledge is vital for accurate problem analysis and effective solutions (cf. Grabill and Simmons; Swan). However, over the course of her study, Cushman observed practices that elicit this kind of knowledge just once, when Mr. Villups "cleared a rhetorical space for [Raejone] to bring her community based discourse to bear in a context where fluency in academic English is valued" (Cushman, *Struggle* 187). Designed to mediate the social world as it is and the possibility of a better one (cf. Branch 190), institutional pedagogies insinuate inventive practices into institutional settings in attempt to bridge the lived experiences of community residents and the policies of public institutions.

Cushman's insight into the agency of others is "built on the kind of knowledge normally available only to the attuned ethnographer, confidant or friend [. . .]" (Flower, "Intercultural Inquiry" 197). Institutional pedagogies ask what it would take for students to learn to identify and to represent the agency and knowledge of others within the institutional contexts they will occupy in future professional capacities. Thus, institutional pedagogies focus on institutional change: how classroom pedagogies can circulate professional practices that are more rhetorically sound than those Cushman typically observed in Quayville—more responsive to intercultural differences and more attuned to the situated knowledge of community residents. Some exemplars include the following:

- a technical writing course at Texas A & M University (Cárdenas)
- a public-policy seminar at CMU (Swan)
- a web-design project at Georgia State University (Grabill "Writing the City"; see also Grabill and Simmons)
- a service-learning course at the University of Central Florida (Scott).

Institutional pedagogies portray students as professionals in training. Students in these courses go public in their professional roles; likewise, these pedagogies promote social change by altering the rhetorical practices students take with them into the workplace.

1. *Students note the ethical implications that technical communications carry.*

The communications that institutions circulate often distance ordinary people from decisions that affect the quality of their lives. Yet because many public institutions and social service agencies are grounded in a history of genuine concern for people's well-being—and students, likewise, may be eager to launch careers that do good (Cushman, *Struggle* 223)—these implications can be difficult for students to identify.

What teachers can do to help:

. . . *Address these implications directly with students.* This is what Diana Cárdenas does in her technical writing class where a good many students aspire to the kinds of public-sector jobs that caused residents in Quayville so much grief, including "criminal justice majors who will work with juvenile and adult probation departments, child protective services, border patrol, and immigration services" (Cárdenas 121). Cárdenas addresses the ethical implications of technical communications directly with her students. Assignments "take [students] into their future workplaces to learn the literacy of the work environments" (121). In addition, she talks with students "about being empathic to the 'clients,' about understanding the factors that create their situations, and trying to intervene to change those factors" (121). She challenges students "to identify community needs that must be solved" (121).

. . . Challenge the norms for relating to clients as inscribed by bureaucratic institutions. John McKnight would probably try to deter students from entering human-service careers in the first place—indicting gatekeepers of the same ethical violations as the well-intentioned "bereavement counselor" whose "new tool [. . .] cut[s] through the social fabric, throwing aside kinship, care and neighborly obligations," leaving finally even the bereavement counselor bereft of the "[. . .]possibility of restoring hope in clients [. . .] with nothing but a service for consolation" (266). However, institutional pedagogies challenge educators to join students in negotiating this terrain. The ethics of going public are not unique to advanced professional communication courses. Even at the most introductory level, rhetorical pedagogy "produces, circulates, and delivers communicative souls to the discourse of a public" (Greene 434). What *does* distinguish courses like Cárdenas's, however, is that they replace the norms of "stranger relationality" (Warner 74–76) that Quayville embodied with the expectation of becoming "knowledgeable advocates and fair judges" (Cushman, *Struggle* 187).

2. Students interrogate asymmetrical relationships as institutional arrangements with complex histories and important social implications.

Whether students are planning careers as technical communicators, social workers, or medical professionals, they face a similar problem: asymmetrical relationships—the power differentials that position professionals and community residents in a "one-up/one-down" relationship (Tannen 24). Good will alone won't level the playing field. Even well-intended "collaboration" or "reciprocity" can't "level the asymmetries of power relations" (Cushman, "Response" 151). Though Cushman addresses implications for researchers, her advice holds for professionals-in-training, as well. She suggests that researchers "open[ly] negotiat[e] with participants the terms of give-and-take" ("Response" 151)—just as Mr. Villups negotiated rhetorical space with Raejone. But if give-and-take is "tricky, awkward, and at times discombobulating" for the researcher (151), it is all the more so for the gatekeeper-in-training, for whom it means suspending one of the main tools of the trade: control. Institutional pedagogies teach students that engaging in give-and-take isn't a procedure, per se, but a "listening stance" (Grabill and Simmons 427) that attends to "dissensus" as a "heuristic" for listening to the interests of others (Powell and Takayoski qtd. in Cushman, "Response" 152).[2,3]

What teachers can do to help:

... Teach students how to engage in dialogue that negotiates asymmetrical relationships. If you want to change an outmoded practice, you have to replace it with a more robust one. Scholarship describes two techne (or rhetorical strategies) that are particularly well suited to helping students learn to negotiate asymmetrical relationships:

- the rival-reading technique for eliciting alternative interpretations of a cultural artifact—e.g., a housing application form (Flower, *Problem Solving* 415–19; Lawrence)
- the "cultural circuit" heuristic for critiquing "the power relations in which [students' technical communications] participate" (Scott 304).

Susan Lawrence observed that college mentors at Pittsburgh's CLC often assumed the need to find and maintain common ground—to try to level the ground between their teen writers and themselves; the rival reading technique provided an option for more generative conversations.[4] In explaining their rival readings of texts (such as a jeep advertisement in *Ebony* or an image of success in *Fortune*) mentors and teens traded stories that called attention to the differences in one another's social locations and prompted the "moral humility" to listen across difference rather than assume they could fully imagine walking in another's shoes (I. Young, *Intersecting* 168).

While the rival-reading teaches double-sided discourse moves between intercultural partners, the cultural-circuit heuristic examines the consequences of the technical communications students write for the community. Designed for the service-learning classroom, the cultural-circuit heuristic is based on Richard Johnson's model that "tracks the transformation of cultural forms" (Scott 304). In adapting Johnson's cultural theory to service-learning pedagogy, Scott replaces questions that prompt students' personal reflections with those that address "the power relations in which [their texts] participate" (304). Focused on how documents circulate in a web of cultural conditions, such questions include, "How could the texts and their contexts of distribution more respectfully depict the audiences and their needs?" and "How could the text be more responsive to the audiences' and community's needs, values, and contexts?" (305). Scott suggests that such a heuristic "can push students past purely practical and uncritically empathetic stances, help them account for the fuller circulation and effects of their texts, and enable them to more strategically intervene in problematic cultural practices" (304).

Such a heuristic can make or break service-learning curriculum. So writes Nora Bacon in her review of service-learning textbooks. Writing in 2004, Bacon observed a tendency in service-learning textbooks to treat writing for the community as an entirely vocational endeavor carried out to hone students' technical proficiencies. Such textbooks discourage students from participating in community organizations outside their assigned roles as professional writers and restrict engagement with community residents beyond the executive directors who give students their writing assignments. While Bacon acknowledges these restrictions "makes sense in terms of project management" (366–67), such a curriculum also restricts students from more significant public engagement. Bacon states her priority this way: "If my students could take only one service-learning course, I might prefer that it be one where their *range of contacts* in the community and the *range of critical questions* raised about the experience were broader" (367, emphasis added). Pedagogical practices that teach students how to structure and to conduct rival readings or to interrogate cultural circuits (especially by considering Scott's questions with community residents themselves) can help students take the public turn that Bacon envisions.

The rival-reading technique and the cultural-circuit heuristic are informal and flexible techne that students could adapt to many rhetorical situations. The next move ratchets up institutional pedagogies. Here, formalized community-based research methods serve as the cornerstone for how students learn to carry out their work as professionals.

3. Students learn professional research methods for seeking out the perspectives and situated knowledge of community residents.

There's all the difference in the world between advocating for community-based practices ("you should!") and eliciting the situated knowledge, interests, and concerns of ordinary people as a matter of course (Grabill and Simmons 437). In the professional roles they will assume as graduates, professionals-in-training are in a unique position to bring community-based research methods to institutions that are accustomed to bypassing community perspectives. As Grabill and Simmons note, students' effectiveness will turn on their ability not to strike a didactic or defensive stance but a procedural one that goes about structuring participatory processes as a function of how they carry out their work as professionals.

What teachers can do to help:

. . . *Teach research methods that incorporate community residents' interests and expertise into the institution's decision-making process.* Such methods include:

- human-centered design principles for technical communicators (Grabill and Simmons)
- community problem-solving strategies for public-policy professionals (Swan)
- the collaborative-inquiry communication model for medical providers. (A. Young and Flower)

Human-centered design principles include "a range of contextual interviewing and observation practices [. . .] that necessitate researchers work with audiences in the construction of knowledge" (Grabill and Simmons 432). They embody a critical rhetoric for technical communication and can be used, for instance, to assess and to communicate environmental risks (Grabill and Simmons), to design institutions responsive to community interests (Grabill *Community*), and to design computer interfaces that make data accessible and useful to community residents involved in policy decisions about their communities (Grabill "Written City").

The CLC's problem-solving strategies described in chapter 7 provide another set of inquiry methods for eliciting and representing the situated knowledge of community residents. In Swan's study of a public-policy course at CMU, graduate students used the story-behind-the-story, rivaling, and the options-and-outcomes strategies to study a proposal for an urban renewal project. The strategies prompted the graduate students to listen to the perspectives of local residents and urban teenagers and to draw on that expertise to qualify the positions of academic experts and to build more robust representations of urban problems and more comprehensive proposals for urban renewal.

These same problem-solving strategies inform collaborative inquiry, a rhetorical model that engages both health-care providers and patients in a shared process of interpretation and deliberation (A. Young "Patients"; A. Young and Flower). Adapting the same rhetorical problem-solving strategies that Swan's public policy students used to build alternative discourses to deliberate over shared problems, collaborative inquiry functions rhetorically as a heuristic that allows "patients to represent their medical problems in the context of their life experiences and to define, both for themselves and for the provider, the logic that directs their health care decisions" (A. Young and Flower 79). Likewise, collaborative inquiry is adaptable—both to "short, structured conversations" and "extended dialogue between a health educator and a patient in a clinical setting" (83). Collaborative inquiry creates a new rhetoric for patient-provider interaction that prioritizes "creating new knowledge, participating in a problem-solving dialogue, creating partnerships, and sharing knowledge" (86).

. . . *Anticipate forces that militate against collaborative practices by providing more and more frequent explicit instruction and, when possible, by designing and conducting courses with off-campus partners.* In some formal domains, "mere awareness" seems to be all it takes for people to go public (Warner 60). But Ronald Greene suggests "[t]he standard of 'mere attention' applies a thinner ethical subjectivity than that increasingly imagined by rhetorical studies" (441). "Mere awareness" was certainly insufficient for graduate students in the public policy course Swan studied. Ultimately, their grasp of the problem-solving strategies was no match for the "pull of genre expectations" and their "very real need of soon-to-be-graduates to be seen as policy professionals" (106). Yes, students became adept at using rhetorical problem-solving strategies to conduct their interviews—and, thus, accessed knowledge that wouldn't have been available to them otherwise. But when it came to writing their results of their inquiries, students had difficulty figuring out how to use the community knowledge so opted, instead, for discursive moves—from sentence structure to graphic organizers—that muted ordinary people's voices and overlooked local insights in favor of discursive moves that complied with conventional, disciplinary standards of validity, rigor, and authority. Even at the sentence level they had trouble doing justice to the agency and expertise of others. Swan explains: "The grammar of the students' research project usually located agency in academic experts, the public policy students, or their research projects" (99). When they did represent the agency of youth, for instance, youth were represented in the aggregate, in a graph, but not in "their own words" (99).

In light of the disciplinary pressure that thwarted students' efforts to incorporate community residents' expertise into their proposed urban renewal projects, Swan speculates that a "new [research] method" could improve the situation: "What may be called for is a new method constructed outside any specific academic genre or discipline, situated in the community, and performed collaboratively [with community residents] throughout the entire process" (106).

Institutional pedagogies promote social change by insinuating into professional settings rhetorical practices that recognize and represent the agency and expertise of community residents. In contrast, as we see next, tactical pedagogies tend to defy formal, public institutions and to capitalize on the capacity of indecorous and hostile counterdiscourses to upset the status quo.

TACTICAL PEDAGOGIES

Tactical pedagogies prioritize that students learn to produce and to circulate their own public writing. The tactical shadow system that Cintron used to interpret Angelstown's everyday public culture (chapter 8) is most evident in Welch's "Living Room: Teaching Public Writing in a Post-Publicity Era," but it operates in other tactical pedagogies as well. Exemplars include the following:

- Aphrodite's Daughters—a women's studies seminar at the University of Vermont (Welch)
- Curriculum for community studies as proposed in *Class Politics: The Movement for the Students' Right to Their Own Language* (Parks)
- Introduction to Black World Studies at Miami University (Pough)
- Literatures of Homelessness offered in conjunction with a writing project called Kids' 2 Cents in Boston (Mathieu *Tactics*).

As the pun on "living room" in her article's title indicates, Welch orients public writing less in the domesticated kitchens and rented rooms of Ann Ruggles Gere's extracurricular rhetoric and more in the workings of the shadow system: "in city streets, public parks, on picket lines and graffitied walls" (474). To identify fissures in the dominant discourse, Welch looks for topoi, including many on Cintron's list: order vs. disorder, civilization vs. barbarism, deliberative citizen vs. threatening mob (Welch 482). Mimicry of "rhetoric from above" serves as a heuristic for Welch and her students' public displays of social criticism and protest (478). Rejecting formal argumentation for proving ineffective in her university's current organizational climate, Welch modeled tactical literacies that include a cake sale that critiqued the university's employment practices, including "Rice Krispie Temps ('cheaper by the dozen') and Vice Provost Cupcakes ('Now 40 percent more!')"; a map of Iraq that traded the name of prominent cities for U.S. corporations under the banner "Neo-Liberated"; an anti-war flag that usurped the U.S. flag's position on the campus green; and graffiti that changed campus stop signs into STOP BUSH signs (484, 488).

It was not only Welch who cast Aphrodite's tactical pedagogy as a shadow system; her students did as well. For instance, a student called Katie dressed in black and lurked downtown at night to post ransom-note-style poetry in undesignated areas. In sparking these "arresting moments," students flirted with, tested, and defied the police's version of law and order, as did RavenLight (bearing her mastectomy scar) and Angelstown's street gangs (holding picnics two thousand strong in public parks in a defiant display of nationhood) as described in chapter 8. In the same cadence that Cintron uses to ask how "one acquires respect *under conditions of little or no respect*" (183), Welch asks how ordinary people find "visibility, voice, and impact against the powerful interests that seek to deny visibility, voice and impact" (476). The conclusion she reaches is also the same: by enacting tactical literacies the system world considers "dangerous indeed" (Welch 486).

Tactical pedagogies teach students to circulate counterpublic discourses as expressions of students' social and political views. One measure of the discourses' rhetorical effect is that university administrators often find them offensive. Tactical pedagogies also situate counterpublic discourses in a larger historical narrative of radically progressive social change. These two features—a countervalent rhetorical force and a highly charged historical narrative—infuse both the distinct ways students go public in such courses and the ways teachers support students' efforts to do so.

1. *Students place their own public writing within a larger historical, sociopolitical context.*

Students in Aphrodite's Daughters positioned their writing in terms of the twentieth century working-class struggle, specifically "capitalism's long history [. . .] of the creative and persistent ways in which ordinary people have organized to claim living room" (470). It's not class struggle but Black Power that was the theme of Gwendolyn Pough's Introduction to Black World Studies. Students positioned their exposés of campus race relations as an extension of the political demands of the Black Panther Party's (BPP) political platform. For instance, students updated and localized the BPP's "What We Want, What We Believe" to make ten "demands for a more diverse academic and social climate" (481). The shared history between the twentieth century American labor movement and the Black Power movement drives the community-studies curriculum Park proposes in the concluding chapter of *Class Politics: The Movement for the Students' Right to Their Own Language.* He commends "a multidisciplinary program linked to the community"—where students use a range and combination of discourses—from SWE to any number of street vernaculars—to engage in and study the possibilities of progressive social change (246). Similarly, in Literatures of Homelessness, students contextualized not their own tactical texts but rather those of other younger writers. In a sixteen-paged issue of *Spare Change,* college students "contextualize[d]" young writers' first hand accounts of homelessness with various "articles," "book reviews," and "background pieces" (Mathieu, *Tactics* 109).

What teachers can do to help:

. . . Teach the history of powerful social movements—and assign key documents from these movements—as bodies of rhetorical knowledge. For Welch, rhetoric is most productively viewed not as "a specialized techne [. . . and the] property of a small economic and political elite" but as a "mass popular art" (474). The history of twentieth century working-class struggle provides "clues about working with others to create rhetorical space while anticipating the resistance that comes from [trying to do so]" (475). To educate ourselves about this history and the tools it embodies, Welch recommends her colleagues read and share with their students *Detroit, I Do Mind Dying,* "an account of the League of Black Revolutionary Workers" and *Teamster Rebellion,* the

story of how truckers instituted "the nation's first daily strike newspaper" (480).

For Pough, it was the rhetoric of the BPP that motivated her teaching. Like Welch, she reached back in history to teach students to critically examine contemporary social issues and to imagine rhetorical responses to them. Used to interpret the current demographics at Miami University, BPP documents fueled "disruptions in the academy through public debate and protest" (468). Both Welch and Pough position their courses in relation to America's history of radical progressive social change and urge educators to make the rhetorical significance of such movements accessible to students.

. . . Show students how current economic and political conditions thwart ordinary people's efforts to go public. As Welch sees it, "this latest wave of economic privatization" has suppressed "public voices and rights" (470). It's not just that publics are inherently difficult to construct, which was the lesson that Wells took from President Clinton's failure to find a responsive public to deliberate health care reform. Rather, institutional and political forces make it all the harder for ordinary people to do so. From Welch's perspective, Clinton never intended for his appeal for broad-based public deliberative to take effect; instead, his speech was "designed to hide from public view the powerful private interests that had already set with Clinton the health-care agenda for the 1990s" (489). Welch stresses that in order for students to use tactical literacies to go public, they need first to understand the larger "discursive and extradiscursive obstacles" that regulate public discourse and restrict access to it (474).

2. Students adapt the counterpublic discourses of radically progressive social movements to their own rhetorical purposes.

Students in Aphrodite's Daughters found—and constructed, when needed—the venues they used to go public. Typically, the genres they used were not the formal essay and stylized debate of the academy but rather the "placards, poetry, murals, chants, handbills, [and] slogans" of class struggle (Welch 480). These genres performed social action not only by communicating their stated messages, but also by creating a "palpable tension between individual and mass, legislative and extralegislative, and ruling-class and working-class argumentative forums and forms" (478). Similarly, students in Introduction to Black

World Studies "could not wait to have the chance to write things that would have a larger impact" (Pough 474). Students' newspaper editorials "sparked a wave of controversy" (479) punctuated by "class walkouts, building takeovers, marches, and protests" (480).

What teachers can do to help:

. . . *Teach a contemporary take on the canon of delivery.* For Welch, rhetorical education in tactical literacies requires "students and teachers to ponder in the fullest way possible the rhetorical canon of delivery" (478). Welch suggests "training in civil disobedience or at the very least a guest lecturer from the ACLU" (478). In *Community Action and Organizational Change,* Faber offers what could serve as the curriculum for such lectures: "show how special interests achieve political goals [and . . .] teach how to read a situation and determine the roles power, rhetoric, and change are playing and how strategic players may be able to influence these roles" (136). By associating tactical literacies with the rhetorical canon of delivery, both Welch and Faber reinforce Carolyn Rude's argument in "Toward an Expanded Concept of Rhetorical Delivery" that "[p]reparing students for civic engagement requires new knowledge about the uses of documents for advocacy and social change" (271).

3. *Students know they don't "have to go it alone."*

The students in Introduction to Black World Studies organized. They initiated the Black Action Movement (BAM) on campus to carry out the political actions discussed in class and to respond to their consequences. Pough explains that BAM was a "response to Miami's lack of diversity and to the telephone threats to an African American male student by alleged members of the Ku Klux Klan" (480). Students from Pough's class provided BAM with key leadership.

Such solidarity was missing among students in Aphrodite's Daughters. Too often, Welch reflected afterward with remarkable candor, students "risk[ed] penalties for their words, and [. . .] felt (in a class drawing out no specific lessons to the contrary) that going public means going it alone" (477). For Welch, this is a lesson learned. Next time she teaches the course, she'll take measures to ensure individual students don't take unnecessary, uncalculated risks to go public.

Juxtaposing Aphrodite's Daughters and Introduction to Black World Studies suggests that the African American students who en-

rolled in Pough's course may have come to class better prepared to organize as a collective body (e.g., BAM). It also suggests that they used
assigned readings—the platform and autobiographies of the Black
Panthers—to imagine tactical literacies as decidedly *collective* acts of
political resistance.

What teachers can do to help:

. . . *Interrogate the image of the edgeworker.* The dominant popular image of the ordinary person who goes public is the "anarchic 'edgeworker'" (Welch 484). Aphrodite's Daughters didn't do enough to challenge
this dominant image. This image makes the individual responsible for
all the risks of going public. Welch notes: "It's much easier [. . .] for a
university administrator to sanction one student for her speech than
to sanction one hundred" (476). But it also erroneously applies Nike's
"'Just-Do-It'" shoe campaign to local political life (Welch 484). Next
time Welch teaches a course like Aphrodite's Daughters, she says she'll
draw upon the history of class struggle to help students to interrogate
the image of the edgeworker, to explore "the limits of a poetics/politics
fixated on solitary acts of writing" (485), and to imagine creative and
timely acts of political solidarity.

Tactical pedagogies encourage students to find their own venues
for going public. Because tactical pedagogies are rooted in the history
of American resistance, students typically use these pedagogies to go
public in bursts of what Cintron calls "persuasive displays"—in-your-
face mockery of the status quo (*Angels' Town* 174–76). But in some
circumstances, students in such classrooms construct venues for going
public that prioritize extended and focused deliberative inquiry. For
instance, a student called Cassie from Aphrodite's Daughters organized a forum that more than 70 people attended to discuss the consequences of welfare reform. Such a forum requires the ability to engage
multiple perspectives in sustained dialogue. This rhetorical capacity is
most directly supported by inquiry-driven pedagogies.

INQUIRY-DRIVEN PEDAGOGIES

Inquiry-driven pedagogies support discursive spaces where students
work with intercultural partners to inquire into and deliberate about
pressing social problems, working toward both personal and public
change. Readers will note that many institutional pedagogies share

this commitment to inquiry. In fact, the rival-reading technique (Lawrence) and collaborative inquiry (A. Young and Flower) belong to a family of practices that are central to this discussion. But the focus of inquiry pedagogies is not to prepare students for future professional careers, but to engage them in contemporary public action here and now and as part of their civic education. Intercultural pedagogies respond to the interests and expertise of community residents; they reposition members of a university not as experts with the answers but as committed and concerned citizens who bring to the table particular kinds of resources, including the ability to elicit and to document multiple kinds of knowledge. In inquiry-driven courses, college students learn to participate with other people and perspectives in problem-focused dialogue. Exemplar include:

- Community Leadership in Bronzeville Public Schools, Phases Two and Three of the community-based IPRP at IIT (Coogan "Service Learning")
- the Community Literacy Seminar at CMU sponsored in conjunction with the CLC's literacy programs for urban teens (Flower "Literate Action"; Flower "Intercultural Inquiry"; Long "Mentors Inventing")
- the Rhetoric of Making a Difference at CMU sponsored in conjunction with Community Think Tanks (Flower "Intercultural Knowledge"; Flower and Heath; www.thinktank.cmu.edu).

These examples embody the dynamic tension between the rhetoric of consensus and a rhetoric of difference explored in chapter 7—but now in terms of options for students' public action and the instructional practices that support it. In the analysis that follows, I move between two sets of pedagogies—materialist rhetoric and intercultural inquiry—to highlight the pedagogical implications that follow from different conceptions of public deliberation. table 8 and the brief overview below may help readers follow the discussion.

Materialist Rhetoric: Realizing Practical Outcomes through Consensus

Coogan's Community Leadership in Bronzeville Public Schools enacted a materialist rhetoric, teaching students to develop arguments to

Table 8. A comparison of materialist rhetoric and intercultural inquiry.

Features / Exemplars	Sponsor	Inquiry Method	Aim of inquiry	Students' off-campus role	Off-campus text and forum	Students' on-campus final project
Community Leadership in Bronzeville Public Schools	Office of Community Development at IIT and Urban Matters	materialist rhetoric: ideological analysis	consensus; practical, institutional outcomes	public advocate and rhetorical analyst	research report; meetings	project-management reports
Community Literacy Seminar	CMU and Pittsburgh's CLC	community problem-solving strategies	deliberative inquiry that turns critical reflection and personal exploration into rhetorical action.	writing mentor for urban teen	newsletter; community conversation	multi-voiced inquiries
The Rhetoric of Making a Difference	CMU			community researcher	critical incident interviews; community think tank	

achieve consensus. Much like the knowledge activism of Goldblatt's community organizing, materialist rhetoric engages students in the process of forging consensus among disparate stakeholders. Although the activist practices of Alinsky date back to the 1930s, applications for such a rhetorical pedagogy have been articulated much more recently in Coogan's 2006 article "Service Learning and Social Change."

You'll recall reading about Phase One of this IPRP under interpretive pedagogies. In that phase, students shadowed community leaders and wrote leadership portraits for Urban Matters. Coogan revised the next iterations of the IPRP—the ones discussed here—to "teach[. . .] students how to position themselves on the ideological battleground of claims and warrants on public issues facing our communities" (669). The IPRPs had two components, fieldwork and coursework. For their fieldwork, students worked as a team of "public advoca[tes]" conducting rhetorical analyses and, on the basis of their findings (689), compiled a research report recommending arguments to create the conditions for a diverse set of stakeholders to "organize *for* something"—in this case, the reform of Bronzeville's public schools (689). For their coursework, students wrote a final reflection paper explaining how their team managed the demands of the year-long research project.

INTERCULTURAL INQUIRY: RESTRUCTURING DELIBERATIVE DIALOGUES AROUND DIFFERENCE

Inquiry-driven pedagogy developed at the CLC transforms personal and public knowledge by re-structuring deliberative dialogues among individuals and groups across lines of difference (Higgins, Long, and Flower). Like the community think tank described in chapter 7, this pedagogy emphasizes intercultural difference as a resource for problem solving. The phrase *intercultural inquiry* describes both the alternative model of deliberative inquiry developed at the CLC and the distinctive pedagogy that makes it possible (cf. Peck, Flower, and Higgins 209). Grounded in the theory behind several dozen literacy projects, university seminars, and think-tank initiatives, this pedagogy emphasizes intercultural inquiry and typically engages college students either as writing mentors for urban teens writers (cf. Flower "Literate Action"; Long "Mentors Inventing") or as researchers investigating and documenting the problems and perspectives that launch community think tanks.

These courses include both an off- and an on-campus segment, both of which circulate alternative public texts and practices. The off-campus segment positions college students as supporters, learning to elicit and to help document the situated knowledge of community residents. For instance, in the Community Literacy Seminar, sponsored in partnership with the CLC in the 1990s, college students served as mentors trained in collaborative planning to support urban teenagers who wrote newsletters that provided the basis for projects' culminating community problem-solving dialogues (cf. Flower, *Construction* 141–49; Flower, Wallace, Norris, and Burnett). Similarly, the Rhetoric of Making a Difference continues in conjunction with Community Think Tanks, and Literacy: Educational Theory and Community Practice brings urban teens with learning disabilities to campus for Decision Makers. In these iterations, college students conduct critical-incident interviews with stakeholders in order to write problem narratives like the one described in chapter 7 about Melissa negotiating the gaps in her on-the-job training.

As a complement to such fieldwork, the on-campus segment initially teaches students problem-solving strategies and provides relevant scholarly background. Then, after the community think tank, students use the design of previous *Findings* (organized around a scenario, decision points, and a discussion of options and their outcomes) to orchestrate an event and create a text that replicates some of the dialogic dynamics of the community think tank. Back on campus, students consolidate and represent the critical statements they heard during the think tank sessions. Their work informs the formalized *Findings* published for that think tank. In addition, for their final projects, students synthesize their fieldwork, readings, and reflections in the form of a "multi-voiced inquiry" in which students deliberate culturally loaded open questions with teen writers or other community partners (Flower, *Problem Solving* 421; "Intercultural Inquiry"). These inquiries "put charged issues like [. . .] justice, success, responsibility, emancipation, or role models [. . .] on the table as open questions" where they "become[. . .] qualified, conditionalized concept[s . . .] for both the teenager and the mentor" (Flower, "Intercultural Inquiry" 197).

1. *Students position themselves as members of a local public deliberating with others across boundaries of difference into a pressing social issue.*

In learning new rhetorical skills and gaining new intercultural competencies, students become members of a community—one that exists to deliberate a pressing social issue. Material rhetoric evokes a conventional model whereby stakeholders come together to deliberate claims and evidence in order to reach decisions for future joint action. Students position themselves as rhetors in the local public that resembles the discursive site of community organizing. Here, they "listen[. . .] closely to [. . .] community partners" in order to identify claims and warrants that had (and hadn't) worked in the past and those that have the best chance of securing agreement under the current circumstances (Coogan, "Service" 690).

In contrast, intercultural inquiry invites students to participate in a transformed model of local public talk. Given intercultural inquiry's search for alternative perspectives, student position themselves as supporters and participants in the local public of a community problem-solving dialogue. Here, students develop their intercultural competence by learning to listen imaginatively across cultural difference. They actively seek out difference (in the form of diverse perspectives, rival hypotheses, situated stories behind the story), put inquiry before advocacy, and engage collaboratively in problem-solving dialogue. They also prompt other participants to do the same, so the focus isn't solely on what the students can learn but also on the public interaction they help create.

What teachers can do to help:

. . . *With community partners, assess the rhetorical situation.* In classical rhetorical theory, deliberation begins at the point of stasis; however, "in diverse communities, such argument seems premature; the problem space itself has not been defined" (Higgins, Long, and Flower 35). Consequently, both materialist rhetoric and intercultural inquiry—despite their different aims—stress that deliberation begins with the initial work of discovering with community partners the nature of problems and thus plausible responses to them.

With consensus as its aim, a materialist rhetoric looks for an argument that a community partner needs to win—one whose impact stands to improve the lives of urban residents—and one for which it is reasonable to assume that college students' research projects can make a significant, if modest, contribution. For instance, Coogan started assessing the rhetorical situation with his community partners in advance of the school year. Initially, he and community leader Mrs. Brown identified the need for a "network" of community organizers and parents to work together—"independent" of the school system—

to "improve all Bronzeville public schools" (681). This assessment posed the question: *What kind of an argument would mobilize such a network?* Producing viable alternatives and testing their impact are part of Coogan's materialist method, so over time, he and his partners refined this initial assessment and refined their guiding questions and shifted their focus accordingly.

Intercultural inquiry also stresses that analyzing the rhetorical situation is an ongoing, collaborative process. It identifies four activities central to this process:

- configuring the *problem space* or object of deliberation
- identifying relevant *stakeholders* in the community
- assessing existing *venues* for public problem solving and
- analyzing *literate practices* used to represent and address problems and the way these practices structure stakeholder *participation* (Higgins, Long, and Flower 11).

Assessing the rhetorical situation entails both identifying the exigency (the perceived problems) and audience (the potential stakeholders addressed) and also critically reflecting on the process of problem solving itself, the ways in which existing practices and histories of decision making and argument might privilege or exclude important stakeholder groups. Literacy leaders, researchers, and student mentors who work in community-literacy projects contribute not by defining the problem for others or offering prepackaged responses but by helping groups articulate, document, and update their sense of the rhetorical situation as it unfolds and develops.

In diverse settings, assessing the rhetorical situation means engaging as part of a team, not an observing ethnographer, objective consultant, or professional facilitator (cf. Faber). Inquiry-driven pedagogies stress that all stakeholders have knowledge, cultural capital, material resources, and experience that contribute to a robust assessment of the rhetorical situation.

. . . With community partners, create a local public for the purpose of joint inquiry and social change. You'll recall from chapter 7 that the community-organizing effort and the community think tank offer alternative images of local public deliberation: the former focuses on generating talk and text to secure agreement; the latter also depends on text, but

its purpose is to enact an alternative public discourse where ideas and identities are argued and performed in the hybrid discourse of community literacy. This distinction explains the underlying logistical differences in how educators use materialist rhetoric, on the one hand, and intercultural inquiry, on the other, to support students' public action.

A materialist rhetoric focuses on argument—particularly, how argument works in community settings and what it takes to secure the kind of agreement among diverse parties that can change institutional policies and practices. If assessing the rhetorical situation is the preliminary work required in order for university partners to participate intelligently with community partners and to incorporate students in the mix, then creating the local public is the deliberative process of securing the desired agreement. Like Goldblatt in "Alinsky's Reveille," Coogan documents the rhetorical traction required to mobilize a local public that reaches toward consensus. He and his community partners mobilized a local public once they focused on the right question, not how to advocate local control over all of Bronzeville's public schools— as they had initially framed the question—but what it would take to increase parental involvement in fewer and more needier schools. College students participated in this local public by attending "formal meetings with the teachers, staff and parents to brainstorm appropriate programs for parent involvement" (Coogan, "Service" 689) and conducting field research to determine "the needs and current resources" of individual schools (689).

From an intercultural perspective, a local public is a problem-solving dialogue that reaches not for consensus but a working resolution that acknowledges the need for continued negotiation in the face of reasonable difference. You'll recall how findings from the think tank embodied this contingent resolution by using an inventive "mix of narrative, argument, evidence, testimony, and practical plans" (Flower, "Intercultural Knowledge" 255) to capture "the abstract voices of published reports, data and policies found in the literature, the rich specifics of critical-incident interviews, the interpretations drawn from rival readings of problem cases, and the action plans of decision-making dialogues" (266). Creating such a local public means designing a discursive site where college students join other members of the community to seek out rival perspectives on a shared problem and to put these perspectives into generative dialogue. Computer technology can support such public dialogue.

Computer-supported dialogue. The local public that developed from the CLC is the community problem-solving dialogue. In the context of both the Community Literacy Seminar and the Rhetoric of Making a Difference, these dialogues are actual forums, the culmination of extended projects. As a metaphor, however, the concept of a problem-solving dialogue affords the possibility of teachers and students of rhetoric using computer technology to create local publics in other venues, as well. Consider, for instance, Amanda Young's interactive multimedia tool *What's Your Plan?* To support decisions about safe sex and abstinence, the computer interface brings to life the faces and voices of multiple boyfriends and girlfriends as well as teens' moms, older friends, and medical advisors. In Young's study, physicians and counselors used the software to engage young women in conversations "to develop strategies for effective contraceptive use or for maintaining sexual abstinence" (A. Young and Flower 90). But the concept applies to rhetorical education, as well. To explore a pressing social issue in their community, college students, for instance, could research multiple perspectives—using the same critical-incident technique that students in The Rhetoric of Making a Difference have used to elicit the situated knowledge of welfare-to-work recipients and nursing aides. Students could also design the software interface to reflect the complexity of the issue and to engage participants in actively negotiating the competing perspectives. First, students would be designing a virtual local public encapsulated in the computer program. In addition, their work would come to life when they use that interface to host problem-solving dialogues with other members of the community. In such a venue, the local public would be the intercultural relationships and focused inquiry that such an interface supports among those whose conversations it helps to structure.

Digital storytelling offers another option for using computer technology to create local publics. Wayne Peck and Jan Leo's *Telling Our Stories* provides an example. The core concept here is the *audio tour* that one finds at technologically equipped art installations. (In structure, the set up reminds me of wandering the wheat fields of St. Remy, France, with headphones on my ears—listening to excerpts of Vincent Van Gogh's biography while looking at Plexiglas-protected reproductions of the art he produced inspired by a given wheat field or haystack.) But *Telling Our Stories* is a traveling exhibit with a decidedly counterpublic purpose: to bring to light the stories of the Presbyterian gay, lesbian, bisexual and transgendered (GLBT) community. The exhibit travels to the sanctuaries of "more light" congregations affiliated with the Racial and Social Justice and Reconciliation Ministry Team of the Pittsburgh Presbytery. On easels stand portraits of people who have gone public with their stories, compiled and entitled *Voices from the GLBT Community*. On MP3 players equipped with headphones are state-of-the-art radio stories on par with National Public Radio's *StoryCorps* and *This American Life*. These stories tell of the pain of exclusion and call into question homophobic practices and attitudes that marginalize church members based on their sexual orientations. Entitled "A Couple's Story," "One Man's Story," "A Sister's Story," for instance, participants' stories go in many directions, given their own experiences and perspectives, but each is a problem narrative that culminates in a statement that speaks to divisions in the church at large and create paths toward healing and reconciliation. The stories are edited into segments; the printed subtitles are listed on the right-hand bottom corner of each portrait. This feature allows listeners to select the parts of the storyline that strike them as most interesting. It is my observation, however, that people tend to listen to stories in their entirety.

Though the focus here is telling stories of exclusion to a homophobic public, the rhetoric of this digital storytelling program could be adapted to any number of community issues and community-literacy courses, as well. With sufficient support, students could learn to conduct the interviews and to edit the digital radio stories that community members use to go public with their stories. Likewise, students in community-literacy courses could use such digital-story telling techniques to host similar forums—with the portraits, easels, digital recordings, and follow-up dialogue of their own.[5]

Readers interested in digital storytelling will take inspiration from DUSTY, as well—University of California at Berkeley's multi-media, multi-modal outreach project. Housed in the basement of a community center amidst the urban poverty of West Oakland, DUSTY asks participants "to articulate pivotal moments in their lives and to assume agentive stances toward their present identities, circumstances, and futures" (Hull and Katz 44).

2. Students structure inquiry with others, using tools attuned to their rhetorical goals.

In the face of pressing social problems, conversation alone is often insufficient to bring about either personal or social change. Rather than relying solely on default strategies in such situations (e.g., establishing common ground or magnifying differences), students use inquiry pedagogies to structure dialogue as a dynamic process of engagement and learning. Expandable and exportable, the methods that students use are also attuned to off-campus partners' perspectives and priorities and the particular deliberative aims associated with the given local public.

What teachers can do to help:

. . . *Develop rhetorical capacities.* Inquiry-driven pedagogies emphasize that deliberating with community partners is a demanding activity that merits its own name and requires its own rhetorical method. Two techne that develop specific rhetorical capacities are ideographic analysis and community problem-solving strategies.[6] Ideographic analysis helps participants to conduct the following public work:

- to discover the arguments that already exist as ideographs in a community
- to analyze the effectiveness of those arguments
- to collaboratively produce viable alternatives with community partners and
- to assess the impact of these interventions (Coogan, "Service" 668).

Community problem-solving strategies support the following abilities:

- to elicit situated knowledge
- to engage difference in dialogue and
- to construct and to reflect upon wise options (Higgins, Long, and Flower 19–29).

Both methods develop participants' capacities to navigate the complex terrain of local public deliberation. However, ideographic analysis charts a more specified "path from rhetorical discovery to practical outcomes" such as policy changes within specific institutions (Coogan

"Service" 668) while the community problem-solving strategies open up the possibility for "personal and public transformation" (Higgins, Long, and Flower 29).

Emphasizing the historical and political context of public arguments, materialist rhetoric asks students to use ideographic analysis to investigate "the larger rhetorical history that has shaped—and is likely to continue shaping—deliberations" on a given problem in a given community (Coogan, "Service" 668). Such analysis involves ferreting out "the ideographs" that circulate in the larger culture—fragments of cultural codes and concepts that carry persuasive power. It reveals how institutions exercise authority. For instance, in Community Leadership in Bronzeville Public Schools, an ideographic analysis revealed that beneath seemingly persuasive arguments for "local control" was a history of fractious political positioning in Bronzeville's ongoing debate over school reform. The analysis suggested that a more productive tack would shift the focus from "local control" to "local responsibility." With this new focus, students were able to help mobilize alternative rhetorical strategies for securing agreement and instigating action among diverse stakeholders to institute specific policy changes.

In contrast, intercultural inquiry develops students' rhetorical capacities for deliberating across lines of hierarchy and difference in order to arrive at more nuanced understandings of complex public issues. As pedagogy, intercultural inquiry develops the same rhetorical capacities that allow community think tank participants to engage one another in dialogue, as described in chapter 7. Intercultural inquiry teaches students to serve as collaborative planning partners, how to rival, and how to prompt for the story behind the story. Its problem-solving strategies are adaptive heuristics for treading into unfamiliar intercultural waters and interpreting, then circulating, the products of joint inquiry.

3. Students circulate alternative texts and practices.

In inquiry-driven community-literacy courses, students translate their inquiries into purposeful public documents that respond to rhetorical goals and social exigencies.

Students use materialist rhetoric to work simultaneously as public advocates and rhetorical analysts, listening to clients' needs and crafting any number of texts in attempt to meet them (Coogan, "Service" 682). In the Community Leadership project, for instance, students' most effective contributions were their "formal, group-written reports" that followed from their ideographic analysis. These reports made specific recommendations for parent-involvement programs in each of the partnering schools (689).

In a pedagogy based on intercultural inquiry, students circulate both alternative texts and inventive intercultural practices. Consider, for instance, the rhetoric of mentoring. In the Community Literacy Seminar, mentors forged working relationships with their teen writers—relationships based on inquiry into community issues. Building these relationships was an inventive act of intense negotiation of competing priorities, values and goals (Flower "Literate Action"; Long "Mentors Inventing"). So, foremost, these relationships were sites of mutual learning and shared respect—rhetorical achievements in their own right. In addition, they provided valuable support for teen writers articulating their experiences and expertise publicly in newsletters and community conversations.

Students working in conjunction with the community think tank also participate in the circulation of public texts. Consider, for instance, a think tank designed in response to a local, unresolved crisis in staffing at long-term care facilities. The think tank gave voice to the insights of low-wage nursing aides, the women, usually African American, who worked at the bottom rung of the medical establishment's intensely hierarchical system. For two semesters, students in The Rhetoric of Making a Difference conducted critical-incident interviews, scripted problem scenarios, and worked with small groups to draw out "stories-behind-the story," all of which went into a briefing book that was distributed first at a series of think tank sessions with nursing home staff and management and later in a city-wide session with stakeholders from hospitals, agencies, government, policy research, medical education, and nursing homes. This led to the more formal publication and distribution of the *Carnegie Mellon Community Think Tank Findings on Healthcare: The Dilemma of Teamwork, Time, and Turnover* (see www.thinktank.cmu.edu).

What teachers can do to help:

. . . *Set expectations for the public documents students write, and teach strategies for meeting these expectations.* Engaging in inquiry with community partners is one thing; turning material from that research into texts capable of accomplishing cultural work is quite another.

Intercultural inquiry teaches the inventive use of text conventions in order to draw readers into the issue at hand while inviting readers to negotiate and integrate rival perspectives from the text for themselves. Like the think tank's findings, students' end-of-term multi-voiced inquiries, for instance, don't "add up" to a tidy thesis but "confront [. . .] contradictions" and "invit[e] rivals [. . .] through the eyes of difference" (Flower, "Intercultural Inquiry" 187). Intercultural inquiry invites students to explore the tendency of conventional academic research conventions to absorb difference, contradiction, and complexity—making it hard to express the tentative, experiential, or unresolved aspects that arise when students engage difference in dialogue. It encourages students to draw upon "techniques [they] know from creative writing and expressive document design" to juxtapose alternative perspectives while offering a running commentary that interprets these voices and their significance to the inquiry (Flower, *Problem-Solving Strategies* 421).

. . . *Provide structure and opportunity for feedback from real readers.* An important component of text production in both materialist rhetoric and intercultural inquiry is reader-based feedback (Schriver 160–62). In Coogan's materialist pedagogy, a community-based "approval process" structured the means by which students refined their reports prior to publication ("Service" 689). Similarly, CLC college mentors sat next to teen writers to listen to visiting readers respond to the teens' drafts before final versions were sent to the printers. Based on these exchanges, the mentors prompted the teens to fill in gaps in the story line and to articulate the otherwise hidden logic to make the documents accessible and comprehensible to a broad range of readers.

Community think tanks provide other opportunities for reader feedback, but here readers include stakeholders with whom students conducted critical-incident interviews. College students typically launch the first phase of a think-tank dialogue by performing the scenarios (or playlets) they have written on the basis of their critical-incidents interviews. The audience includes the very the people whom the students have previously interviewed. Their responses indicate how well students have represented their versions of the problem.

. . . *Provide venues for students to circulate the fruit of their inquiries.* No matter how educational the inquiry process itself may have been, a goal of inquiry-driven pedagogies is for students to circulate the fruit of their research (Coogan, "Service" 686). To support students' circulation of public writing, inquiry-driven pedagogies provide several options. One option is to let the larger rhetorical exigencies determine, by and large, the venues students will use to go public. In advance of the academic year, Coogan worked behind the scenes to figure out how to position the IPRP within the community. But once the project began, the collaboration process identified the research problem students would pursue (e.g., "'the sort of parent involvement programs [that] work in low income, African-American urban communities'") and the writing students would produce, ranging from "a guidebook for parents of school-age children; a PowerPoint presentation on how to read and interpret a school budget; and flyers, posters, even magnets advertising upcoming meetings" to a research report on their rhetorical analyses (682).

Intercultural inquiry provides other venues for circulating texts. Implications for the off-campus segment of a course are obvious—with its emphasis on eliciting and documenting the situated knowledge of community residents through newsletters, community conversations, and think tanks. But the multi-voiced inquiries students complete for the on-campus component also circulate beyond a given classroom. A website posts selected student inquiries. Students in subsequent community-literacy courses then read from these posts as a regular assignment. The Intercultural Inquiry website also links selected inquiries to the project's findings, the CLC archive, printed dialogues, pertinent research, and the community think tank homepage.

Performative Pedagogies

In Heath's description of Trackton's public stage (chapter 4), local public performance was an end in itself. Trackton's boys "handle[d] their roles by getting their cues and lines straight and knowing the right occasions for joining the chorus" (Heath 79). Performative pedagogies capitalize on the dramatic aspects of public performance, particularly the capacity to call a public into being. However, just as the shadow system complicates the theater as a metaphor for local public life, so, too, pedagogical practices broaden performance beyond its dramatic connotation. At question is the relationship between inquiry and performance in daily deliberations over human affairs—the capacity of people to figure out what to say and how to say it in the presence of strangers. You'll recall that inquiry wasn't the focus in Trackton. Heath observes: "None of these daily situations [such as Aunt Bertha's eviction notice] brought a lot of talk about why they happened or what was needed to set things straight. People [in Trackton] just waited quietly or acted quietly [. . . . F]or a change to come along, they often had to wait a long time" (66). In stark contrast, emerging performative pedagogies are intensely interested in the connections among inquiry and performance, invention and participation, wisdom and action. But, as we'll see, this interest pushes performative pedagogies to the borders of contemporary rhetorical theory.

Performative elements permeate many of the pedagogies reviewed earlier. Tactical pedagogies—particularly their persuasive displays—typically have a dramatic quality. Intercultural inquiry is also a rhetoric of performance. But to signal distinctive performative pedagogies, Flower invokes a decidedly rhetorical interpretation, one that depicts members of marginalized communities circulating ideas that lead to dialogue, deliberation, and social action (*Community Literacy*). Likewise, material rhetoric cultivates not "expert dissectors of texts" but "*agile performers* who cue their audience with a 'dense reconstruction' of the fragments" (Coogan, "Service" 671, emphasis added).[7] In addition to those discussed previously, exemplars include the following:

- TeenTalk and similar programs featured in Art*Show* (Flower and Heath; McLaughlin, Irby, and Langman; Smyth and Heath)
- The New Ghost Dance, a model of intercultural dialogue that recognizes the rhetorical sovereignty of indigenous peoples (Lyons).

Equally helpful to this discussion are emergent theories of rhetorical performance, including:

- *Community Literacy and The Rhetoric of Engagement* (Flower)
- "Sophists for Social Change" (Coogan)
- "Toward a Civic Rhetoric for Technologically and Scientifically Complex Places: Invention, Performance, and Participation" (Simmons and Grabill).

To synthesize this discussion, I begin with a pedagogy that cultivates the dramatic aspect of public performance. I then describe a pedagogy that draws on Stephen Greenblatt's notion of *performatives*—indicators of the rhetorical agency required to chart literate social action amidst competing, legitimate alternatives. Finally, I describe practices that recast and reinvent the sophistic paideutic tradition as a contemporary performative rhetoric—engaging citizens in cultivating the practical wisdom required to build inclusive communities for effective problem solving in a complex world.

1. Students capitalize on the dramatic aspects of performance, the poetic world making that Warner—writing about text—associates with style.

Wells had hoped that deciding what we want from public writing would let educators shift their attention away from the vexing issues of identity politics and instead direct their attention "to the connection between discourse and action" (337). However, Stanford University's longitudinal study of writing suggests that because of the world-creating capacity of style and style's affiliation with expressions of identity, students often develop their repertoires as public rhetors through "live enactment of their own writing," often publicly performed identity narratives (Fishman et al. 244). This version of performance stresses the theatrical dimensions of local public life such as those Heath identifies with Trackton where verbal challenges called a public into being, transforming "the plaza" into "a stage for [. . .] performers making entrances and exits" (Heath 72).

Students in Stanford's longitudinal study of writing reported that a similar dramatic quality was central to much of the writing they did out of class and contributed to their growing repertoires as rhetors capable of calling a public into being—what Warner describes as "the reflexivity by which an addressable object is conjured into being in order to enable the very discourse that gives it existence" (67). Consider, for instance, the spoken poetry artist Mark Otuteye featured in the study. Otuteye performed his slam poetry differently whether it was staged in a coffee shop, a professor's office, or a conference session. The differences constituted a "performative reinvention of writing" based on "the decision he ma[de] in response to the actual scene of enactment: his spontaneous adjustment of words, gestures, and voice in response to heads nodding, feet tapping, and the intangible, yet palpable energy of a full room" (Fishman et al. 244). These adjustments—Fishman et al. suggest—capture poetic world making in the making. In the same study, a student named Beth McGregor deliberately adapted improvisation techniques learned in drama class to quiet her internal editor and cultivate the character of Elizabeth, a competent, knowledgeable college-level writer (236). Encouraged to reflect on the rhetorical decisions required to adjust individual performances "to the rhetorical situation at hand" and "to such physical logistics as acoustics, space and time," student writers develop their own working theories of how to bridge gaps in one's knowledge and to transfer rhetorical expertise to new terrain in order to create a public for their self-performed writing (Fishman et al. 227, 232).[8] By performing their writing for "external audiences, especially public rather than personal ones," students in Stanford's study reported that their writing took on some distinct—and distinctly rhetorical—characteristics. Such writing was "purposeful[. . .]"; it encouraged them, as rhetors, to find the "courage" to take risks (231).[9]

What teachers can do to help:

    . . . Look to drama theory to set standards for what constitutes decidedly public performance and how to support its claims for social change. Fishman et al. stress that educators need to set standards for what distinguishes public performances from those that are primarily literary or entertaining. Performance "on a public-scale" is "something efficacious or capable of producing change" (Sedgwick qtd. in Fishman et al. 232).[10] But in relation to the college classroom, what constitutes efficacy and change depends on how educators (and other stakeholders) configure the public sphere. Drama theory suggests students' performances might interrogate existing social hierarchies or explore the possibility of alternative configurations (cf. McKenzie 31); or combine social critique and resistance (cf. Pineau 41). To bring drama theory into the composition classroom, Fishman et al. urge compositionists "to define a rhetoric (or several rhetorics) of performance" and "to develop strong rubrics for evaluating the different 'writing' performances that our students complete for our classes" (246).

2. *Students develop the reflective, rhetorical agency that Greenblatt calls performatives.*

Amanda Young uses the term *performatives* to describe the rhetorical agency of the young women who used *What's Your Plan?* to make deci sions and negotiate expectations, needs, goals, and preconceived ideas about sexual behavior. She borrows the term from Greenblatt's observation that words can perform actions—the premise of any self concept or belief system. Different in content but not in structure, equally strong performatives operated for college mentors in the Community Literacy Seminar who negotiated alternatives for linking literacy and social justice in their work with urban teen writers. But here, mentors negotiated not the voices of safe sex ("'Ever heard of Aids?'"), but the disciplinary debate in rhet/comp over how to link literacy and social justice. As documented in the self-interviews they conducted and audiotaped following afternoon writing sessions at the CLC with their teens, the college mentors wrestled with *how* to make good on the promise of literacy as a tool for social justice. Upon reading about their work, Ross Winterowd appraised the CLC mentors' performatives this way:

> [The] outline of issues, as developed by the college mentors, is enough to occupy the thoughts and nightmares of a compositionist for at least the interlude between one CCCC convention and the next. Emphasize grammatical correctness. Support emancipation. Invite free expression. Support action-oriented problem-solving. For each of these items, we could supply a plethora of citations, festoons of allusions, long bibliographies. *The point, though, is that the issues arose from the work of nonexpert mentors.* (371–72, emphasis added)

Mentoring positioned college students in the vortex of rhetorical activity: contingent choices among competing alternatives for purposeful action. In negotiating this terrain, mentors engaged in the very problem that characterizes the nature of human affairs:

> If we approach the debate over literate social action by holding out for universal truths, we will end up empty-handed. And if we are content merely to analyze the reasonableness of competing claims, literate social action will remain a theoretical construct that never moves outside the walls of the library. (Long, "Rhetoric" 314)

By moving beyond text-based alternatives, mentors "drew from the disciplinary debate to make judgments about what *to do* as literacy mentors" (emphasis added, 314). Combining Greenblatt's terminology and Flower's theory of negotiated meaning making, we can say that the college mentors' performatives were sites of negotiated conflict and risk—the conflict and risk that comes with building inclusive communities. Students' performatives allowed them to take action and be accountable to that action.

What teachers can do to help:

. . . *Structure reflection.* Face-to-face interaction with teen writers was imperative to the mentors' rhetorical agency. Just as important were the structured reflections that prompted mentors at the CLC to attend to competing goals and priorities. The Community Literacy Seminar assigned students to conduct and to record structured self-interviews back in their dorms following each literacy session. The open-ended self-interview questions asked:

- What were your expectations for the session?
- In what way were they met or complicated?
- What did you and your writer accomplish? and
- What other issues are on your mind that you'd like to explore here? (Long "Intercultural" 113)

Structured reflection helped to focus students' attention on the competing priorities, goals, and values they brought to their roles as mentors. It also served as a catalyst for students to actively negotiate these competing voices, to build richer interpretations of their roles and ways to enact them (cf. Flower "Literate Action"; Long "Intercultural"). As a pedagogical practice, structured reflection provided the basis for electronic bulletin board discussions and group reflection meetings. On a theoretical level, reflection was also the primary catalyst that developed the rhetorical agency that college students needed to navigate (in their working relationships with teens, as well as in their minds) the unfamiliar terrain of community literacy.

3. Students perform contemporary paideutic rhetoric by standing for something with others across difference.

The term *paideutic* refers to the "promise" of classical rhetorical education: "the making of good citizens" (Coogan "Service" 667; cf. Fleming "Rhetoric"). A question for today's educators is how classical rhetoric can inform performative rhetorics of contemporary local public life. Relevant classical concepts include the following:

- Aristotle's heuristics—strategies for making deliberate rhetorical choices and for responding to their outcomes (cf. Flower *Community Literacy*)
- Isocrates's paideutic rhetoric—a *progymnasmata* for cultivating good citizens (cf. Coogan "Service")
- The sophists' emphasis on practical wisdom—a model for taking action in the face of incomplete knowledge—the conundrum of human affairs (cf. Coogan "Sophist"; Flower *Community Literacy;* Flower "Intercultural Knowledge").

However, to be useful, these concepts must be recast in light of the dynamics that distinguish contemporary public life from its counterparts in ancient Greece and Rome, dynamics reflecting the prophetic commitments of progressive activism, the African-American freedom struggle, and the intellectual tradition of prophetic pragmatism (cf. Flower *Community Literacy*); the fragmentary nature of contemporary culture (cf. Coogan, "Service"); and the demands that scientific and technological complexities place on public deliberation (cf. Simmons and Grabill). As I write this chapter, a contemporary theory of rhetorical performance is still very much under construction—as Simmons and Grabill note when they write: "We use the term *performance* along with writing and composing in this article because *we are unsure what, precisely, to call what we see* in communities and how to name what people can make with advanced information technologies" (443, emphasis added). In sum, their approach suggests "a more theoretically informed notion of performance" (443).

Thus far, efforts to articulate a contemporary rhetoric of performance tend to pursue two projects. One project describes the synergy between rhetorical inquiry and rhetorical performance, particularly how specific inquiry practices inform specific kinds of public performances. This is Lyons's purpose in describing the Native American New Ghost Dance. As an image for rhetorical education, the New Ghost Dance evokes performance (communal prayer, protest, and

dance) in relation to inquiry that "locat[es] history and writing instruction in the powerful context of American rhetorical struggle"
(465). The connection between performance and inquiry also drives
Simmons and Grabill's interest in software interface design. In order
for community residents to do the science increasingly required for
public deliberation, computer interfaces must be designed to support
rhetorically astute data analysis.

The second project is to revise the liberal humanist notion of the
lone rhetor delivering a persuasive speech to a larger audience from
behind his podium.[11] Simmons and Grabill observe it no longer makes
sense to theorize the individual rhetor but rather organizations. Organizations read. Organizations distribute and orchestrate knowledge.
Flower speaks for another alternative—one that recognizes not only
the collaborative and relational quality of community literacy but also
the inseparable individual and social nature of literate action.

In the spirit of this theory building, this chapter's final entry does
less to maintain a sharp division between students and teachers and
more to convey the synergy among design literacies (cf. Flower "Intercultural Knowledge"), institutional organization and innovation
(cf. Simmons and Grabill), and the capacity of people as rhetors with
something to say and the right to say it in the presence of strangers (cf.
Hull and Katz). These design literacies, inspired contexts, and rhetorical agents are highlighted in the following discussion of Art*Show* and
the community think tank.

What teachers can do to cultivate contemporary paideutic rhetoric:

. . . *Support students as they move between performative literacies that
call a public into being and inquiry literacies that support deliberation
over complex issues—treating performance and inquiry not as mutually
exclusive literate forms but as complements to local public life.*

Art*Show* and the community think tank have used performance
to introduce and to dramatize issues that—in the same public event—
were focal points for public deliberative inquiry. Regarding the performative qualities, dramatic descriptors are inherent in Art*Show*'s
program design. The youth group was comprised of "a drama team"
who wrote "scripts" to be performed "as dramas" (Flower and Heath
48). In Art*Show,* for example, dramatic performance had a single goal:
to "bring audiences to a tense edge of understanding" on issues "of

peak concern in their communities" (Flower and Heath 48). Performance is especially adept at calling local publics into being.

Quite separate from their dramatic performances but as part of the same event, Art*Show* drew others into inquiry around issues that the forum was designed to address. For Art*Show*, actors choreographed the moment that they dramatically turned their backs on their audience, snapped their fingers, or left the stage to signal that their scripted performance was over and that it was time, now, for audience participation. In this second phase of activity, actors posed questions to the audience to engage them in careful consideration of the information and perspectives that the drama presented. To prepare for such performances and discussions, youth had worked with subject-area experts to develop their scripts. Orchestrating performance and inquiry, the youth were more than conduits for this information. In appraising Art*Show*, Flower and Heath distinguish between performance ("dramatic form") and inquiry ("sensitive insightful discussions") even as they commend their complementary relationship: "For many audiences, university experts could not have gotten either information or persuasive arguments across. Young actors could—for many groups that would never listen to adult experts" (50). The actors in Art*Show* knew that performance, not academic analysis, would draw audiences into the heat of controversy that makes the influx of illegal drugs and the spike in suspension rates complex social issues. But the point isn't that performance *wins the day* over inquiry or that community discourse is *intolerant* of careful analysis. Rather, to put analytical strategies to work, these rhetors needed first to establish the complexity of the terrain they urged the audience to consider. Such complexity is best embodied not in isolated facts but in the details of lived experience dramatized in performance.

Likewise, the critical incidents that students research for community think tanks move students from inquiry to performance and back to inquiry. As part of their course in community outreach, students learn the distinguishing features of the critical incident (cf. Flanagan) and practice strategies for eliciting such information from those whom they interview (cf. Flower, *Problem-Solving Strategies* 340, 368). For example, for a series of think tanks focused on the workplace/worklife issues of healthcare workers, students interviewed "food service workers, cleaning staff, nursing aides" (Flower and Heath 52). Students then experience the world-creating capacity of performance when they perform—as the catalyst that launches a think tank's first phase of dialogues—the scripts they have written on the basis of their critical-incidents interviews. Of all the tools that community think tanks employ—the cribsheets, the briefing books, the strategies—no tool has rivaled the power of dramatization to focus participants' attention on real problems.

CONCLUSION

The practices reviewed in this chapter radically depart from the "warped" image of citizen-as-consumer so prominent in mainstream culture (Cintron 126). Far from simply advocating politically correct consumer choices, these practices ask students to take risks, to build new kinds of working relationships, to venture into spaces they've never gone before, to tax their writing skills like nobody's business, to think long and hard about the challenges and possibility of social change, and to act. But that departure also means that the pedagogies described here reflect very different images of local public life than students in all likelihood bring with them into the classroom. The bigger difference between students' preconceptions of public action and our public pedagogies, the more disconcerting students may find what we ask of them (cf. Deans 137–38). Of course, there's nothing wrong with cognitive dissonance. But the fact that we can predict—or "pre-interpret"—such dissonance from students puts us, as rhetors, in an especially interesting place (Faber 101).

On the one hand, in anticipating such dissonance, we may be tempted to pull out more tools of the academic trade: more and lengthier syllabi, lectures, and assignments. The practices reviewed in this chapter suggest that while such tools may provide valuable clarity, they are likely insufficient to support students' public action.

Nor will it do simply to amend this list of pedagogical practices. Instead, what I think might benefit students and community partners most of all is for each of us to figure out how to invest such pedagogical practices with the world-creating power of style.

In part, I'm suggesting that *in ways reflective of the images of local public life that drive our pedagogies,* we need to become what Heath might call "smart-cat Darrets" for those looking to us for cues about going public. From the dramatic accounts in "Living Room," I sense that Welch is particularly good at using style to bring to life with and for students a distinct and knowable discursive space, as well as the working theory of public rhetoric that governs that space.

But the politics of community literacy also quickly complicate this focus on the teacher-as-world-creator. Coogan alerts us to the fact that the rhetorical traditions operating in the community may differ from those recognized and valued in the academy. He reminds educators "to stay grounded in the rhetorical practices of the communities we wish to serve if we are to have any hope of successfully partnering with these communities" ("Counterpublics" 468). Likewise, Flower warns us against "wrap[ping] ourselves in the purple robes of human agency [. . .]" ("Intercultural Inquiry" 198).

Ultimately, this chapter's list of practices calls us, as educators, to create *with community partners and students* at once tangible and poetic interpretative schemas to guide our participation in local public life. The previous chapters bear witness to what Warner might call the world-creating power of "style" in community-literacy studies (129). Through metaphor, Heath, Brandt, Heller, Cintron, and others capitalize on this world-creating power of style. In academic publications, scholars use figurative language to bring new images and working theories to life for themselves and one another—to create a discursive space (a public) for the study of local public rhetoric. I'm less confident that we always know how to do this performative work in conjunction with our community partners and in relation to our community-literacy courses. In light of the previous chapters, I would suggest it is probably not enough for students to go to new places or to work with others in new ways—as important as these moves may be.

As Cintron's critical ethnography attests, students are, like the rest of us, symbolic beings who depend upon interpretative schemes to make sense of complex and contradictory experience and to take action in the face of such complexity. With studies of situated literacies as a benchmark, we need to construct with others compelling, tangible interpretative schemes that are capable of describing and responding to the demands of contemporary local public discourse. And we need to articulate the working theories that support these interpretative schemes. Finally, we need to continue documenting such collaborative efforts and sharing them with interested colleagues in and outside the academy. To be sure, this work will be as invigorating as it will be worthwhile.

10 Glossary

Alternative discourse—A mix of discursive forms no longer affiliated with given homeplaces or public institutions. As inventive hybrids, alternative discourses lace together discourses of the street and school, policy talk and political activism. It is helpful to think of discourse not as a monolithic entity, but as a constellation of related practices that bear a family resemblance and that invoke different kinds of strategies and habits of mind that distinguish them from other families of practice. Though discourses associated with formal institutions are often the most rigorously enforced, the inventive capacity of rhetoric makes alternative discourse possible—though always in relation to contextual conditions and constraints.

Autonomous model of literacy—An understanding of literacy prominent through the 1970s that took reading and writing to be generalizable skills that foster levels of abstract thinking and critical analysis unavailable to the oral mind. The model assumed that literacy could be packaged and transported from one setting to another for equal effect. The model pinned the hope of a developing country's institutional and economic autonomy on its general population attaining a certain rate of literacy.

Collaborative planning—A technique for rhetorical invention that structures the rhetorical thinking typical of experienced writers. The supporter prompts the writer not only to consider content or topic knowledge (the point at which inexperienced writers typically start and stop), but also to construct a more rhetorically astute plan by actively thinking about key points and purpose, the needs and anticipated responses of readers, and alternative text conventions that might support this increasingly elaborated network of goals, plans, and ideas. Developed by Flower and her colleagues, the strategy has been used in a number of academic and community settings to teach writing, to support classroom inquiry by teachers and students, and to conduct research into students' rhetorical strategies. Because this process of articulating a plan makes thinking "more visible," collaborative planning is a useful research tool that captures something of the social cognitive interaction at play when people engage in rhetorical planning.

Critical-rational discourse—See *rational-critical discourse*.

Communicative democracy—A model for public deliberation that attempts to correct for the exclusionary features of rational-critical discourse. Associated with Iris Young's political philosophy, communicative democracy values not only argument, but also narrative and the broader range of communicative styles that disenfranchised people may prefer to use to interpret their own, and their communities', lived experiences and to advocate for change.

Community organizing—A grassroots political practice that leverages connections and resources for the good of local neighborhoods. Based on the practical theory of Alinsky, co-founder of Back of the Yards Neighborhood Council, community-organizing efforts typically organize large groups of people to execute subversive tactics against big business and stagnant government agencies and have sponsors who provide an institutional base as well as systematic training.

Community think tank—A forum designed to support intercultural inquiry into complex social issues. A permutation of the problem-solving dialogue at Pittsburgh's Community Literacy Center (CLC), the community think tank deliberately reorganizes community, academic, professional, and vernacular discourses to ask how people can use their differences to construct realistically complex understandings of pressing social issues in order to support expanded sets of options in their own spheres of influence.

Counterpublic—A subaltern public that shelters oppositional identities and interests. A counterpublic deliberately circulates discourse outside the counterpublic in attempt to persuade others to think differently about its members.

Cultural agency—The capacity of institutions to circulate resources to bring about social change by endorsing specific literate practices and incentives for using them. Compare to *linguistic agency* and *rhetorical agency.*

Cultural appropriation—The means by which a subaltern makes new meaning by taking symbols from the dominant culture and ascribing to them new significance that reinforces the internal integrity of the subaltern. The process of appropriation renders the original symbol unrecognizable to the dominant culture.

Cultural imaginary—Postmodern terminology referring to the ideological landscape that links cultural forms and the political unconscious to specific material conditions.

Deliberation—The public practice of decision-making associated with rational-critical discourse, for instance, the jurisprudential practice of securing warranted assent or the give-and-take of a well-functioning committee. Conventional deliberation strives for consensus and dictates rules for participation.

Design literacies—Theory-driven rhetorical interventions that structure local public discourse to achieve aims not readily accomplished in other forums.

Discourse—The whole discursive kit and caboodle that distinguishes one set of social practices from another; includes not only habits of reading and writing but also social roles, values, and body language—or what John Paul Gee calls "writing-doing-being-valuing-believing combinations" (6). Discourse is associated with Gee's notion of an "identity kit" and the distinction between primary, capital-<u>D</u> Discourse into which one is born and secondary discourses into which one is socialized over a lifetime.

Domains—A sociolinguistic term referring to distinct terrains that structure the social purposes that literacy serves and how it is learned. Domains are affiliated with a society's institutions. The domain of the home, for instance, is largely structured by the social institution of the family; likewise, the domains of schools, hospitals, and courtrooms are affiliated with educational, medical, and legal institutions, respectively.

Dominant discourse—Prestige literacies that carry out the purposes of social institutions. Dominant discourse is affiliated with mainstream culture. It helps to circulate a system of rewards to those who abide by its codes and conventions and, thus, who serve the system's interests. Contrast with *vernacular literacy.*

Economy of efficiency—A context for literacy learning characterized by a dearth of readily accessible resources. An economy of efficiency demands that learners resourcefully transform familiar practices in order to respond to new rhetorical exigencies. The distinction between economies of *efficiency* and *excess* is central to Brandt's account of the increase of literacy rates among African Americans in times of political and economic duress.

Economy of excess—a context for literacy learning characterized by a plentitude of resources. In such a context, learners benefit readily from a host of sponsors who offer incentives for learning to read and write.

Formal public—A discursive entity that exists in relation to texts and their circulation. Warner stipulates seven features of a formal public, emphasizing, for instance, stranger relationality and mere awareness as criteria for public-making. (The complete list is included under Warner's entry in the annotated bibliography that follows. See also *local public.*)

Gatekeeping encounter—A discursive site within an institutional setting where an institutional worker and a community resident negotiate the resident's access to limited resources. Typically, a gatekeeping encounter is a site of political struggle where a resident strives to preserve personal dignity while also securing resources for herself and her family.

Great divide—A gulf said to distinguish literate and oral minds, the former believed to be more intellectually agile, better able to separate fact from myth, and better able to glean abstract principles from concrete experience. Early literacy studies such as the Via Literacy Project (1973–1978) established empirical methods for testing such assumptions. Scribner and Cole found that claims of a great divide are not so much wrong as overstated. A more accurate understanding considers that specific discursive practices carry with them specific cognitive consequences (whether for memorizing, quantitative reasoning, or constructing arguments) based on the social purposes for which literacy is organized, rather than the linguistic system used to encode such practices.

Hidden logic—Often unspoken motives, values, and assumptions that people use to interpret complex situations. People's hidden logic is an important resource for building realistically complex representations of complex social issues.

Hidden transcript—An unarticulated running commentary that indirectly opposes and critiques racist and classist assumptions of the institutional worker's public transcript.

Ideological model of literacy—A view of literacy associated with New Literacy Studies that works from the premise that literacy is always already a contested site of meaning making, not a neutral cognitive tool. The ideological model emphasizes that the institutional practices that structure and reward (or discourage) literacy's use in specific social and cultural contexts determine its meaning and social value.

Inspired context—A context for literacy learning that cultivates people's capacity to transform their literate repertoires to address new exigencies under conditions of scarcity and stress. It compensates for the toll that poverty and other forms of social neglect—in including diminished opportunities for literacy learning—take on people's lives.

Institution—An organization that holds the power to make and to enforce policies. An institution perpetuates processes for producing and distributing knowledge. Within studies of community literacy, *public institution* often refers to the wide range of social service agencies that distribute resources within a society, such as regional branches of the Department of Social Services, the Housing Authority, and the criminal justice system.

Institutional workers—Gatekeepers who operate and represent the interests of public institutions by determining who accesses the limited resources they oversee.

Intercultural inquiry—A willingness, a capacity, and a rhetorical method for exchanging perspectives and seeking out commonalities, differences, and gaps in interpretations. Intercultural inquiry helps participants critically assess and expand their knowledge of a problem in personally and socially significant ways. It includes rhetorical tools for understanding one's own situated knowledge in terms of the larger social landscape—for recognizing that the starting point from which others join a conversation is different from one's own. Intercultural inquiry seeks not consensus among disparate parties, but makes difference a resource for personal and public transformed understanding.

Knowledge activism—The means by which a writing program administrator facilitates the collaborative process that community partners use to determine the shape of a shared project and to craft the documents that articulate this project and move it toward fruition. The knowledge activist takes his or her cues from Alinsky's practical theory of community organizing.

Linguistic agency—The rhetorical decisions that community residents make to navigate encounters with institutional workers. Includes the resident's capacity for critical analysis, particularly the ability to evaluate the effectiveness of her decisions within a gatekeeping encounter and to retool accordingly. Since such encounters are co-constructed in the language of both parties, however, a community resident can not control for the institutional worker's response but rather can only hope to improve the likelihood that the institutional representative will respond in a desired manner. Thus, linguistic agency also acknowledges that a resident's agency is limited by situational constraints and how a given encounter unfolds.

Literate act—Since the late 1970s, literacy scholars have worked to distinguish the study of literacy from literary scholarship that associates writing with textual product. Readers interested in these initial efforts will find useful the references that Heath provides in footnote #2 on page 386 of *Ways with Words*. This and the next four entries highlight key distinctions in this effort—distinctions that not only prioritize certain aspects of literacy but also evoke different conceptual frameworks for its study. Within this discussion, then, *literate act* is a unit of analysis within Flower's socio-cognitive theory of writing, a perspective that is especially attuned to the constructive process through which writers actively and intentionally transform what they know and adapt discourse conventions to carry out personally meaningful, goal-directed uses of literacy. The concept of a literate act calls into question descriptions of literacy predicated on discrete and stable practices and highlights instead the dynamic process through which writers often negotiate complex, even contradictory, rhetorical goals.

Literacy event—A unit of analysis associated with sociolinguistic studies of literacy, often in educational settings. As an object of study, the literacy event focuses attention on those occasions where one or more persons engage a text, whether to comprehend an existing text or to compose a new one. Literacy events carry with them rules of engagement that regulate how people talk about the text at hand. As evident in Heath's *Ways with Words,* the study of literacy events has documented the interdependent nature of literacy and orality.

Literate (rhetorical) performance—Literate action situated in decidedly public arenas where rhetors speak with others for values and ideas. Associated with Flower's rhetorical theory of social engagement, literate performances are relational in that rhetors actively engage with others and respond to the intended and unintended consequences of their discursive decisions. Literate performances include strategic inquiry, deliberative engagement, and reflective decision making.

Literate practice (Scribner and Cole)—A unit of analysis associated with anthropological studies of literacy. The literate practice focuses attention on the social purposes that organize patterns of literacy use. Scribner and Cole emphasize four features of a literate practice: as an activity, it is recurrent and goal-driven; it makes use of a particular technology and operates within a particular system of knowledge.

Literate practice (Street)—The ideological model of literacy also describes literacy in terms of practices but now pitched to a higher level of abstraction than Scribner and Cole's definition focused on goals, technology, knowledge and skills. A leader of NLS, Street focuses on the ways that literacy participates in overlapping systems that distribute institutional power. In this framework, *literate practice* refers to activities that are embedded in institutional contexts and, thus, implicated in wider social, economic, and political processes.

Local public—The community in community literacy. At once discursive and material, local publics are the sites that people devise to address distinct rhetorical agendas that range from socializing children into appropriate uses of language to drawing upon stakeholders' differences as a resource for addressing shared problems to demanding respect under conditions that yield little of it. Local publics are often the form of public life that ordinary people access most readily; thus, they are sites where ordinary people tend to develop their voices and repertoires for going public.

Local public framework—A five-point heuristic for comparing accounts of how ordinary people go public. Focuses attention on the researcher's *guiding metaphor* for describing the discursive space, especially the metaphor's distinctive features; *context,* including issues of location, as well as other context-specific factors that give public literacies their meaning; the *tenor of the discourse,* or register, that makes for the distinctive affective quality of the discourse; the *literacies* people use to organize and carry out their purposes for going public; and *rhetorical invention,* the generative process by which people respond to the exigencies that call them together as a local public. The local public framework highlights implications that follow from alternative accounts of local public life, particularly how rhetorical invention translates into choices, practices, and actions for educators, learners, community partners, activists, and researchers.

Materialist rhetoric—an inventional technique aimed at identifying the fragments of argument—or ideographs—most likely to secure agreement among diverse constituencies.

Mestiza public—An image of an inclusive local public inspired by Gloria Anzaldua's descriptions of mestiza consciousness. In the name of social justice, this public borderland creates a community-based intercultural dialogue that extends across borders of race, class, status, power, and discourse to accommodate multiple discursive codes.

Negotiation—The process through which the writer provisionally resolves the conflict among competing rhetorical goals in order to construct inventive and purposeful literate action. An observation-based account of literate action grounded in Flower's socio-cognitive approach to rhetorical inquiry, negotiation theory offers a plausible explanation of how socially situated individuals make difficult decisions in the face of multiple, internalized competing public voices. Negotiation lets people build more robust working theories of the problem and, thereby, draw on these revised, enhanced working theories to respond to similar versions of the problem when it arises for them in the future.

Network—Social relations within and among domains through which people carry out shared literate activity. Nodes of a network represent different stakeholders who come together around a social problem to protect their own interests.

New Ghost Dance—A contemporary version of the Native American practice that exercises and celebrates communal integrity at the same time that it invites cultural difference and supports inquiry. A performative public rhetoric, the New Ghost Dance is at once a right, a theory, a practice, and a kind of poetry. Lyons urges other educators to engage students in this practice by teaching treaties and federal laws as rhetorical texts and by situating classroom inquiry in relation to larger historical trends relevant to their educational context.

New Literacy Group (NLG)—Sponsors of the ideological model of literacy and situated studies of literacy. The NLG launched numerous cross-cultural comparisons and similar studies of minority-group practices here in the United States.

New Literacy Studies (NLS)—An approach to the study of literacy grounded in a broad understanding based not on reading and its purported psychological consequences but on the study of literate practices in their social and cultural contexts. NLS defines literacy as a constellation of local, situated practices that are shaped by institutional power and responsive to changes across time and place. This body of scholarship demonstrates how literacy participates in the construction of ethnicity, gender, and religious identities by structuring and sustaining power dynamics within institutional relationships.

Prophetic pragmatism—An intellectual stance affiliated with the moral philosophy of West. Prophetic pragmatism calls people to recognize and to work to dismantle the causes of social misery. It informs the strong rival-hypothesis stance as the basis for intercultural inquiry within the CLC's rhetorical model of community literacy.

Public—see *formal public*.

Public transcript—The language the institutional worker uses to carry out the business at hand. The public transcript typically follows the grand narrative of mainstream ideology, enshrining the authority of the gatekeeper as the morally upright helper and community resident as the quite possibly shifty seeker-of-services.

Rational-critical discourse (also appears in scholarship as *critical-rational discourse*)—A model for public deliberation based on formal argumentation, particularly that which privileges general *truth* over particular *experience*, authoritative *facts* over *emotion*, and reasoned *positions* over *narrative*. Rhetoricians further distinguish *rationality*, which assumes the merit of a claim to be self evident given the internal logic of its appeal from *reasonableness*, which recognizes that what counts as a compelling argument must be negotiated with other members of the discourse community. On the one hand, rational-critical discourse is often portrayed as the enemy of inclusive democratic practice because of its tendency to disguise social privilege in the rules it embodies for what counts as rigorous thought and valued social contribution. But as West argues in *Democracy Matters,* when it comes to complex social issues (such as those that drive community literacy) there is a place for disciplined, "rational" contributions and respectful civil exchange. The point is that in the effort to foster inclusive democratic practices, users of rational-critical discourse should not get to determine the rules of the game and who gets to play but, instead, expect to find their place along side the other perspectives and communicative styles at the table.

Rhetorical agency—A capacity of the non-authoritative writer to take meaningful rhetorical action by actively engaging with contested issues and ideas in order to conduct inquiry, to seek rivals, and to construct a more expansive and shared intercultural understanding. A visible feature of rhetorical agency is public performance—the act of engaging others in actual dialogue in effort to broaden one another's understandings of the issue at hand. Rhetorical agency is the basis of Flower's rhetoric of engagement.

Rhetorical intervention—Any one of a number of action-research methodologies (often expressed as design literacies) that activist rhetoricians use to work with community partners to shape the discursive space in which they work together on a shared problem.

Rhetorical invention—The generative aspect of discourse through which people discover how to respond to new exigencies. Accounts of ordinary people's inventive processes reflect researchers' working theories, such as Cushman's description of the *evaluative process* by which community residents assess and refine the institutional literacies they use to navigate gatekeeping encounters; Flower's theory of *negotiation* by which people turn some level of attention to those voices that complicate their initial understandings of a pressing social issue; and Cintron's understanding of *appropriation* by which gang members mimic mainstream cultural codes, making them unrecognizable to mainstream culture and a display of identity for members of street culture.

Rhetorical sovereignty—The right and ability of minority cultures to represent themselves, their needs, desires, and interests in public and to use their own communicative styles in order to do so. Rhetorical sovereignty underscores the important function that writing plays in acts of self-definition and -determinism for minority cultures.

Rhetorics of sustainability—Working theories of local publics and their future trajectories. Competing rhetorics of sustainability turn on different understandings of conflict and its relationship to rhetorical intervention, the discursive engine that lets ordinary people go public. These rhetorics also nominate alternative sets of priorities and practices for maintaining a given local public and its distinctive activities.

Sponsor—The institutional relationship that provides cultural and material support to literacy learners, including explicit instruction, technological support, and social incentives. Sponsorship is associated with Brandt's study of how ordinary Americans born between 1895 and 1985 responded to changes in the meaning and methods of literacy learning.

Sustainability—Expressed in the maxim, "Without margin, there is no mission." In community work, sustainability is the capacity of a community organization to keep life and limb together, to maintain a strong sense of purpose and to secure the requisite funding and personnel needed to flourish.

Techne—A technique or strategy used to chart deliberate rhetorical action. In *Rhetoric Reclaimed,* Atwill observes that this special class of productive knowledge is "stable enough" that people can grasp them as specific strategies and transfer them to new contexts but "flexible enough" to be useful in specific situations and for particular purposes (48).

Topoi—In the postmodern parlance of Cintron's rhetoric of everyday life, these are the commonplace binaries through which ideology structures the interpretative landscape. Topoi comprise the fund of cultural meanings from which a shadow system manufactures its own subterranean and esoteric meanings. The power of a topos is its capacity to invoke its opposite—for example, tame vs. wild, respect vs. disrespect, and rationality and order vs. madness and disorder.

Transformed understanding—Grounded in Flower's social cognitive rhetoric and research documenting that people build mental representations of problems as a first phase in rhetorical problem solving. These flexible, mutable multi-modal mental networks can direct people's decisions and actions and, thus, inform the kind of wise judgment that takes into account multiple (and often competing) accounts of lived experience.

Vernacular literacy—Ways with words affiliated with the home and neighborhood. Vernacular literacies tend to be informal and flexible in contrast to the uniform and inflexible literacies that structure institutional practices. Also referred to as *hidden literacies* or *nondominant discourse.*

Working theory—From Flower's social cognitive rhetoric, the internal representation that a person constructs to interpret and to carry out complex rhetorical activity—whether teaching a course as a classroom teacher or navigating police presence as an urban teenager. Different from both informal lore that circulate in support of alternative practices and from formal theories that exist as propositions in published text, a working theory is a social-cognitive interpretative scheme that mediates, interprets, and guides activity.

11 Annotated Bibliography

Scholars have contributed to community-literacy studies by pursuing a range of interests. For some, that interest has been community action (e.g., Faber); for others, intercultural inquiry (e.g., Flower). Some have contributed to community-literacy studies by pursuing an interest in children's language acquisition (e.g., Heath); others, in adult literacy (e.g., Howard). As a composite, this bibliography underscores the range of theoretical frameworks, methodological approaches, and scholarly purposes that now inform inquiry into the vast array of issues that relate to and extend the question of how ordinary people go public.

Adler-Kassner, Linda, Robert Crooks, and Ann Watters, eds. *Writing the Community: Concepts and Models for Service-Learning in Composition*. Washington, DC: American Association for Higher Education, 1997.

Writing the Community: Concepts and Models for Service-Learning in Composition situates the discipline's growing interest in public writing in relation to writing theory, the writing-across-the-curriculum movement, and service-learning. The volume is first in a series that the AAHE sponsored to promote service learning across academic disciplines. In the introduction, Adler-Kassner, Crooks, and Watters make a strong case for public writing as productive knowledge that defies reductive distinctions between theory and practice. They identify institutional structures within higher education that need to be changed to facilitate service-learning initiatives, including course/term structures, disciplinary and departmental structures, and evaluation procedures for assessing students' work. The collection is a snapshot of second generation service-learning curricula. As such, authors of several articles describe iterations of course design, documenting their efforts to make good on the promise of public writing within local contexts that makes such learning both possible and problematic.

The volume includes "Partners in Inquiry: A Logic for Community Outreach." Here, Flower elaborates the logic of inquiry that drives community literacy as an alternative discourse for intercultural deliberation. Toward this end, she describes features of the community problem-solving dialogue and offers suggestions for incorporating such a practice within "ordinary" writing courses. Flower observes that what often foils community-university partnerships are the logics motivating them: for instance, the logic of cultural mission that puts patronizing distance between the university "doer" and the community "receiver"; the logic of technical expertise that assumes the discourse and tools of the university provide the only viable ways to frame solutions and structure relationships; and the logic of compassion fostering an "intensely individual consciousness" quite separate from "public action" (100). The logic of inquiry casts public writing as an innovative rhetorical activity in which students develop rhetorical capacities for engaging with others in dialogue about pressing social issues.

The volume reprints Bruce Herzberg's often cited article, "Community Service and Critical Teaching." It also includes an annotated bibliography that Bacon and Deans compiled, documenting a decade of disciplinary discussion linking composition and community service.

Anderson, Jim, Maureen Kendrick, Theresa Rogers, and Suzanne Smythe, eds. *Portraits of Literacy Across Families, Communities, and Schools: Intersections and Tensions.* Mahwah: Lawrence Erlbaum Associates, 2005.

Representing some of the most inventive inquiries in NLS to date, *Portraits of Literacy Across Families, Communities, and Schools* interrogates domains of school, family, and community and their influence over what gets defined, taught, and learned as literacy. Employing a cross-cultural perspective associated with NLS, the volume features studies from Karachi, Pakistan; to Cape Town, South Africa; to the Manitoulin Island in northern Ontario, Canada. The tenets of NLS that frame the introduction also inform the researchers' largely anthropological research methods.

Part I is focused on how various configurations of *family* shape language learning. This section focuses on children's language learning, but also attends to that of immigrant parents, for example, and the ways in which effective family-literacy programs can create synergy with teachers who learn, in turn, the literacies their students practice at home. Part II addresses the literacy learning of youth, with an emphasis on the capacity of young people to work in multimodalities, often with a propensity for combining literacies across domains. Part III focuses on adult and community literacy, and Part IV considers implications at the level of educational and public policy.

Themes threaded throughout the collection's diverse research studies coalesce around the volume's key arguments. One such argument is that effective literacy curricula respond to the values and practices of local communities. The volume also argues that people's literacies are often rendered invisible by the social hierarchies that structure formal institutions. Explored in several chapters, this theme is most explicitly addressed in David Bloome's chapter, "The People Write Back: Community Literacy and the Visibility of the Ordinary Writer." Bloome argues that obstructive institutional hierarchies need to be dismantled so more people can access the tools they need to position themselves as legitimate meaning makers in the workplace.

The volume's final theme is the contested connection between literacy and social justice. In the book's final chapter, "Connecting the Local and the Global: A Pedagogy of Not-Literacy," Elsa Auerbach charges that claims for literate social action are another version of the literacy myth. Instead, Auerbach promotes not-literacy programs affiliated with specific social movements. In a review of this book (*Reflections: A Journal of Writing, Community Literacy* 6.1 (2007): 185–89), Higgins responds to Auerbach's argument by pointing out that social movements are themselves literacy sponsors—often sponsoring and leveraging, for instance, the rhetorical capacity to participate in forums addressing problems in one's community. Higgins notes that several studies in *Portraits of Literacy Across Families, Communities, and Schools* document people constructing alternative literacies in order to subvert moves in dominant discourse that would dismiss their expertise. Higgins's reading of *Portraits of Literacy Across Families, Communities, and Schools* affirms that specific literate practices can, indeed, make beneficial differences in people's lives.

Barton, David, and Mary Hamilton. *Local Literacies: Reading and Writing in One Community*. New York: Routledge, 1998.

Community residents have a host of reasons for using literacy in their communities. In *Local Literacies: Reading and Writing in One*

Community, Barton and Hamilton identify the top six, including keeping in touch with friends and carrying out leisure activity. Based on extensive ethnographic research including twelve case studies in a neighborhood called Springside in Lancaster, England, in the 1990s, Barton and Hamilton observe that community residents with shared interests may organize themselves in groups and use literacy to support shared aims; for instance, members of a knitting club read, wrote, and calculated to adjust the sizes of the sweater patterns that they circulate among themselves. From time to time, such groups may find themselves contacting public institutions, as in the case of a stamp-collecting club writing to the postal service for an official album. Most demanding of all, residents may draw on their literate resources to contact public institutions for the purpose of social action.

Barton and Hamilton offer a rich analytical vocabulary for studying everyday literacies, including ways in which the private-public distinction exposes the complex relations between and among domains. The distinction highlights differences between domains, the ways that they encroach on other spaces, and ways that domains blend and overlap, for instance, when a family uses a household literacy (for instance, an affinity for producing puppet shows) to recast a classroom assignment (from a book report, say, to a script for a puppet show) or when a literate behavior constructs a private space in public (for instance, when a commuter in a crowded subway car props up a newspaper to create privacy).

By situating their literacy study in a less conventional domain than the school or workplace, Barton and Hamilton assert that their research agenda reflects a political commitment to document hidden literacies that are often devalued and overlooked. Their commitment to Springside's locale is also a theoretical argument about where literacy itself is located, or resides—not as individual property in individual's heads (an argument that they contend leads to unfounded public claims about cognitive deficits of non-mainstream and working-class learners) but as a resource enhancing community life.

Branch, Kirk. *"Eyes on the Ought to Be": What We Teach When We Teach About Literacy.* Cresskill: Hampton P, 2007.

In *"Eyes on the Ought To Be": What We Teach When We Teach About Literacy,* Branch argues that any literacy program is geared toward a given vision of the future. What is unique about Highlander Folk

School—the focus of Branch's fourth chapter—is that throughout its history it has openly recognized the persuasive dimension of the social contract it has offered its learners. Branch contrasts the Highlander Folk School's crisis education, in place from 1932-1961, with the discourses of contemporary correctional education, vocational education, and No Child Left Behind legislation—all of which are predicated on allegedly self-evident social agendas and scientifically based and, thus, ideologically neutral educational practices. Rather than seeing educators as inextricably trapped within oppressive regulatory systems, Branch suggests the metaphor of the trickster who looks for gaps in the system in order to participate creatively and productively in social change.

Brandt, Deborah. *Literacy in American Lives.* Cambridge, UK: Cambridge UP, 2001.

Literacy in American Lives studies the conditions in which ordinary Americans learned to read and write in the previous century. Taking a cohort analysis approach to the study of literacy, Brandt interviewed 80 people born between 1895 and 1985 from south central Wisconsin and listened to what they remembered about learning to read and write. Brandt's study attends to the role of sponsors, those agents who set the terms for literacy learning, offering incentives for learners to practice reading and writing in particular ways. While some sponsors use coercive tactics and others more hospitable methods, all sponsors have self interests that implicate sponsors in the learning relationship and the versions of literacy they endorse and perpetuate.

Literacy in American Lives traces the forces that make literacy an elusive resource. Because of economic conditions that have tied literacy increasingly closer to the country's forms of consumption and production, literacy in America is in flux. Increasingly over the 20th century, learning to read and write has required learners to engage with this flux, for it permeates the materials used to read and write, the structure of the relationships in which that learning takes place, and the tools that shape and constrain the purposes that literacy serves. Flux carries economic consequences as evidenced in the changing conditions in which successive generations of a single family learn to read and write. As Brandt's analysis documents, on the one hand, each member of a family may inherit a "higher pile" of literacy resources; however, the social currency affiliated with these literacies becomes increasingly short lived. Thus, what distinguishes contemporary literacy is the capacity for "amalgamation"—the ability to reconfigure sets of old practices (each set likely bearing its own historical and ideological traces) for new purposes.

Lest the reader conclude that literacy leans faithfully toward the future, Brandt also documents that histories of older institutional practices continue to hold some sway over the value and meaning of literacy despite the pull of emerging economic forces. This explains the status that reading continues to enjoy in many formal and informal contexts—affiliated as it is with earlier religious functions and the genius of literary artists. Conversely, writing continues to be associated with mundane work despite the demand that the current economy makes on writing.

Literacy in American Lives documents the "ideological congestion" that permeates moments of literacy learning. Brandt also observes that many everyday literacies languish because of insufficient encouragement. Brandt urges educators and policy makers to be more conscious of these and other intricacies of literacy learning in the effort to equalize chances and rewards for learning to read and to write—whereby making literacy a genuine civil right.

Cintron, Ralph. *Angels' Town: Chero Ways, Gang Life, and Rhetorics of the Everyday.* Boston: Beacon P, 1997.

This critical ethnography asks, *how do people demand respect under conditions that offer little of it?* Observing Latino street life from the late 1980s to mid-1990s in an industrial city just west of Chicago, Cintron documents rhetorical tactics and interprets their political implications. Take, for instance the *albures*—or jokes—that Don Angel told using Spanish expressions and bawdy humor to disrespect white class privilege. Testament to his verbal wit and intellectual prowess, the *albures* showcased his unique talents to his compadres and, consequently, created conditions of respect. Other men in Cintron's study demanded respect by circulating hyperbolic displays of iconography affiliated with dominant culture. Graffiti is the most obvious example, but the hyperbolic was also evident in the images that a young man circulated about himself in a collage decorating his bedroom wall. Images of the military, European sports cars, and sports heroes created a hyperbolic display of strength and neatness that defied the dominant culture's messages of raggedness and humiliation that otherwise threatened to define him, his family, and his neighborhood.

Cintron argues that the politics of location figured prominently in Angelstown. For instance, the city's revitalization project streamed funds into a nearby commuter train station. The new station's architecture rendered the Latino section of Angelstown invisible and irrelevant to the city's identity and future—a move which Cintron describes as the ultimate act of humiliation. The ideological implications are clear. In the city's efforts to project an image of civic prosperity and mobility, the new train station and railway created a barrier to conceal that which it considered "ugly, dirty, and threatening" (50).

Cintron also argues that the ideology of the local has immediate consequences for practices of social justice. For Cintron, theorists like Fraser promote "a big-picture version of social justice" with their critiques of a restrictive public sphere and counter theories that legitimate subalterns. The problem is that the "big picture" can be so vague that it lacks meaningful application. But the flipside, the local, has its own problems. For Cintron, the local is the site where mainstream culture exercises its domination, promoting its response to a problem as "the only 'real' solution." The challenge, Cintron argues, is "to argue critically for a big picture of social justice and simultaneously find solutions that make sense from the perspective of the local" (196).

In his analysis of graffiti, thumper cars, and *albures,* Cintron never legitimates criminality, but he also thinks past classic liberal politics that would fail to take seriously both the transgressive valence of many everyday literacies and the social conditions responsible for them.

Coogan, David. "Community Literacy as Civic Dialogue" *Community Literacy Journal* 1.1 (2006): 96–108.

In "Community Literacy as Civic Discourse," Coogan observes firsthand the power of civic discourse to open up a space for intercultural inquiry in ways that neither the ardent stance of advocacy (favored in community organizing), nor the decisive stance of critique (favored in the university), readily supports. Several sites of controversy arose over the course of the community-writing project that Coogan designed at IIT, a university on the south side of Chicago that borders the impoverished neighborhood of Bronzeville. The sites of conflict ranged from community organizers' skepticism—even contempt—for the project's initial design to an African American student's difficulty representing in text the discourse of the African American community resident whom she interviewed for the project's publication, *Digital Stories in Bronzeville*. Coogan analyzes such sites of conflict in order to consider a public not as a spatial forum but as a discursive "tethering" that links people across otherwise often divisive material and institutional boundaries—such as the grand narrative that circulated on the college campus about neighboring housing projects and those who live there. Toward this end, the community-writing project successfully "performed" a political critique of racism and criticism by circulating more informed representations of Bronzeville and its residents—constructions that circulated and sustained a public discourse grounded in empathy, dialogue, and understanding.

Cushman, Ellen. *The Struggle and the Tools: Oral and Literate Strategies in an Inner City Community*. New York: SUNY P, 1998.

The Struggle and the Tools: Oral and Literate Strategies in an Inner City Community presents the linguistic agency that community residents exercise while navigating gatekeeping encounters—politically charged meetings with institutional workers who broker resources such as public housing, food subsidies, and child support. Cushman models an activist methodology emphasizing dialogue, collaboration, and reciprocity with the community residents involved in the study. Conducting her ethnography from 1993 to 1996 in an industrial city in the northeastern United States, Cushman worked most closely with two families—primarily the women who headed the households—to identify features of institutional literacy, to understand situations in which this literacy is used, and to interpret the ideological implications of both institutional literacy and the situations that call for it. The study revealed a three-phased cycle through which community residents developed their linguistic repertoires. During the acquisition phase, community residents learned linguistic moves for handling themselves in gatekeeping encounters. Then in the transfer phase, residents applied strategies from their repertoires to new situations. In the final evaluation phase, residents critically appraised how the encounter unfolded, including the politics that played out and the effectiveness of their linguistic moves—all with an eye toward next time.

Attending to both oppressive daily politics and the rhetorical strategies that residents used to negotiate them—the struggle and the tools—Cushman critiques political theories that assume false consciousness and assess agency in terms of measurable, sustained outcomes, and large-scale social movements. Cushman argues that gatekeeping encounters are sites of daily political struggle for respect, as well as resources. Moreover, she maintains that critical consciousness is not a fixed state of awareness but a stance that shifts and changes in light of one's age, experience, and gender.

Cushman, Ellen, Eugene R. Kintgen, Barry M. Kroll, and Mike Rose, eds. *Literacy: A Critical Sourcebook*. Boston: Bedford/St. Martin's P, 2001.

Literacy: A Critical Sourcebook offers thirty eight landmark selections in the study of literacy. Instrumental in staking the intellectual claim for the study of community literacy, its predecessor *Perspectives on Literacy*, published in 1988, identified "community" as one among four kinds of perspectives (along with theoretical, historical, and educational) for conceptualizing literacy. More comprehensive, the *Sourcebook* pulls together a larger number of works that have defined literacy studies as a distinct field of inquiry. In doing so, the *Sourcebook* both traces various disciplinary interests in literacy, and it documents the wide range of research methodologies that have informed how literacy is currently understood. The *Sourcebook* organizes the scholarship it surveys across seven interrelated categories: (1) technologies for literacy; (2) literacy, knowledge, and cognition; (3) histories of literacy in the United States; (4) literacy development; (5) culture and community; (6) power, privilege, and discourse; (7) mobilizing literacy: work and social change. The *Sourcebook* features many of the same theorists and key works featured in this volume (such as excerpts from Heath's *Ways with Words* and Brandt's *Literacy in American Lives*) and contextualizes them within the broader historical, interdisciplinary landscape.

Deans, Thomas. *Writing Partnerships: Service-Learning in Composition*. New York: NCTE, 2000.

Deans argues that community-university partnerships provide educators in English studies opportunities not only to contribute beyond their universities' walls, but also to test and to extend claims central to the discipline itself: that writing is socially relevant; that audience and purpose transform content knowledge; and that rhetoric is ultimately the art of intervention, not only interpretation. *Writing Partnerships* offers a pluralistic framework for understanding service-learning initiatives and for making informed curricular decisions. Deans's heuristic distinguishes service-leaning initiatives that ask college students to write *for, in,* or *with* the community, and he features exemplars of each approach.

In the writing-*for*-the-community model, students work for local community organizations, writing the kinds of documents (proposals, newsletters, brochures) that such agencies need to carry out their work. Featuring Laurie Guillon's course in Writing in Sports Management, Deans shows how students' writing projects (informational brochures and office memos, for example) positioned them in a web of social interactions. Deans underscores the value of critical reflection in such courses, particularly assignments that ask students to interrogate the power dynamics they observe and how the documents they write participate in those dynamics.

In the second approach, students write *about* the community. Here, students engage—typically as tutors—in community settings and then reflect on those experiences to write academic essays on a relevant topic. The chapter features Herzberg's service-learning course for which students served as writing tutors in the community and drew on their experience to interrogate the politics of schooling. Deans values the neo-Marxist critical stance that drives Herzberg's class. He also challenges educators to use critique to inform deliberate community engagement rather than stop short of rhetorical intervention.

The third approach, writing *with* the community, focuses on community literacy and the practice of intercultural inquiry. Featuring Pittsburgh's CLC and an interview with Flower, Deans describes college and graduate students' collaborative inquiry with teen writers, local activists, and community residents. Deans cautions that writing with the community can be so demanding and so unprecedented within students' lived experiences that cognitive dissonance can undercut students' engagement. Deans argues that at its best service learning brings together Dewey's model of reflective inquiry and Freire's critical praxis.

Faber, Brenton. *Community Action and Organizational Change: Image, Narrative, Identity.* Carbondale: Southern Illinois UP, 2002.

In *Community Action and Organizational Change: Image, Narrative, Identity,* Faber argues that an organization's identity is created through its internal stories. As long as an organization's internal stories are consistent with its external story, the organization's identity is coherent and useful. However, when internal stories contradict the external stories that circulate, the organization's identity becomes conflicted and counterproductive. Organizational change, Faber argues, is the process of aligning an organization's conflicting narratives.

In part, *Community Action and Organizational Change* is itself the story of Faber constructing an interventionist method grounded in "[e]mpirical-yet-activist discourse about change and community action" (6). By focusing on narrative as the nexus of change, he worked as an "academic consultant" to facilitate responsive organizational change in a variety of locales—from a neighborhood bank to a community-owned cemetery to a local political campaign. Some attempts failed, and others succeeded. What Faber offers is not some sure-fire formula for success but a context-sensitive, critically astute, rhetorically robust probabilistic method for facilitating productive organizational change among diverse stakeholders. Faber demonstrates that if academics are to work effectively with community members to understand organizational problems and to effect progressive social change, they have to engage as team members, not as observing ethnographers, objective consultants, or professional facilitators.

For readers interested in the complex relationship among publics, the texts they circulate, and social change, the fourth chapter, "Narratives and Organizational Change: Stories from Academe," is especially instructive. The trade school where Faber served as a change-management consultant was a tough nut indeed. Despite the high-flown language of the school's mission that hung printed and framed on the president's wall, the administration, faculty, and students had braced themselves in a nasty set of antagonistic relationships. Faber listened attentively to their various perspectives. Drawing on a range of critical theories and rhetorical principles, he then composed a new policy handbook that offered a more generative narrative about the institution and community members' places within it. Faber explains the rhetorical judgments that shaped the content of the handbook. Even more significantly, he documents how the school's new leadership used the handbook to institute and to reinforce new policies and practices that reconstituted the working relationships of the people who participated in the life of the organization.

Flower, Linda. *Community Literacy and the Rhetoric of Engagement.* Carbondale: Southern Illinois UP, 2008.

In *Community Literacy and the Rhetoric of Engagement,* Flower argues that the promise of community literacy lies in its ability—as a cultural, discursive, and intellectual practice—to support people standing *with* others *for* something—as a powerful alternative to rhetorical traditions that emphasize speaking *up* or speaking *against.* This relational stance emphasizes not only the collaborative and relational quality of community literacy, but also the inseparable individual and social nature of literate action. Central to community literacy is the practice of intercultural inquiry that calls partners to interpret the conflicts and contradictions that inform their readings of a shared issue. Not limited to finding a voice, intercultural inquiry creates a space for dialogue and deliberation in which everyone who engages in this process is recognized as a legitimate partner in discovery and change.

Portraits of teen writers, community activists, and college writing mentors provide a richly complicated image of community literacy. Teen writers like Mark and Shirley featured in chapter 4 respond to problematic experiences by building negotiated understandings of the issue at hand and by going public in acts of dialogue and transformation.

Against these stories, Flower tests what a social cognitive can illuminate about rhetorical engagement. Dramatizing the approach's explanatory power, Flower shows in specific instances of intercultural inquiry the role of task representations, the presence of hidden logics, and the process of negotiated meaning making. Together, these features of a social cognitive theory of writing provide an observation-based account of *how* community literacy works to transform understanding.

Throughout, Flower reflects critically on what community literacy contributes to a new cultural politics of difference that affirms the agency, capacity, and ability of people who have been degraded, oppressed, and exploited by the status quo. Flower argues that community literacy makes manifest the rhetorical agency of everyday people in two ways: both in the capacity to construct a negotiated understanding and in the willingness and ability to go public in dialogue and deliberation. One of the critical roles for partners from places of privilege, Flower argues, is to become rhetorical agents who do not speak for others but rather affirm, nurture, document the rhetorical agency of marginalized people. This act of engagement supports the counter-public work of fostering participants' transformed understanding.

Flower, Linda "Talking Across Difference: Intercultural Rhetoric and the Search for Situated Knowledge." *College Composition and Communication* 55.1 (2003): 38–68.

In "Talking Across Difference: Intercultural Rhetoric and the Search for Situated Knowledge," Flower shows how situated knowledge motivates the need for intercultural inquiry. Her inquiry rests on the socio-cognitive assumption that people's knowledge of complex cultural issues is largely experiential and operates tacitly unless people are compelled to articulate it—thus the need for purposeful dialogue and for rhetorical problem-solving strategies. "Talking Across Difference" tests the capacity of this situated knowledge to provide rich frameworks for interpreting the kinds of issues that bring together concerned city residents—not in the stable and homogeneous context that Habermas idealized as the bourgeois public sphere but across intercultural differences that characterize community problem-solving dialogues at Pittsburgh's CLC.

Taking a newly instituted city curfew as a case in point, Flower builds a case for intercultural rhetoric and its central outcome: transformed understanding—the rhetorical capacity to actively negotiate competing interpretations of a problem in order to build a more realistically complex and grounded representation of the issues involved. For eight weeks, teens at the CLC had studied the city's decision to institute a city-wide curfew. The project culminated in a community conversation where teens dramatized in text and on stage what the city's curfew could mean in the lives of its urban youth. An African American named Andre, for instance, recalled being detained by the police because his hair (an ordinary afro) bore resemblance to that of a crime suspect. The dramatization elicited a series of responses from the audience. A city council member argued that the curfew was in violation of established American civil rights. A father argued that overseeing the behavior of his child was his right—not the city's. A police sergeant described plans for a curfew center that would offer teens a safe alternative to the city's night-time streets. A single mother said she welcomed support from the wider community to safeguard her son.

Analyzing this dialogue, the teens' written document *Raising the Curtain on Curfew,* and the final inquiries of college mentors' involved in the CLC project, Flower contends that what circulated most productively within and across these contexts were multiple situated representations of curfew and its projected consequences in the city. The study shows the need for an intercultural rhetoric that can put alternative readings of the world into purposeful dialogue.

Flower, Linda, and Julia Deems. "Conflict in Community Collaboration." *New Perspectives on Rhetorical Invention.* Ed. Janet M. Atwill and Janice M. Lauer. Knoxville: U Tennessee P, 2002. 96–130.

"Conflict and Community Collaboration" studies rhetorical invention in the context of an urban community group called together to address landlord/tenant disputes in the Pittsburgh neighborhood of Perry Hilltop. Based within an ARGUE project at the CLC, the study interrogates the bias toward consensus in community work, particularly how the drive for consensus can undercut the deliberative process that sustains inquiry. The group of four community leaders, representing a range of landlord and tenant perspectives, did not share the same vision of *the* problem, let alone agree upon a single process for addressing it. But that does not mean their work together was unproductive. Rather, Higgins, ARGUE's facilitator, structured the process through which the group used rhetorical strategies to invent, design, and compose a Memorandum of Understanding, a multi-vocal document representing multiple views and articulating legitimate, alternative courses of action. Organized as a series of problem scenarios, the document blended or realistically modified actual events from anecdotes and personal experience in order to illustrate four "typical" conflicts that could serve as cases against which the memorandum's authors tested their proposals for change.

As participants in the study knew first hand, talk at community-organizing meetings is often ephemeral, and divergent viewpoints can easily be dismissed or left out of the public record. As a result, difference gets lost or ignored as quickly as it is generated. As an antidote, the study emphasizes the value of rhetorical invention in community-literacy programs where participants come together as writers to develop a rhetorical plan that acknowledges their divergent perspectives while at the same time supports agreement—not over specific ideas, but rather about the decision to act.

Flower, Linda, Elenore Long, and Lorraine Higgins. *Learning to Rival: A Literate Practice for Intercultural Inquiry.* Mahwah: Lawrence Erlbaum Associates, 2000.

Focused on African-American college students and inner-city teenagers, this study shows how the interdisciplinary literate practice of "rivaling" (taking a rival-hypothesis stance) alters in relation to its context of use and how in learning to rival, in school and out, students must often encounter and negotiate conflicts the instructor never sees.

Learning to Rival: A Literate Practice for Intercultural Inquiry began as a study of the rival hypothesis stance—a powerful literate practice claimed by both humanities and science—that posed two questions:

- How does this stance define itself as a literate practice as we move across the boundaries of disciplines and genres, of school and community?
- How do learners (who will be crossing these boundaries) interpret and use this family of literate practices—especially in situations that pose problems of intercultural understanding?

Over the course of the project, the generative connection between the rival-hypothesis stance and the process of intercultural inquiry emerged as one of the most powerful and compelling results of the inquiry, posing in turn a new question:

- How can the practice of "rivaling" support the difficult and essential art of intercultural interpretation in education?

Learning to Rival describes a community-crossing practice that is at once deeply embedded in its contexts, owned by its distinctive communities, and still recognizable as a distinctive, interdisciplinary intellectual stance and practice.

Learning to Rival addresses the very difficult question of how people might negotiate and use difference to solve problems. Rivaling is a practice and set of strategies for thinking and writing that can enable this work. In taking this approach, Flower, Long, and Higgins define a new agenda for rhetorical education—what they call *interculturalism.* Unlike most accounts of multicultural classrooms or minority student programs, the study focuses on an intercultural inquiry which (instead of describing differences) invites people to use difference collaboratively to understand common problems. The rival-hypothesis stance provides a techne for such inquiry, and the book is an example of how to conduct research based on this same intercultural, multiperspectival analysis.

George, Diana. "The Word on the Street: Public Discourse in a Culture of Disconnect." *Reflections: A Journal of Writing, Community Literacy* 2.2 (2002): 5–18.

In "The Word on the Street: Public Discourse in a Culture of Disconnect," George studies the process not of *place*-making, but of *public*-making, particularly in local, everyday contexts. Providing a genealogy of literate social action dating back to Dorothy Day, founder of the Catholic Worker Movement, and the origins of *The Nations Magazine,* George interviews local activists who identify themselves at some level as writers within Day's rhetorical tradition. George studied how their publications were produced and circulated, on whose behalf, and toward what ends. Questioning Wells's claim that teachers and students often seek to engage the larger public but don't know how to access it, George argues that the problem may be with how we, as theorists, define public address. The activist writers whom George interviewed intentionally sought to call into being small, focused—and intensely energized—local publics. George argues that the "cheaply produced, often unprofessional looking" newsletters which she studied defy mainstream culture and, instead, offer ordinary people the opportunity to take significant rhetorical action (8).

Goldblatt, Eli. "Alinsky's Reveille: A Community-Organizing Model for Neighborhood-Based Literacy Projects." *College English* 67.3 (2005): 274–94.

"Alinsky's Reveille: A Community-Organizing Model for Neighborhood-Based Literacy Projects" asks what it would take for community-university partners to work together in a mutually beneficial relationship. To direct his steps toward such a partnership, Goldblatt looked to the legacy of Alinsky to find ways to support writing and discussion among community partners. Together, they constructed a shared vision for community-literacy consortium, a collaborative called Open Doors. The final outcome of their meetings was a written purpose statement uniting the partners around shared action plan which Goldblatt hopes will eventually improve the training of community educators in North Philadelphia, as well as the way that students at his university participate as writing tutors at neighboring community centers.

Grabill, Jeffery T. *Community Literacy Programs and the Politics of Change*. Albany: SUNY P, 2001.

Grabill's *Community Literacy Programs and the Politics of Change* is an extended argument for how to make institutional systems visible, how to locate spaces for change, and how to enact an alternative institutional design that actively involves program participants in the design of the community-literacy programs in which they enroll. Grabill's study is a response to the documented gap between adult literacy programs' offerings and learners' own senses of what they need such programs to deliver. Demonstrating the institutional case method, Grabill situates his study of community literacy in the context of Western Distinct, a state-funded Adult Basic Education program. He asks of this program: *What counts as literacy here? Who decides? In whose interests are such decisions made?* Central to his analysis are two adults, Seldon and Gertrude, who were more or less satisfied with the tutoring they received—thanks largely to the individual tutor providing instruction rather than to specific features of the state-funded institution supporting the program. Yet Grabill argues that to be even more liberatory, programs like the Western District Adult Basic Education Program should draw from the field of information design to incorporate users—in this case, adult tutees—into the process of designing the programs they seek.

Grabill documents the ways in which state legislation institutes a cycle of policy decisions, educational practices, placement methods, and assessment routines quite separate from learners' own needs and expectations. As a corrective that would, instead, deliver programs to correspond with the meaning and value of literacy in learners' daily lives, Grabill commends a participatory design method. Based on principles of human-centered design, such a process gives preference to the less powerful. Participatory institutional design structures a process not only for eliciting residents' local knowledge of their community's assets and needs, but also for integrating that knowledge into the form and function of future literacy programs.

Greene, Ronald Walter. "Rhetorical Pedagogy as a Postal System: Circulating Subjects through Michael Warner's 'Publics and Counterpublics.'" *Quarterly Journal of Speech* 88.1 (2002): 434–43.

In "Rhetorical Pedagogy as a Postal System" Ronald Greene considers the pedagogical implications that follow from Warner's argument that a public exists not as a material body, but through the process of circulation—the flow, cycling, and transformation of discourse. Conceptualizing public discourse in this way challenges educators to prepare students not only to communicate with others but also to circulate their texts. Greene argues that conventional rhetorical education invokes an interactive model of communication highlighting the dynamic between the communicating Self and the listening/responding Other. In *Publics and Counterpublics,* Warner casts this dynamic in the public realm and refers to it as *stranger relationality.* Greene argues that while Warner's theory recognizes stranger relationality as one feature of public life, its contribution to rhetorical education is the emphasis it places on preparing students to circulate texts. This shift attends to a whole set of additional communication competencies and sensibilities for entering a discursive sphere not unlike a postal system. (See Trimbur, John. "Composition and the Circulation of Writing." *College Composition and Communication* 52.2 (2002): 188–219.)

Harris, Joyce L., Alan G. Kamhi, and Karen E. Pollock, eds. *Literacy in African American Communities.* Mahway: Lawrence Erlbaum Associates, 2001.

Literacy in African American Communities responds to the institutionalized racism in the United States that perpetuates an achievement gap among African American children and the associated restrictions of serious health conditions, low socioeconomic status, and limited life choices. The book is a thirty-year retrospective on literacy research since the 1970s when Dell Hymes launched the idea of the citizen scholar. The collection of essays celebrates work from this era, including William Labov's "Academic Ignorance and Black Intelligence" published in 1972 in the *Atlantic Monthly* and Smitherman's testimony later that decade on children's behalf in the case of Martin Luther King Junior Elementary School Children et al. v. Ann Arbor School District. However, researchers contributing to *Literacy in African American Lives* also concede that less progress has been made in the effort to improve the education of African American learners than Hymes and his colleagues had hoped.

Challenging readers to draw on research to inform classroom practices, community-literacy initiatives, and public opinion, the volume's contributors stress several claims. First, public intellectuals, linguists, language educators, and compositionists have a responsibility to honor the linguistic integrity of local languages. Second, the more just the public policy, the more the language of the policy and the practices that follow from it take into account local values and practices. (For instance, in the book's foreword, Heath asserts that everyday people rightly hold an authority over how language is used in their communities; likewise, every community assigns authority to those who best master the activities and skills it values. Thus, educational policies should reflect the authority of this local knowledge.) Third, effective local literacy innovations should inform broad-based educational reforms. Finally, local literate social action relies on linguistic tools, but not necessarily in the form of standard correctness, the fetish of public opinion.

Heath, Shirley Brice. *Ways with Words: Language, Life, and Work in Communities and Classrooms.* New York: Cambridge UP, 1983.

A landmark study in the cultural dimensions of literacy, Heath details the various reading, writing, and speaking practices she observed while studying two rural communities in the Piedmont Carolinas in the 1970s. Central to her analysis are the interactions that socialize children into a community's ways with words. In the white community called Roadville, language instruction was a private endeavor, primarily the domain of a child's own mother and geared toward preparing the child for school. In contrast, in the African American community of Trackton, language learning was a social—even public—event that rewarded the most adept for their competitive word plays and stories. Using the literacy event as a primary unit of analysis, Heath documents the interdependent relationship between literacy and orality and shows that even practices not valued in the mainstream are culturally adaptive and operate in socially meaningful ways.

Heller, Caroline E. *Until We are Strong Together: Women Writers in the Tenderloin.* New York: Teachers College P, 1997.

In *Until We are Strong Together: Women Writers in the Tenderloin,* Heller chronicles the life cycle of the Tenderloin Women Writer's Workshop in one of San Francisco's roughest neighborhoods. Central to the ethnography are the workshop's participants who gathered weekly to find expression for their insights and life experiences—participants including the group's visionary, Mary TallMountain, a prolific writer whom Heller portrays in stunning color. Heller also documents the leadership styles of workshop facilitators and contextualizes her own observations against a rich backdrop of fellow travelers, from Nathaniel Hawthorne and Emily Dickinson to bell hooks and Clifford Geertz. Heller conveys the dignity, strength, and voice that the workshop afforded women amidst their personal struggles for health, housing, and social stability. Heller analyzes the workshop for its social, political, spiritual, and educational implications and documents how the workshop's sponsor, Tenderloin Reflection and Education Center, combined Freirian emancipatory pedagogy and the expressivist tradition to support adult practices for social justice here in the United States.

Higgins, Lorraine, and Lisa D. Brush. "Personal Experience Narrative and Public Debate: Writing the Wrongs of Welfare." *College Composition and Communication.* 57.4 (2006): 694–729.

"Personal Experience Narrative and Public Debate: Writing the Wrongs of Welfare" reports findings from a community-literacy project that called together eight current and former welfare recipients to shift public discussion away from policy analysts talking among themselves or tax payers pitching insults at welfare recipients towards a local public that puts into conversation a range of perspectives and possibilities.

Higgins and Brush argue for the generative role of narrative in public dialogue. They document narrative's persuasive power that can help unfamiliar audiences identify with the teller's perspective in a way that abstract and generalized positions or claims do not. However, the study shows that crafting narratives to interpret a problem in the service of joint inquiry is not something that necessarily comes naturally or easily. To interpret policies for welfare reform in the context of their own lives, the welfare recipients in the study had to avoid the default schema of popular hero or victim, handy narratives which threatened to erode the writers' credibility by masking the complexity of their lives and decisions. In the face of such rhetorical challenges, the participants benefited from explicit support, especially since their initial stories tended to be under-elaborated, making it hard for readers to understand the motivation behind a narrator or character's actions, her reasoning, or interpretation of the situation. Higgins and Brush report that visual organizers such as timelines helped writers remember and organize the chronology of their life events for unfamiliar readers. Likewise, collaborative-planning supporters provided incentives for writers to explain the logic of their experiences to readers unfamiliar with their stories—and often ready to judge and condemn what they don't understand.

Higgins and Brush argue that the intellectually and emotionally demanding rhetorical work of transforming personal narratives for public inquiry can lift the level of public dialogue. For instance, on the basis of the reasoning the group had articulated over the project's sixteen sessions, its concluding document addressed the most egregious assumptions about welfare recipients that commonly circulate in the dominant discourse. The writers then used the document to talk back to these charges, complicating these claims with counterexamples and rival interpretations that had become shared over the course of the project.

In addition to reporting the results of their action research, Higgins and Brush also promote the role of the activist rhetorician and offer a fine-grained description of this practice. The activist rhetorician, whom Higgins and Brush describe, actively designs and explicitly teaches rhetorical strategies that writers can use to cross publics without being co-opted by the dominant discourse and its prevailing attitudes.

Higgins, Lorraine, Elenore Long, and Linda Flower. "A Rhetorical Model of Community Literacy." *Community Literacy Journal* 1.1 (2006): 9–42.

"A Rhetorical Model of Community Literacy" develops a rhetorically-centered model of community literacy in the theoretical and practical context of local publics—those spaces where ordinary people develop public voices to engage in intercultural inquiry and deliberation. Drawing on fifteen years of action research in the CLC and elsewhere, Higgins, Flower, and Long characterize the distinctive features of local publics, the deliberative intercultural discourses they circulate, and the literate practices that sustain them. The model uses writing to support collaborative inquiry into community problems, calls up local publics around the aims of democratic deliberation, and transforms personal and public knowledge by re-structuring deliberative dialogues among individuals and groups across lines of difference.

The article describes four critical practices at the heart of this model of community literacy. First, assessing the rhetorical situation involves configuring the problem space or object of deliberation, identifying relevant stakeholders in the community, assessing existing venues for public problem solving, and analyzing literate practices used to represent and to address problems and the way these practices structure stakeholder participation. The authors stress that in an intercultural context, this practice is intensely collaborative, for when writing about community problems, all participants enter a discourse and address a situation they do not fully understand—including groups with direct experience, experts who have studied the problem, political leaders with the power to shape public policy, and literacy workers who are there to support change. What's required is genuine collaboration across groups to elicit the relevant cultural capital, material resources, and experience of all stakeholders—knowledge critical to assessing the rhetorical situation.

The second practice entails creating local publics. By this, the authors mean something more than the public meetings or think tanks they have supported in community centers, church basements, health clinics, and college auditoriums yet something less broad than the imaginary national "public" of the media or the demographic units targeted by marketers. Instead, they have in mind a rhetorical creation called into being by being addressed as a body (i.e., as a public) of interested participants. Third, the model identifies rhetorical capacities that help participants co-construct the alternative discourse needed in order to deliberate across lines of hierarchy and difference. The model defines these capacities as the ability to articulate, elaborate, and circulate situated knowledge—both one's own and one another's; the ability to engage difference in dialogue by predicting and engaging rival perspectives; and the ability to construct and reflect upon wise options by specifying the consequences that might reasonably ensue based on the knowledge they have gleaned from their work together.

The article offers theory-based strategies that participants have used to enact these capacities. Finally, the model supports social change by circulating alternative texts and practices. As a transformative counterpublic, this model of community literacy circulates a deliberative practice in which marginalized knowledge enters discussion as a sought out, valued (but not privileged) understanding or interpretation that a deliberative democracy needs to consider.

Howard, Ursula. "History of Writing in the Community." *Handbook of Research on Writing: History, Society, School, Individual, Text.*

Ed. Charles Bazerman. Mahwah: Lawrence Erlbaum Associates,
2008. 237-54.

Concerned primarily with England, Howard traces the historical roots
of community-based writing. Synthesizing insights from several hundred empirical studies, as well as from cultural theories and primary
sources, Howard shows that from the outset community writing has
operated in tense relation to formal institutions, especially the church,
school, and workplace. Taking into account the problems of evidence
that thwart a conclusive historical account, Howard convincingly argues that the history of community writing is the story of the democratization of cultural practice.

While "History of Writing in the Community" focuses on the
nineteenth century and the complex socioeconomic developments that
circulated literacy to ordinary people, it does so in relation to significant developments from the previous millennium. From sixth century
monastic transcriptions to tenth century English biblical translations,
religious writing spawned practical uses of literacy in ordinary households. During the two hundred years following the imposition of the
Doomsday Book in the eleventh century, literacy took hold as the
trusted medium for documenting commercial transactions and the
ownership of property. Over the next several hundred years, the printing press circulated inexpensive reading material to a reading public.
Much of this material was political in content, generated in response
to the social changes brought about by the Industrial Revolution.
Throughout the seventeenth and eighteenth centuries, community-
based writing practices emerged for the purpose of political protest
and social movement.

In the nineteenth century, community literacy was pushed and
pulled in many directions. This era in British history saw an unprecedented growth in public institutions that formulated their own literate
practices. On the one hand, institutional practices sought to measure,
regulate, and control people and, thus were sites of resistance. On
the other hand, these practices circulated and provided incentives for
learning a host of literacies—legal, literary, scientific, among others.
While opportunities were never distributed evenly and were in especially short supply for laborers and women, these institutions planted
the seeds for alternative forms of self expression, political organization, and practical application that continue to characterize community writing.

Hull, Glynda A., and Mira-Lisa Katz. "Crafting an Agentive Self: Case Studies of Digital Storytelling." *Research in the Teaching of English* 41.1 (2006): 43–81.

"Crafting an Agentive Self: Case Studies of Digital Storytelling" provides a framework for understanding agency that extends beyond textual expressions of selfhood. Hull and Katz argue that theories that are sensitive to the ways social, political, and economic conditions constrain human activity often fail to convincingly illustrate what it might mean to exercise agency within highly constrained contexts. They seek an alternative framework, and West Oakland provides a provocative test case. Plagued with poverty and the trappings that come with it, West Oakland is not a place one might readily expect to find young people eager to share compelling personal narratives of what they are up to in life. Nor is it a place where one might readily identify acts of agency unless equipped with a robust interpretative framework for recognizing them. Hull and Katz's interpretative lens emerges from their action research, a framework that synthesizes recent scholarship on narrative, identity, and performance. They focus this framework on DUSTY, University of California at Berkeley's computer-based outreach project in West Oakland that offers youth the opportunity to communicate in multiple modalities.

The first case study features Randy, a multi-modal artist who extracted images and texts from their original contexts and repositioned them into his own digital stories, for his own purposes. In repositioning cultural images, Randy narrated pivotal movements in his life and a trajectory for the future. In a second case study, a teenager named Dara crafted digital stories to interpret her life and the life around her. In the process of scripting and configuring these digital stories, Dara engaged in social critique and participated as a valued expert among her peers and mentors from U. Cal. Berkeley. Hull and Katz argue that given the kind of community support and social scaffolding that characterize DUSTY, community-university partnerships can create public forums where young writers develop the capacity to perform multi-modal narratives that exemplify key features of an agentive self.

Kells, Michelle Hall, Valerie Balester, and Victor Villanueva, eds. *Latino/a Discourses: On Language, Identity and Literacy Education*. Portsmouth, NH: Boynton/Cook. 2004.

Latino/a Discourses: On Language, Identity and Literacy Education asks compositionists to re-imagine their classroom practices in order to honor the linguistic diversity Latino/a students bring to writing classrooms and to challenge the linguistic racism that still permeates mainstream culture. Setting the collection's tone, Guerra's "Emerging Representations, Situated Literacies, and the Practice of Transcultural Repositioning" advocates *transcultural repositioning*, the deliberate process by which members of minority culture move among diverse dialects, social classes, and aesthetic forms. Exploring the ideological problems of naming an ethnic *community* and the almost equally daunting challenges of defining *literacy*, Guerra commends rhetorically attuned code-switching as a way for all students—especially the Latino/a students with whom the volume is concerned—to exercise greater degrees of self-determinism and personal freedom. Also critiquing institutional racism but through the lens of critical ethnography, in "Valerio's Walls and the Rhetorics of the Everyday" Cintron interrogates both the assumptions that underlie and the implications that follow from the psychosocial label *learning disabled*. Adapting "A Boy and His Wall" from *Angels' Town,* Cintron shows the disconnect between the performative and dialogic ways that a young man named Valerio used discourse at home, on the one hand, and the meta-discursive, fill-in-the-blank exercises that defined and measured literacy at his school, on the other.

The volume explores implications for public discourse. Viewing literacy learning as social engagement, in "Creating an Identity: Personal, Academic, and Civic Literacies" Cárdenas describes the course projects she designed for a technical writing class to engage students in local community issues. Especially for the Latino/a students with whom she identifies most strongly, Cárdenas argues such writing projects reinforce connections to the community, whereby revising an academic relationship that students otherwise often experience as agonistic to familial and communal ties. In "Keepin' It Real: Hop Hop and *El Barrio,*" Jon Yasin employs an alternative logic to curricular design. Importing hip hop music that circulates publicly, he asked students to help him adapt this musical genre to his course objectives focused on the writerly practices of brainstorming, drafting, revising, and editing.

Connections between linguistic diversity and public discourse are most explicitly addressed in the section that follows the eight essays, the section entitled "Tertulia," a site for public discussion similar to the French salon. Here, Beverly Moss and Flower contend that notions of *identity* and *empowerment* are not as stable as readers might conclude from reading the previous eight essays. Rather, in various public discussions, competing interpretations of identity and empowerment circulate rather vigorously. Flower urges practitioners to consider the various outcomes that follow from these competing interpretations. In doing so, educators would likely encounter yet another view of linguistic empowerment—rhetorical social action. In this version, identity is less an interpretative label and more a rhetorical "action practiced in the world that lets students talk *across* differences" (131).

Victor Villanueva concludes the volume. He celebrates the capacity of discourse to bear witness to diverse cultural legacies. Recognizing the multiplicity of differences across Latino/a discourses, he urges readers not only to honor differences but also to bear witness to shared experiences of struggle, exile, displacement, and servitude. In coming together to understand their Latino/a discourses, Villanueva argues that he and other readers of *Latino/a Discourses* can receive the respect that is rightly theirs.

Long, Elenore. "The Rhetoric of Social Action: College Mentors Inventing the Discipline." *Inventing a Discipline: Rhetoric Scholarship in Honor of Richard E. Young.* Ed. Maureen Daly Goggin. Urbana: NCTE, 2000. 289–318.

Reporting on a study of college students mentoring teen writers at Pittsburgh's CLC, "The Rhetoric of Social Action: College Mentors Inventing the Discipline" argues that the act of mentoring positioned college students in the vortex of rhetorical activity: contingent choices among competing alternatives for purposeful action. The study reveals that the college students actively grappled with a question at the heart of rhetoric and composition: how to connect literacy to social justice. As part of the Community Literacy Seminar at CMU, students conducted and recorded structured self-interviews back in their dorms following each literacy session. Rhetorical analysis of these taped transcripts revealed that students arrived at the CLC with competing images for how literacy should support social justices. Over the course of their mentoring sessions, they actively wrestled with conflicting priorities, from teaching grammatical correctness to supporting emancipation to inviting free expression to encouraging action-oriented problem solving. Mentors drew from the disciplinary debate to make judgments in the face of often intensely conflicting alternatives—judgments not just

about what *to think* or *say* about literacy but also about what *to do* as
literacy mentors.

McComisky, Bruce, and Cynthia Ryan, eds. *City Comp: Identities,
    Spaces, Practices.* Albany: SUNY P, 2003.

City Comp: Identities, Spaces, Practices contributes an emergent rhetoric
of place-making, what Flower calls in the book's foreword "the rhetoric of real places" (xi). City comp is the discursive act of negotiating
the myriad competing discourses that collide in urban spaces that support writing within and outside university walls. In "Speaking of the
City and Literacies of Place Making," Marback offers an accessible,
yet highly nuanced, explanation of how this place-making occurs in
the histories, actions, objects, and words that shape what we know and
experience as city life.

Increasingly, disciplinary histories trace the public turn in rhetoric and composition, as well as the field's interest in everyday rhetoric
and attention to community literacy, to changing admissions policies
at urban universities in light of the civil rights movement and the G.
I. Bill. *City Comp* addresses what that history means today as urban
universities realign and renew their institutional missions. The first
section, "Negotiating Identities," addresses the identities urban students negotiate as writers, both their own identities and that of their
cities. In "Not Your Mama's Tour Bus," Mathieu and her students
construct a mobile local public to dramatize the stories of local homeless and low-income writers. Paving the way to her book-length *Tactics of Hope: The Public Turn in English Composition,* in *City Comp*
Mathieu urges urban educators to embrace the radical insufficiency
of community literacy. Likewise, Swan draws on community-literacy
pedagogy to construct a local public within a composition classroom
at CMU where college students engaged with food-service workers in
Pittsburgh to consider their difficult socioeconomic realities.

The second section, "Composing Spaces," examines the material
constraints and conditions that shape city comp. In "A Place in the
City: Hull House and the Architecture of Civility," Van Hillard examines how the Hull House and the American settlement house tradition
constructed a rhetoric of civic discourse that prepared working-class
families—especially women and children—for public life. In "The
Written City Urban Planning, Computer Networks, and Civic Liberties," Grabill teaches design practices to technical writers who, in turn,

use these practices to design a software interface that helps community residents access the data they need to participate in public discussions of a community planning project.

The final section, "Redefining Practices," urges educators to support urban writers as they negotiate the multiple identities of self, place, and purpose that circulate in contemporary urban life. This section extends the theory of place-making launched in the introduction and sustained throughout the previous sections. In "Composition by Immersion: Writing Your Way into a Mission-Driven University," David Jolliffe, for instance, describes a curriculum that takes students to the streets to investigate what the Jesuit tradition of tolerance and community outreach means to contemporary life in the city of Chicago and to students' lives as members of DePaul University. The curriculum models an alternative to other critical pedagogies that pit students in ardent tension with formal institutions. Along with the other four practitioners in this section, Jolliffe argues for and instantiates composition pedagogy as localized, situated practice.

McLaughlin, Milbrey W., Merita A. Irby, and Juliet Langman. *Urban Sanctuaries: Neighborhood Organizations in the Lives and Futures of Inner-City Youth.* San Francisco: Jossey-Bass, 2001.

Urban Sanctuaries reports the results of a five-year study of urban youth that features teenaged "hopefuls" and the neighborhood-based organizations that made a difference in their lives. These organizations include a gymnastics team, a Girl Scout troop, and TeenTalk—a youth-based actors guild addressing pressing urban issues. Following teens' own judgments of where they wanted to spend their time, McLaughlin, Irby, and Langman document how such sites were conceptualized, organized and sustained.

The core of the book is dedicated to six "wizards"—leaders of effective teen-centered community organizations. While these leaders approached their work differently—and from different social locations within and outside their communities—what distinguished them as wizards is their success capturing the imaginations, talents, commitments, and energy of the teens in their communities when other organizations had failed. The authors' document ways in which wizards set expectations for youth and involved teen members in holding each other accountable to these expectations. Wizards also tenaciously promoted neighborhood teens, often including gang members whom public opinion had cast as irredeemable. The ethnography also documents a shared problem the wizards faced: recruiting and retaining capable and committed staff.

For readers concerned with institutional sustainability, chapters 9 and 10 are especially illuminating. These chapters document the circuits of resources—personnel, capital and commitment—that the wizards relentlessly marshaled toward their organizations. What transforms a neighborhood-based organization into an urban sanctuary is the wizard's intensive strategic knowledge of how the immediate community and the larger city operate.

Mathieu, Paula. *Tactics of Hope: The Public Turn in English Composition.* Portsmouth: Boynton/Cook, 2005.

Mathieu's sensitivity to academic hubris leads her to commend a tactical approach to community literacy over sustained, systematic—or strategic—approaches. What Mathieu has in mind are "clever uses of time" that erupt in the politically charged spirit of the moment and often influence public opinion in ways that not only defy easy prediction and measurement but are themselves "mysterious and unknowable" (48). *Tactics of Hope: The Public Turn in English Composition* offers a postmodern reading of rhetorical techne grounded in the work of de Certeau. Mathieu urges socially concerned academics to consider "questions of time, space, credibility, knowledge, and success" (21)— or "Who speaks? Who pays?" (66). These questions are designed to spark tactics of hope—rhetorically responsive actions grounded in moral humility, persistence, and courage.

Moss, Beverly J. *A Community Text Arises: A Literate Text and a Literacy Tradition in African-American Churches.* Cresskill: Hampton P, 2002.

A Community Text Arises: A Literate Text and a Literacy Tradition in African-American Churches circulates the results of Moss's five-year project studying literacy events at African American churches. Grounded in ethnographic analysis of three churches in Chicago and one in Columbus, Ohio, Moss demonstrates how a cultural institution shapes literate practices across locations. Three features characterize literacy in the African American church: the participation of multiple people within a literacy event; intertextual relationships that allow for the dynamic interplay between orality and literacy and fluidity among participants' roles as speakers, writers, listeners and respondents; and the formative influence of cultural norms rooted in a shared belief system. Distinguishing among a manuscript minister who composed his sermons in their entirety, a non-manuscript minister who rarely relied on notes, and a partial-manuscript minister who composed about a quarter of any given sermon, Moss draws connections between preaching styles and composing practices, and she highlights the dynamic and interdependent relationship between written and oral discourse within African American churches.

The literacy events that surround the sermon provide another window into the interplay between written and oral discourse within the church. Focusing on the church bulletin, for instance, Moss argues that its design not only disseminates information about the worship service and concerns of the community, but it also endorses specific ways of interacting with text in the context of church. Expressed through an identifiable set of cultural practices, a collective identity circulates this shared knowledge. To sustain this collective identity, ministers in Moss's study deployed rhetorical strategies that let them participate as both leaders and fellow church members—strategies including code switching to intensify their identification with church members and call and response to encourage their active engagement in the co-construction of sermonic discourse.

The study identifies a number of implications for the composition classroom. Moss's analysis of shared knowledge and collaboration complicates more static, academic notions of plagiarism and ownership. She asks educators to support African American learners as they apply what they know about literacy from their participation in church to college writing. She argues that the burden should not be entirely on the students; rather, educators need to help students develop the tools to discern how literacy is configured across the two domains.

Nystrand, Martin, and John Duffy, eds. *Towards a Rhetoric of Everyday Life: New Directions in Research on Writing, Text, and Discourse.* Madison: U of Wisconsin P, 2003.

Towards a Rhetoric of Everyday Life: New Directions in Research on Writing, Text, and Discourse brings together nine essays investigating how ordinary people use language to construct their social realities. The collection begins with an historical account of the social and intellectual forces that made everyday discourse a prominent focus of research and theory-building in rhetoric and composition studies. In "Introduction: The Sociocultural Context for the New Discourse about Writing," Martin Nystrand and John Duffy trace historical events that awakened the field to issues of cultural difference and the relevance of theorists such as Kenneth Burke and Mikhail Bakhtin. Of course, much of everyday discourse attends to issues not overtly public in orientation—as Caroline Miller shows in "Writing in a Culture of Simulation." In her study of rhetorical constructions of intimacy within computer simulations, Miller argues that concerns over ethos are intensified not lessened in cyberspace. Here as elsewhere, the rhetoric of the everyday is concerned with inventing alternatives: "alternate worlds, alternate selves, alternate modes of belief" (78).

Ralph Cintron, David Fleming, and John Ackerman directly explore rhetorical implications of everyday public life. In "Gates Locked and the Violence of Fixation," Cintron argues that the ideology of vengeance operated as much within statesmen's responses to Angelstown's "gang problem" as within the gang members' decisions to annihilate anyone who disrespected them, their cars, their iconography. Demonstrating the synergy between rhetoric and anthropology and the interplay between "presence" and "partiality" in everyday discourse (21), Cintron poses the possibility of an alternative public discourse that would have recognized gang members and authorized them to speak publicly. Cintron argues that the dialogue would have had to venture into territory that at the time of his study was decidedly off limits: serious consideration of how the economic conditions that marginalized Latinos in Angelstown also perpetuated the revenge cycle that undermined the quality of daily life for everyone in the city.

In "Subjects of the Inner City," Fleming likewise describes an alterative public rhetoric, one where the city serves as a school of public discourse. Fleming studied a campaign to revitalize Cabrini Green in downtown Chicago. In the more than 200 documents he analyzed, public discussions cast urban-housing residents as threats to social order, emphasizing pregnant or truant youth, unfit parents, and alcoholic adults. Fleming's point is not that residents of Cabrini Green were unaware of these representations or that they fell entirely victim to them, but that the discourses in which residents represented themselves were "marginal in the overall discussion" (238). Furthermore, these representations didn't reinforce the concept of resident as citizen. Fleming observes that the few times *citizen* did appear in discussions of public housing in Chicago, it impugned the character of urban residents rather than engaging them in public deliberation on issues affecting their live.

In "The Space for Rhetoric in Everyday Life," Ackerman urges rhetoricians to turn their attention from text to social space. Drawing on Henri Lefebre's *The Critique of Everyday Life,* Ackerman describes a rhetorical techne that renews the vitality of public life and subverts the consumerism of mass culture. He finds evidence of such rhetorical ingenuity in the architectural sketches of a graduate student named Marty who proposes a homeless shelter in the space between a viaduct and a highway overpass—translating an urban landscape into a site of inquiry and reflection regarding the distribution of a city's resources and the possibility for local social reform.

Peck, Wayne, Linda Flower, and Lorraine Higgins. "Community Literacy." *College Composition and Communication* 46.2 (1995): 199–222.

Defining community literacy as a distinctive area of inquiry within rhetoric and composition studies, this article has invited others in the field to locate the profession's work more broadly in the public realm. The authors locate their own projects not in schools or workplaces (at the time, typical sites for composition scholarship and pedagogy), but in the CLC, a multicultural urban settlement house and place of community building where private lives and public agendas often merged during social gatherings, youth programs, and community meetings. Even more than an argument for new sites for research, however, Peck, Flower, and Higgins coined the phrase *community literacy* to refer to a new kind of rhetorical *activity* encompassing a unique set of goals, literate practices, resources, and relationships. Here, community literacy is "a search for an alternative discourse" (205), a way for people to acknowledge each other's multiple forms of expertise through talk and text and to draw on their differences as a resource for addressing shared problems. Foremost, Peck, Flower, and Higgins affirm the social knowledge and rhetorical expertise of community residents. They argue that literacy should be defined not merely as the receptive skill of reading, but as the public act of writing and taking social action. Toward this end, the authors test four principles of literate social action: a dedication to social change and action; support of intercultural inquiry and collaboration; a commitment to strategies for collaboration, planning, argument, and reflection that are intentionally taught and deliberately negotiated; and a commitment to a mutually beneficial community-university partnership that supports joint inquiry.

Simmons, W. Michele, and Jeffery T. Grabill. "Toward a Civic Rhetoric for Technologically and Scientifically Complex Places: Invention, Performance, and Participation." *College Composition and Communication* 58.3 (2007): 419–48.

Here, Simmons and Grabill argue that the ability of ordinary citizens to go public in technologically and scientifically complex places hinges on their capacity for rhetorical invention—the ability to make and to circulate new, relevant knowledge. This is especially so, given the "indirect exclusions" and asymmetrical relationships that characterize contemporary public forums (420). Their argument centers on three examples. The first features a birth records database. Reflecting a trend to provide community residents with information about their communities, the database could provide community residents with valuable knowledge. However, the interface for this one dumps the user into a confusing cyberspace, populated with long tables and pressing choices about eliminating or selecting variables in order to generate more tables. Without meaningful interpretative cues, the user has no means for drawing useful conclusions. From this example, Simmons and Grabill argue that computer interfaces must construct a rhetorical space in which users can effectively "access, assemble, and analyze" information (419).

The second example is a database that uploaded thousands of documents that had previously lain unlabeled and disorganized in a couple dozen boxes in a town office. Again, the idea of a website is commendable. But this one had to be searched by date. That is, the design assumed that users would approach the website with knowledge of the dates of environmental incidents they wanted to research. This overarching search narrative eliminated the possibility of other search strategies. Simmons and Grabill argue for designing dynamic software interface to help citizens find relevant, useful information.

The third example shows a community organization successfully doing science. The organization's members research relevant problems, read extensively, and follow up with experts cited in the publications they have read. Members report to one another and summarize and distribute their findings to a larger constituency. The organization has had some success halting an initiative to dredge a nearby harbor—a project that poses several environmental threats. From this example, Simmons and Grabill argue for a civic rhetoric that offers a techne for rhetorical invention in community contexts. Simmons and Grabill conclude their article with implications for research and teaching. They emphasize the need for more empirical work documenting the complex literacies required to participate in technologically and scientifically complex public forums. They also call for rhetorical pedagogies that teach information literacy.

Squires, Catherine. "Rethinking the Black Public Sphere: An Alternative Vocabulary for Multiple Public Spheres." *Communication Theory* 12.4 (2002): 446–68.

In "Rethinking the Black Public Sphere: An Alternative Vocabulary for Multiple Public Spheres," Squires argues that the standard vocabulary for describing counterpublics is inadequate for differentiating among alternative publics. She argues that historically black public spheres have configured themselves in different ways to respond to different kinds of social threats. Chief differences include how these alternative publics performed in wider publics (e.g., whether they employed public transcripts or exposed hidden ones) and the sanctions they risked in doing so (e.g., from dismissal from dominant publics to the threat of violence). Squires offers a flexible vocabulary for distinguishing *enclaves* (safe spaces deployed in conditions of intense oppression where interaction with dominant publics is highly scripted) from *counterpublics* (marginal publics that produce discourses that travel outside the enclaved safe space to promote group interest), and *satellites* (separatist entities marked by sporadic engagement with wider publics).

Swan, Susan. "Rhetoric, Service, and Social Justice." *Written Communication* 19.1 (2002): 76–108.

"Rhetoric, Service, and Social Justice" documents the disciplinary pressure that can thwart intercultural inquiry. Drawing on work at Pittsburgh's CLC, Swan advocates the community problem-solving dialogue as a forum for intercultural inquiry, and she adapts such a forum to the academic classroom, in this case a graduate course in public policy. Students used rhetorical strategies to investigate with urban residents pressing local issues, including a proposal for an urban renewal project to revitalize a run-down inner-city neighborhood and the dearth of meaningful, available work for urban youth.

Students in Swan's study became adept at using rhetorical problem solving strategies to conduct their interviews—and, thus, accessed knowledge that would not have been available to them otherwise. But when it came to writing their results of their inquiries, students had difficulty figuring out how to use the community knowledge so they opted, instead, for discursive moves—from sentence structure to graphic organizers—that muted ordinary people's voices and overlooked local insights, in favor of discursive moves that complied with conventional, disciplinary standards of validity, rigor, and authority. For instance, when the graduate students did represent youth, they did so in the form of a graph, not in their own words, even though the interviews with teens had been extensive and insightful.

Swan considers ways to reconfigure classroom learning and to assign professional writing to help public-workers-in-training learn to document the expertise of community residents. She challenges socially-minded academics to move their research outside the university so that it can better address community issues. She also suggests that community residents need to be invited to serve as co-authors of assigned documents, and that the audiences need to include readers who matter to these co-authors.

Warner, Michael. *Publics and Counterpublics*. New York: Zone Books, 2005.

In *Publics and Counterpublics*, Warner argues that a public exists not as a material body, but through the process of circulation—the flow, cycling, and transformation of discourse. He identifies seven features that characterize a public:

> 1) A public is self organized; 2) a public is a relation among strangers; 3) the address of public speech is both personal and impersonal; 4) a public is constituted through mere attention; 5) a public is the social space created by the reflective circulation of discourse; 6) publics act historically according to the temporality of their circulation, and 7) a public is poetic world making (67–114).

Against this backdrop, Warner focuses attention on queer culture and the features that characterize counterpublics. In such critical spaces, he argues, subordinated people formulate oppositional identities, alternative discourse, and competing worldviews. Moreover, they do so through "poetic world making" (114), resisting the exclusionary norms of rational-critical discourse and creating a space for performative world making.

Weisser, Christian. *Moving Beyond Academic Discourse: Composition Studies and the Public Sphere.* Carbondale: Southern Illinois UP, 2002.

In *Moving Beyond Academic Discourse,* Weisser credits radical educationists with turning attention in rhetoric and composition to public writing. Weisser argues that over the past forty years, the discipline has shifted the focus of its attention, first from the individual writer to the social construction of facts, selves and writers; then to concerns for power and ideology in discourse, particularly ways in which discourse sanctions who is to speak and about what kinds of issues. Now that Freire and his followers have put the issue of public writing on the table, the challenge is to incorporate ideas from public-spheres theory into writing instruction in thoughtful and substantive ways. Weisser offers a way forward. He highlights a set of public-spheres scholars and their scholarly contributions. For instance, Richard Sennett's explanation of the complex social, historical, and cultural factors gave rise to the bourgeois public sphere and its consequent decline, forfeiting concern for public deliberation with a fascination for public personalities. Habermas's institutional criteria described an ideal bourgeois public sphere that valued open participation, addressed issues of shared concern, and was accessible. Oskar Negt and Alexander Kluge's image of a proletariat public sphere allowed everyday people to draw on the idioms of their discourse in order to address issues of shared interest. And finally, Fraser's rethinking of the public sphere exposed ways that deliberation can mask domination.

Weisser then applies these key issues to college writing instruction. First, he defines his goal for public writing: helping students develop voices as active citizens capable of engaging in public debate. He stresses that public writing instruction should help students understand the public sphere as a vortex of historically, social, and political forces. He urges compositionists to use public writing instruction to help students attend to issues of difference and the ways that labels of difference are often used to justify dominance of certain groups in public settings. Finally, he challenges compositionists to revise the popular image that associates public writing instruction with the newspaper and its op-ed page. Letters-to-the-editor assignments can reinforce students' sense of the futility of public writing; better alternatives allow students to write for smaller, subaltern audiences in which students can witness first-hand the efficacy of their public voices. Weisser applies public-spheres principles to an advanced composition course he designed, Environmental Discourse and Public Writing. He concludes that tools of their trade equip compositionists to construct distinctive public orientations for their roles as teachers, scholars, and activists—roles that help catalyze broader public discussions and bring about social change.

Young, Amanda, and Linda Flower. "Patients as Partners: Patients as Problem-Solvers." *Health Communication* 14.1 (2001): 68–97.

"Patients as Partners: Patients as Problem-Solvers" intentionally re-invents community-literacy strategies in a medical setting to offer a rhetorical model for patient-provider communication that the authors call Collaborative Inquiry (CI). Observing the emergency department at an urban trauma-level hospital, Young and Flower note miscommunication between patients and health-care providers in three distinct areas: over the meaning of key words, in the framing of the immediate health issue, and over the perceived role of the emergency department. These missed opportunities are the byproduct of a default conversational routine that allows patients and health care providers to carry out the medical encounter without ever comparing and negotiating their competing expectations of one another. CI scaffolds their interaction to build a more comprehensive and coherent representation of the patient's health. CI situates the patient as a problem solver. Unlike the standard medical interview, CI employs heuristics for constructing new knowledge central to both patients' health and the medical providers' sense of satisfaction. In that medical discourse is at once hierarchical and mysterious, any medical encounter can be seen as an intercultural interaction. Used to elicit situated knowledge in the context of other intercultural dialogues, rhetorical problem-solving strategies in the medical setting strengthen the patient-provider working relationship and enhance the patient's sense of control over his or her own health.

Zentella, Ana Celía, ed. *Building on Strengths: Language and Literacy in Latino Families and Communities.* New York: Teachers College P, 2005.

This volume uses socially and politically astute ethnographic observation and discourse analysis to ask what it would take for educators to build on the discursive, emotional, and cultural resources that Latino/a learners bring with them to both formal educational classrooms and less formal educational arenas. If other work in community literacy features rhetorical interventions to support discursive border crossing in the form of community-literacy projects and programs, this work testifies to the many ways ordinary people invent and employ complex rhetorical choices to negotiate cultural borders in the course of their daily lives. Perhaps nowhere are the stakes higher than in the migration raids featured in Lavadenz's *"Como Hablar en Silencio* (Like Speaking in Silence): Issues of Language, Culture, and Identity of Central Americans in Los Angeles." Intensifying the gatekeeping encounter described in Cushman's *The Struggle and the Tools,* Lavadenz shows that in the immigration sweep, the rhetorical challenge is to adjust your vocabulary, pronunciation, and verb forms so that if migration officers notice you, your discourse cues will lead them to conclude you are from Mexico, rather than, say, Guatemala or El Salvador. That way, if you are deported, you'll be sent to Mexico where the living conditions are not quite as harsh as the ones you left in Central America.

Building on Strength is an argument for a transnational perspective on literacy. It demonstrates that there are multiple routes to literacy and education; moreover, it argues that Latino families of all types contribute to this goal. In "Mexicanos in Chicago: Language Ideology and Identity," Marcia Farr and Elías Domínguez Barajas analyze the discourse of Mexican rancheros in Chicago. Farr and Barajas argue that competence in this community means mastering a discourse that is at once direct and jocular. The volume models and advocates a participatory approach to literacy education that engages parents, community leaders, policy makers, and educators in inquiry-driven dialogue about the complexity and variation of language learning. In the afterword, Ana Celía Zantalla argues that given the competing cultural values and social agendas that circulate at sites of language learning, local participatory inquiry is crucial to engender the kind of shared wisdom that educators, parents, and policy makers need to effectively support Latino/a learners.

Notes

Chapter 1

[1] For a review of prominent research methods, see Jill Arola's review essay, "Research Methodologies in Community Literacy."

[2] For instance, Cintron framed his study as "a project in the rhetorics of public culture or the rhetorics of everyday life"—phrasing that orients his inquiry in relation to French postmodernism (*Angels' Town* x). Welch studied how "ordinary people have *organized* to claim living room" (470, emphasis added)—phrasing indicative of her interest in labor politics and class struggle.

[3] The other founder, Joyce Baskins, figures prominently in Flower's *Community Literacy and the Rhetoric of Engagement*. Baskins also co-authored "STRUGGLE: A Literate Practice Supporting Life-Project Planning" with Long and Peck.

[4] Here, I follow Grabill and Simmons's definition of an institution as an "organization [or bureaucracy] with policy and decision making power" (417). As discursive entities, institutions also perpetuate "regular, shared ways of producing and distributing knowledge" that often restrict the access of ordinary people (417).

[5] In response to my presentation of the local public framework at the Western States Conference on Rhetoric and Literacy in October of 2007, Branch nominated another relationship between local and formal public institutions: local publics that seek *to transform* public institutions. As an example, he cited the Highlander Folk School that continues to work to transform racist and other anti-democratic structures operating within the larger society. See chapter 4 of Branch's *"Eyes on the Ought to Be": What We Teach When We Teach About Literacy*.

Chapter 2

[1] The irony in documenting ordinary acts of democracy in the current political milieu was not lost on Iris Young. She wrote *Inclusion and Democracy* "shortly after nineteen of the world's leading liberal democracies have waged a ghastly war [the second war in Iraq] without any of them formally consulting with either their citizens or their elected representatives about whether to

do so" (5). Her purpose in addressing ordinary democracy was directly relevant to community-literacy studies and its effort to theorize how everyday people widen and deepen democracy through practices of inclusion.

[2] For analyses of *ordinary* describing distinct aspects of *people*, see Waller 8; Warner 120; and West, *Keeping* 140–41.

[3] As a category, "everyday literacies" does not necessarily address public-oriented literacies. Michele Knobel's treatment of students' out-of-school literacies does not. For a rich treatment of everyday literacy that does take this public turn, see Martin Nystrand and John Duffy's *Toward a Rhetoric of Everyday Life.*

[4] Flower has addressed the role of working theories in each of these discursive activities: the teaching of writing ("Teachers" 9), composing (*Construction* 260–62), deliberation ("Intercultural Knowledge" 272) and theory building ("Intercultural Knowledge" 6). The concept of a working theory is a central leitmotif in Flower's *Community Literacy and the Rhetoric of Engagement.*

[5] Branch is quoting from Horton, Myles. "Myles Horton's Talk at Experimental Citizenship School Workshop, February 19-21. 1961." Highlander Archives, Box 40, folder 4, 1961, n.p.

[6] Higgins describes how collaborative, community-based problem analysis complicates Lloyd Bitzer's notion of a rhetorical situation (Higgins, Long, and Flower 12–15).

Chapter 3

[1] In "History of Writing in the Community," Ursula Howard brings together empirical research, cultural theories, and primary sources to examine the rise of community writing as a social practice in the 19th century. Though her focus is primarily on the rise of community literacy in Britain, she documents its emergence here in the United States, as well.

[2] Established in 1945 by the United Nations, UNESCO was established as "the flag-bearer of the brave new post-war, post-colonial world from which both economic and cultural poverty were to be eradicated along with illiteracy" (Le Page 4). One of UNESCO's first points of business was to formalize an international position on vernacular literacy education. The resulting 1953 monograph established not just literacy, but vernacular literacy—the ability to read and write in the language of one's home and community—to be a human right (Gardner-Chloros 217). The monograph embodied what Eric Hobsbawm refers to ironically as the Golden Age of the Twentieth Century. The tone of the 1953 monograph is optimistic and sincere—purposeful and hopeful—garnering much of its confidence from the ethnocentric assumptions buried beneath dominant cultures of the time (Fasold 246): that literacy and orality were entirely distinct communicative channels, and that literate cultures were more advanced than oral ones.

[3] In the early 1950s, France, England, and Belgium were extricating themselves from (and, in several situations, were forced from) countries in Asia and Africa that they had previously colonized (Le Page 4). (For a look at the effects of U.S. colonial policies on literacy rates in Puerto Rico, see Zentella.) To rectify at least some of the deleterious effects of colonization, as well as to support previously colonized countries in their own development, many policy makers and linguists in Europe, as well as government officials and educationists in Africa and Asia, promoted the use of vernacular literacy in children's early years of schooling—use, that is, of the mother tongue that children spoke at home. The reason for adopting such policies was twofold. The first was psycholinguistic. When a vernacular language is spoken at home, it's more efficient for a student from that home to learn and, therefore, for teachers to teach, a standard language once the child has learned to read and write in the language of his or her home discourse (Fasold 246). The second—and arguably more pressing—reason was that a literate population was considered the point of entry by which developing countries established their economic solvency (Le Page 9).

[4] For reprints of key arguments in this discussion, see *Literacy: A Critical Sourcebook,* edited by Ellen Cushman, Eugene R. Kintgen, Barry Kroll, and Mike Rose.

[5] Barton and Hamilton are members of the NLG; Barton was also part of the effort to re-evaluate the UNESCO's vernacularization project.

[6] Bruce Horner and John Trimbur argue that these same assumptions must infuse current public discussion if it is to challenge the commonly held misconception that mastery of standard discourse alone provides keys to immigrants' ability to "make good" in the U.S. See also A. Suresh Canagarajah's "World Englishes."

[7] Below is more detail about the circumstances in which IGLSVL documented people using literacy:

- Women in Dakar, Senegal, negotiated with the Dutch embassy to determine the parameters of their literacy project. Enlisting the help of notaries to serve as translators, the women had sought the support of several embassies. Only the Dutch granted their request—on the stipulation that the language of instruction be Wolof. The women agreed. What they really wanted to learn was enough mathematics to keep an eye on their husbands' finances. The literacy project would be a means toward that end (Tabouret-Keller 324).

- Representing numerous vernacular languages, local peasant farmers in North Cameroon reorganized land-management practices for the rice produced in their region. The reform repositioned the peasants more centrally in the rice-production process and "resulted in a total change in the communication system between managers and peasants" (Gerbault 183). One of the farmers' first points of business was to decide among themselves "the 'working language' in which they would be taught to read and write in order to be able to take on their new role" (183).

- Nigerian writer Wole Soyinka devised a pidgin no one actually speaks to reach an audience of readers that crosses linguistic borders, including those in his own country, home to more than 400 vernacular languages (Charpentier 244).

- Portuguese immigrants in France created and published a tri-lingual literary journal, including a written version of a vernacular *immigrais,* "intolerable to purists but understood by the nearly 800,000-strong Portuguese immigrant population in France" (Gardner-Chloros 216).

- Using audiocassettes and tape recorders, members of string bands in the South West Pacific recorded "oral cover letters" to accompany the songs they submitted to Radio Vanuatu for distribution. On first blush, it would seem that writing would have been the medium of choice to compose their songs and letters. For one thing, putting the lyrics in writing would have helped the band members remember them. However, audio recordings had the additional benefit of preserving the songs' "melody and rhythm" (Charpentier 242). Given this advantage, the bands decided against writing cover letters when spoken versions could be included directly on the cassettes.

[8] Such incidents are peppered throughout the IGLSVL's research findings, relayed most often as intriguing vignettes following more systematic treatments of specific vernacularization initiatives. In the strictest sense, such incidents fall outside UNESCO's project, for they don't involve people learning to write a standard language on the basis of knowing how to write in one's "mother tongue." Consequently, the IGLSVL theorized very little about such incidents. For instance, the same sociolinguist warned that the pidgin of novelist Soyinka shouldn't be treated as evidence of some written vernacular—for no one, let alone no group of people, speaks in the discourses of his novels. The sociolinguist referred to the novels as "artificial texts," not examples of "pidgin literature, but research in style" (Charpentier 244)—a claim that a rhetorician may well challenge by noting that it is precisely the strength of the pidgin that gives the novels their reach, permitting them to circulate to strangers and, consequently, to become public documents.

[9] Demonstrating the tension between rights rhetoric and the discourse of research (Bruch and Marback 663), none of the linguistics in *Vernacular Literacy: A Re-Evaluation* overtly rejected vernacular literacy as a human right. But they also went to great lengths to articulate and to document the complexities involved in instituting a policy protecting this right. For one thing, there's the sheer number of vernaculars spoken in a single country, numbering several hundred in Cameroon and more than four hundred in

Nigeria, for example. Then there's the expense, often charged to extremely poor countries, of creating scripts to represent these vernaculars and publishing written materials to use them. In addition, rival orthographies represent not only alternative systems for spelling but also competing political interests. For example, the standard script for Igbo offers twenty-eight consonants, but residents of the Northern Igbo area tend to prefer their own. First, it expresses twelve more consonants than the standard; in addition, it signifies autonomy while the standard exudes imposition and control (Fasold 269). Moreover, the vernacularization project often forced poor countries to make the difficult choice between printing public-health documents in a few dominant languages or reaching the larger population through other means. The dilemma often means that neither priority gets addressed very well, most often to the detriment of the country's poorest populations. (Le Page addresses this dilemma in relation to AIDs-prevention campaigns.)

Furthermore, many children grow up speaking more than one mother tongue; likewise, some countries endorse multiple standard languages, for instance, one for political purposes, another for religious, and a third for commerce. So on what basis do policy makers choose "the vernacular" to use for classroom purposes and "the vector" language to teach as the norm? Migration and travel pose their own complications, with one generation of immigrants experiencing a different set of linguistic norms and needs than the next. In addition, vernacularization is usually the responsibility of the host country, an official body whose interests are not likely those of the immigrant population. Finally, one unintended consequence of writing down vernaculars has been to exaggerate distinctions among spoken languages, whereby destroying the "plurilingual inter-comprehension" that neighboring communities had previously enjoyed (Charpentier 231).

[10] To consider similarities as well as differences between the UNESCO monograph and the SRTOL monograph, see Parks's analysis of the complex set of competing interests that led to the SRTOL, including class politics, the civil rights movement, and efforts within higher education to defy oppressive social structures that reproduce class, race and gender inequalities (7).

[11] The SRTOL was an early harbinger of an extended effort to revitalize rhetoric studies in general and writing instruction in particular by "connect[ing]" these endeavors to "broader rhetorical, social, and civic concerns" (Norgaard 255). Readers interested in this revitalization effort will find a couple of strains of research especially relevant. One strand calls for scholars to anchor contemporary rhetoric in the study of ancient Rome (Fleming "*Progymnasmata*"), ancient Greece (e.g., Halloran "Further Thoughts") and Enlightenment-era Europe (Burton; Fitzgerald), where it was customary for citizens to speak wisely and publicly on issues of shared concern.

Even more relevant to community-literacy studies is a second strand of historical scholarship featuring prominent and less well-known figures who

in their time interjected under-represented cultures, discourses, and inter-
ests into public discussions and social affairs (Villanueva 658). For instance,
Keith Gilyard has studied the protest rhetoric of such giants as Frederick
Douglass and W. E. B. Du Bois, as well as the less well-known contributions
of black abolitionist David Walker and anti-lynching spokesperson Ida B.
Well-Barrett ("African" 626). Keith Miller, David Gold, David Holmes, and
Malea Powell use similar approaches to study the rhetorics of Martin Luther
King, Jr., Melvin B. Tolson, Frances Harper, and Standing Bear, respectively.
Jacqueline Royster notes the play between *ordinary* and the *extraordinary* in
this body of scholarship. The 19th century African American essayists in her
study were at once "unique and exceptional" and "typical and representative"
members of their communities, in that they understood both the power of
language and the injustices inherent in the social contexts into which they
were born (4–5; see also Logan). A related historical approach studies groups
of writers who in their time gained hearings in mainstream circles or alterna-
tively constructed public spaces of their own, as in the case of the nineteenth-
century women in Anne Ruggles Gere's study of writing groups. See also
Patricia Yeager's *Dirt and Desire: Reconstructing Southern Women's Writing,
1930–1990.*

¹² Fraser's "Rethinking the Public Sphere: A Contribution to the
Critique of Actually Existing Democracy" first appeared in *Social Text* in
1990—volume 25/26, pages 58–80. Since then, it has appeared in several an-
thologies. I'm working here from Craig Calhoun's edited volume, *Habermas
and the Public Sphere,* 1993.

¹³ See also Karen Springsteen's and Heather L. H. Jordan's reviews of
Art*Show* and Art*Show 2 Grow.*

¹⁴ Begun in 1974 at the University of California at Berkeley, the NWP
consists of a national network of sites through which teachers throughout the
United States gain access to effective practices and research findings about
the teaching of writing.

¹⁵ Flower references William Labov's *Language in the Inner City: Studies
in the Black English Vernacular.* Philadelphia: U Pennsylvania P, 1972; Henry
Louis Gates's, *The Signifying Monkey: A Theory of African-American Literary Criticism.* New York: Oxford UP, 1988; Carol D. Lee's *Signifying as a
Scaffold for Literary Interpretation: The Pedagogical Implications of an African
American Discourse Genre.* NCTE Research Report, no. 26. Urbana: NCTE;
and Linda Flower's "Negotiating the Meaning of Difference." *Written Communication* 13.1 (1996): 44–92.

¹⁶ For further discussion, see Flower, Long, and Higgins 271–75; Higgins, Long, and Flower 24.

¹⁷ Grabill quotes from page 95 of I. Young's *Justice and the Politics of
Difference.* Princeton: Princeton UP, 1990.

[18] Coogan quotes from pages xii-xiii of Celeste Michelle Condit and John Louis Lucaites's *Creating Equality: America's Anglo-African World*. Chicago: U of Chicago P, 1993.

[19] Readers may wish to compare Atwill's description of techne in *Rhetoric Reclaimed: Aristotle and the Liberal Arts Tradition* (66-69) with Branch's description of métis in *"Eyes on the Ought to Be": What We Teach When We Teach About Literacy* (206-210). Following Atwill's lead, I commend techne as tools for rhetorical discovery that are highly sensitive to contextual differences and, thus, not merely the "hard-and-fast rules" that Branch associates with the term (207). However, I concede that Horton's reluctance to describe and to prescribe a specific methodology sets him apart from other public educators in this discussion who do name and describe the methodological approaches that guide their work. The larger question may be how we, as public rhetors and rhetoricians, find value in the promise of rhetoric—a promise of discovery that ancient scholars commended to readers through terms such as *techne* and *métis*—given the fluidity and Derridian *différance* that characterize local public life in postmodern times.

Chapter 4

[1] These challenge-counterchallenge routines parallel what Thomas Kochman calls "capping" in which each speaker uses wit to overturn the opponent's claim (78). To read more about the cultural dimensions of the literacies that Trackton's children perform, see Elaine Richardson's *African American Literacies* and Geneva Smitherman's *Talkin and Testifyin*.

[2] See also Prendergast's *Literacy and Racial Justice* and Branch's *"Eyes on the Ought to Be": What We Teach When We Teach About Literacy*, 202-03.

[3] Readers interested in the impact of racism on language and literacy may find instructive *Literacy in African American Communities*, edited by Joyce L. Harris, Alan G. Kamhi, and Karen E. Pollock. In the foreword to this collection of studies, Heath implores educators to interrogate classroom practices that perpetuate racism.

Chapter 5

[1] This chapter focuses almost exclusively on chapter 4 of *Literacy in American Lives*, entitled "The Power of It: Sponsors of Literacy in African American Lives."

[2] The feminist nuances of hooks's "homeplace" resonate with Richardson's treatment of "mother-tongue literacy" and the power of black matriarchal epistemology (or mother wit) to critique racism, sexism, and classism and to foster effective public expression. Political implications of public homeplaces are further developed in Mary Field Belenky, Lynne A. Bond, and Jacqueline S. Weinstock's *A Tradition That Has No Name*.

³ Highlighting the political significance of nurturing, contemporary feminists reject the stereotypical image of the self-sacrificing mother whom Virginia Woolf depicted as the Angel in the House, sitting in the draught and relegating the chicken wing to her own plate. In contrast, the cultural womb is a site of preservation and a source from which oppressed people have gathered strength to resist domination. See hooks 42; I. Young, *Body* 146–50.

⁴ Readers may be interested in the shift here from classic feminism that associated nurturing with *labor,* the endless cycle of chores that ties a woman to her home while her male counterpart is out in the world making meaning through his world-building projects, or *work* (de Beauvoir 448). For contemporary feminists like I. Young, reclaiming nurturing has meant acknowledging the transcendent meaning making in much (though certainly not all) of the work that has traditionally been assigned to and taken up by women in their homes. As I. Young observed, "Not all homemaking is housework" (*Body* 138).

⁵ Cultural production theorist Lois Weis, for example, assigns agency to people in the statement: "People are not cultural dupes. [. . .] They do, indeed, exhibit agency, struggle, and imagination as they grapple with the structures wrapped around their located lives. However, they do this in a variety of sites [. . .]" (xii).

⁶ Moss develops a similar argument in *A Community Text Arises: A Literate Text and Literacy Traditions in African-American Churches.*

⁷ Because the congregations of their childhoods had been affiliated with the black church, parishioners held what Moss has called "shared knowledge" through which they exercised their membership (*Community Text* 89). Parishioners of Metro AME described having learned biblical exegesis as children, first by learning to read Sunday school cards "that had the text of the weekly lesson printed out on them" and then by reading Sunday school books as teenagers and adults (Brandt, *American* 115). They drew on these practices to learn to compose the talks that the pastor assigned.

⁸ See Grabill, *Community* 9.

⁹ See Flower's "Literate Acts" and Mathieu's *Tactics of Hope.*

¹⁰ Brandt is careful not to conflate the literacy that the church sponsored in the 19ᵗʰ century with that sponsored by later mass literacy, the black press, or even the civil rights movement itself. Instead, the broad historical framework she sketches identifies intersections among these interdependent systems.

¹¹ See Gorzelsky's *The Language of Experience.*

¹² The workshop sessions were organized around several distinctive practices. Most of all, participants and facilitators offered "constructive criticism" (Heller 74) and "comprehensive editing suggestions" to avoid wordi-

ness (48). Heller records additional practices that organized the give-and-take of the workshop sessions:

- *Close reading:* Textual analysis was used to detect and to diagnose reader's difficulties with specific passages of text (37, 60).
- *Commending, praising, and encouraging:* Motivational feedback ranged from laughter and applause to "confirmation that anxiety is often a necessary and positive ingredient that goes with reading one's work to others" (35).
- *Extrapolating* from the workshop to a larger readership: "With the group acting as a first audience [. . .] a broader public was considered as a future audience as well" (60).
- *Reflecting on, selecting, and synthesizing afterwards:* Mary explained how this practice worked: "'They're my readers. I write down everything they say, and at some point in time, when it's quieter and spiritually proper, when my mind and whole system are attuned to the writing, I go through it'" (26).
- *Rehearsing:* Writers practiced performing their work to one another in advance of public readings (35).
- *Responding:* "The group's reactions always provided vital information for the writers to determine whether their texts were being understood" (60).

These ways of talking about texts endorsed a general process of "writing, reading and rewriting" by which the workshop "built [the women's] skills as writers" (59), permitting the group to "mature to splendor" (28).

[13] Heller quotes from Dorothy Addison's "To Tell the Truth." *Ms.* July/Aug. 1994: 72–75.

Chapter 6

[1] For a discussion of *networks* and their explanatory power in community-literacy studies, see Comstock.

[2] Dueling dualities was the tension in the air, for instance, when the primary representative of the housing office, Kathy Oaks, told Raejone that she would read to Raejone the Section 8 housing application "'because some of the words are tricky'" (Cushman, *Struggle* 157) to which Raejone commented to herself, "'What? Cause I'm poor, I can't read [. . .]?'" (158). Dueling dualities was the tension still in the air as Raejone read ahead (seeing that the fine print stated that providing information about race was optional) and then asked Oakes why she had completed the space for her without reading the fine print to her or asking if she wanted her ethnicity disclosed. Note here how the duel stayed beneath the surface of the encounter. Raejone was careful not to alienate herself from the gatekeeper entirely. "'I could say, 'yo' what's your problem? Gimme my benefits'" (158–59). But in Raejone's estimation, such an approach would have only confirmed Oakes's negative attitude about

her, letting her think, "'Oh, another lazy nigger'" (159). Raejone figured: "'I ain't gonna give them that satisfaction'" (159). For Raejone, dueling dualities was the political act of safeguarding her chance at Section 8 housing while simultaneously refusing to stand for the racist assumptions that structured the gatekeeping encounter.

Chapter 7

[1] For discussions of these distinctions, see Deans 20; Freire 74–90; Weisser 38.

[2] Although Alinsky maintained strong friendships throughout his life, the famous obstructionist was also downright hated. The left hated him for rejecting class analysis, a reactionary militia put a price on his head, and the Ku Klux Klan picketed his arrivals at airports. Alinsky reveled in the hatred he incited. The reaction meant people were paying attention: he and his community organizing tactics really were threats to business as usual (Goldblatt "Alinsky's Reveille"). Studs Terkel provides a lively portrait of Alinsky and his legacy in *Hope Dies Last*. Similarly, Alec Baldwin has produced an engaging documentary entitled *Democratic Promise: Saul Alinsky and his Legacy* (Media Process Educational Films & Chicago Video Project, 1999).

[3] Goldblatt quotes from page 94 of Alinsky's *Reveille for Radicals*.

[4] For other scholarship documenting the rhetorical acumen of community leaders, see, for example, Coogan's "Counterpublics" and the portrait of Alvin Lindsey in Grabill, *Community* 93–98.

[5] Community-literacy research contributes significantly to public-spheres studies in its careful attention to both the limits and potential of down-on-the-ground democratic practice in the lives of everyday people.

[6] Location also sets quality standards for the community think tank. Most think tanks strive "to explain the nature, causes, and likely remedies of problems" (Stone 7). What distinguishes Flower's community think tank as a distinctive source of knowledge is its capacity to provide knowledge that the city of Pittsburgh needs in order to address "timely urban problems" but that isn't otherwise readily available (Flower, "Intercultural Knowledge" 245).

[7] See Flower "Partners"; Flower and Heath; Peck, Flower, and Higgins.

[8] For more on the fit between Dewey's experimental mode and the problem-solving orientation of the CLC, see Deans 114; Flower "Experimental."

[9] Flower quotes from page 29 of Yrjö Engeström's "Activity Theory and Individual and Social Transformation."

[10] In West's words, the "jazz freedom fighter [. . .] galvanize[s] and energize[s] world-weary people into forms of organization [. . .] that promote critical exchange and broad reflection" (*Race* 150).

[11] For further discussion of these rhetorical capacities, see Higgins, Long, and Flower 19–28.

[12] For more about community-based expertise, see Peck, Flower, and Higgins 205; Flower, "Intercultural Knowledge" 245.

[13] Flower quotes from page 13 of Robert Zemsky's *What Employers Want: Employer Perspectives on Youth, the Youth Labor Market, and Prospects for a National System of Youth Apprenticeships*. Philadelphia, PA: National Center on the Educational Quality of the Workforce University of Pennsylvania, 1994.

[14] For reviews of Art*Show* and Art*Show 2 Grow*, see Springsteen; Jordan.

[15] For additional examples of entrepreneurial community-literacy projects, see the descriptions of TeenTalk in *Urban Sanctuaries* and *Telling Our Stories*, both also briefly described in chapter 9 of this volume.

Chapter 8

[1] Cintron quotes from page 37 of Certeau's *The Practice of Everyday Life*.

[2] Judy Holiday uses embodied rhetoric—discussed at greater length toward the end of this chapter in relation to RavenLight's performance in the Toxic Tour—to embrace the value of stepping as public performance. Holiday writes: "I wondered about the embodied effects upon the steppers, particularly the intersection between the public and private regarding rhetorical productivity. For one, as a traveling troupe, the members become publicly recognized and esteemed even while stepping itself becomes sanitized and decontextualized (legitimated)" (Judy Holiday, e-mail to the author, 2 Nov. 2007). I appreciate the qualifications that Holiday's reading places on my own.

[3] Readers interested in the logic of trust will want to read Mathieu's *Tactics of Hope: The Public Turn in English Composition*.

[4] Pezzullo quotes from page 448 of Melissa Deem's "Stranger Sociability, Public Hope and the Limits of Political Transformation," *Quarterly Journal of Speech* 88 (2002): 444–54.

[5] Here Pezzullo quotes from page 17 of Kevin Michael DeLuca's "Unruly Arguments: The Body Rhetoric of Earth First!, ACT UP, and Queer Nation." *Argument and Advocacy* 36 (1999): 9–21.

Chapter 9

[1] Take, for instance, *City Comp: Identities, Spaces, Practices*, edited by Bruce McComiskey and Cynthia Ryan. This chapter's comparative framework would compare the interpretative pedagogy of Joliffe's first-year composition course, Discover Chicago, with the institutional pedagogy that organize Grabill's technical writing class and the performative pedagogy of Mathieu's bus tour.

[2] Cushman quotes from page 419 of Katrina M Powell and Pamela Takayoshi's "Accepting the Roles Created for Us: The Ethics of Reciprocity." *College Composition and Communication* 54.3 (2003): 394–422.

[3] For an extended discussion of "relational patterns" as they relate to community literacy, see Gorzelsky's "Shifting Figures" 92.

[4] For a description of the rival reading technique, see Flower's *Problem-Solving Strategies in College and Community,* 415–18.

[5] For an extended discussion digital story telling and public discourse, see Comstock.

[6] See Simmons and Grabill's "Toward a Civic Rhetoric for Technologically and Scientifically Complex Places" for a community-based inquiry pedagogy that prioritizes information literacy, including the skills required to search and design rhetorically effective databases and to write persuasive public documents that incorporate multiple kinds of evidence.

[7] Coogan cites page 70 of McGee's "Text, Context, and the Fragmentation of Contemporary Culture."

[8] The student, for instance, describes revising her initial conception of "writing as its own thing" and "performance as its own thing" based on a conversation with Andrea Lunsford (Fishman et al. 234). She explains: "My perspective on my own performance and writing was derailed when Andrea Lunsford asserted that all writing is performance. This idea gave me the lens I needed to examine my own writing and acting experience and to recognize some clear connections between them" (235).

[9] Readers interested in students' rhetorical awareness will find of interest Guerra's discussion of "critical practice of transcultural repositioning" (18).

[10] Fishman et al. quote from pages 114–15 of Eve Kosofsky Sedgwick's "Teaching 'Experimental Critical Writing.'" *The Ends of Performance.* Ed. Peggy Phelan and Jill Lane. New York: New York UP, 1998. 104–15.

[11] For analyses that consult classical rhetoric to address challenges of contemporary rhetorical education, see Janet Atwill's *Rhetoric Reclaimed: Aristotle and the Liberal Arts Tradition* and Ekaterina V. Haskins's *Logos and Power in Isocrates and Aristotle.*

Works Cited

Abelson, Donald E., and Evert A. Lindquist. "Think Tanks in North America." *Think Tank Traditions: Policy Research and the Politics of Ideas.* Ed. R. Kent and Weaver and James G. McGann. New York: Manchester UP, 2004. 37–66.

Alinsky, Saul. *Reveille for Radicals.* New York: Vintage, 1946.

—. *Rules for Radicals.* New York: Vintage, 1971.

Anderson, Jim, Maureen Kendrick, Theresa Rogers, and Suzanne Smythe, eds. *Portraits of Literacy Across Families, Communities, and Schools: Intersections and Tensions.* Mahwah: Lawrence Erlbaum Associates, 2005.

Anzaldua, Gloria. *Borderlands/La Frontera: The New Mestiza.* San Francisco: Aunt Lute Book Company, 1987.

Aristotle. "Nicomachean Ethics." Trans. W. D. Ross. *The Complete Works of Aristotle: The Revised Oxford Translation.* Ed. Jonathan Barnes. Vol. 2. Princeton: Princeton UP, 1984.

Arola, Jill. Rev. of *Power and Place: Indian Education in America,* by Deloria Vine Jr. and Daniel R. Wildcat; *Decolonizing Methodologies: Research and Indigenous People,* by Linda Smith Tuhiwai; *Community Action and Organizational Change: Image, Narrative and Identity,* by Brenton Faber; and *Red Pedagogy: Native American Social and Political Thought,* by Sandy Grande. *Community Literacy Journal* 1.1 (2006): 127–31.

Atwill, Janet. *Rhetoric Reclaimed: Aristotle and the Liberal Arts Tradition.* Ithaca: Cornell UP, 1998.

Bacon, Nora. Rev. of *Service-Learning in Technical and Professional Communication,* by Melody Bowdon and J. Blake Scott. *Technical Communication Quarterly* 13 (2004): 364–68.

Barton, David. *Literacy: An Introduction to the Ecology of Written Language.* Oxford: Blackwell P, 1994.

Barton, David, and Mary Hamilton. *Local Literacies: Reading and Writing in One Community.* New York: Routledge, 1998.

—. "The Web of Literacies in Local Organizations." *Local Literacies: Reading and Writing in One Community.* New York: Routledge, 1998. 208–30.

Barton, David, Mary Hamilton, and Roz Ivanič, eds. *Situated Literacies: Reading and Writing in Context.* New York: Routledge, 2000.

Bean, Janet, Robert Eddy, Rhonda Grego, Patricia Irvine, et al. "Should We Invite Students to Write in Home Languages? Complicating the Yes/No Debate." *Composition Studies* 31.1 (2003): 25–42.

Bazerman, Charles. "What is Not Institutionally Visible Does Not Count: The Problem of Making Activity Assessable, Accountable, and Plannable." *Writing Selves/Writing Societies: Research from Activity Perspectives.* Ed. Charles Bazerman and David Russell. Fort Collins: WAC Clearinghouse and Mind, Culture, and Activity, 2002. 428–83. http://wac.colostate.edu/books/selves_societies/

de Beauvoir, Simone. *The Second Sex.* New York: Vintage Books, 1989.

Belenky, Mary Field, Lynne A. Bond, and Jacqueline S. Weinstock. *A Tradition That Has No Name: Nurturing the Development of People, Families, and Communities.* New York: Basic Books, 1991.

Bennett, Susan. *Theatre Audiences: A Theory of Production and Reception.* 2nd ed. New York: Routledge, 1997.

Benson, Chris, and Scott Christian, eds. *Writing to Make a Difference: Classroom Projects for Community Change.* New York: Teachers College P, 2002.

Besnier, Niko. "Literacy and Feelings: The Encoding of Affect in Nukulaelae Letters." *Cross-cultural Approaches to Literacy.* Ed. Brian Street. Cambridge, UK: Cambridge UP, 1997. 62–86.

Biber, Douglas. *Dimensions of Register Variation: A Cross-Linguistic Comparison.* Cambridge, UK: Cambridge UP, 1995.

Bitzer, Lloyd. "The Rhetorical Situation." *Philosophy and Rhetoric* 1 (1968): 1–14.

Bloch, Ernst. *The Utopian Function of Art and Literature:* Selected Essays. Cambridge, MA: MIT P, 1998.

Bourdieu, Pierre. *Outline of a Theory of Practice.* Trans. Richard Nice. Cambridge, UK: Cambridge UP, 1977.

Branch, Kirk. *Eyes on the Ought to Be: What We Teach When We Teach About Literacy.* Cresskill: Hampton P, 2007.

Brandt, Deborah. *Literacy in American Lives.* Cambridge, UK: Cambridge UP, 2001.

—. *Literacy as Involvement: The Acts of Writers, Readers, and Texts.* Carbondale: Southern Illinois UP, 1990.

Brandt, Deborah and Katie Clinton. "Limits of the Local: Expanding Perspectives on Literacy as Social Practice." *Journal of Literacy Research* 34.3 (2002): 337-56.

Britton, James. "Shaping at the Point of Utterance." *Reinventing the Rhetorical Tradition.* Ed. Ian Pringle and Aviva Freedman. Conway, AR: L & S Books, 1980. 61–65.

Bruch, Patrick, and Richard Marback. "Race, Literacy, and the Value of Rights Rhetoric in Composition Studies." *College Composition and Communication* 53.4 (2002): 651–74.

Burke, Kenneth. *Permanence and Change.* Indianapolis: Bobbs-Merrill, 1965.

Burton, Vicki Tolar. "John Wesley and the Liberty to Speak: The Rhetoric and Literacy Practices of Early Methodism." *College Composition and Communication.* 53.1 (2001): 65–91.

Busch, Amy E., and Arnetha F. Ball. "Lifting Voices in the City." *Educational Leadership* 62.2 (2004): 64–67.

Calhoun, Craig. *Habermas and the Public Sphere.* Cambridge, MA: MIT P, 1992.

Camitta, Miriam. "Vernacular Writing: Varieties of Writing among Philadelphia High School Students." *Cross-cultural Approaches to Literacy.* Ed. Brian Street. Cambridge, UK: Cambridge UP, 1993. 228–46.

Canagarajah, Suresh, "The Place of World Englishes in Composition: Pluralization Continued." *College Composition and Communication* 57.4 (2006): 586–619.

—. "Safe Houses in the Contact Zone: Coping Strategies of African-American Students in the Academy." *College Composition and Communication* 48.2 (1997): 173–96.

Cárdenas, Diana. "Creating an Identity: Personal, Academic and Civil Literacies." *Latino/a Discourses: On Language, Identity and Literacy Education.* Ed. Michelle Hall Kells, Valerie Balester, and Victor Villanueva. Portsmouth: Boynton/Cook, 2004. 114–25.

Carrington, Lawrence D. "Social Contexts Conducive to the Vernacularization of Literacy." *Vernacular Literacy: A Re-Evaluation.* Ed. Andrée Tabouret-Keller et al. Oxford, UK: Clarendon P, 1997. 82–91.

de Certeau, Michel. *The Practice of Everyday Life.* Trans. Steven Rendell. Berkeley: U of California P, 1988.

Chaiklin, Seth, and Jean Lave, eds. *Understanding Practice: Perspectives on Activity and Context.* Cambridge, UK: Cambridge UP, 1993.

Charney, Davida H., and Christine M. Neuwirth. *Having Your Say: Reading and Writing Public Arguments.* New York: Pearson, 2006.

Charpentier, Jean-Michel. "Literacy in Pidgin Vernacular." *Vernacular Literacy: A Re-Evaluation.* Ed. Andrée Tabouret-Keller et al. Oxford, UK: Clarendon P, 1997. 222–45.

Cintron, Ralph. Afterword. *Latino Language and Literacy in Ethnolinguistic Chicago.* Ed. Marcia Farr. Mahwah: Lawrence Erlbaum Associates, 2005. 379–87.

—. *Angels' Town: Chero Ways, Gang Life, and Rhetorics of the Everyday.* Boston: Beacon P, 1997.

Collins, Paul. *Community Writing: Researching Social Issues through Composition*. Mahwah: Lawrence Erlbaum Associates, 2001.

Comstock, Michelle. "Writing Programs as Distributed Networks: A Materialist Approach to University-Community Digital Media Literacy." *Community Literacy Journal* 1.1 (2006): 45–66.

Coogan, David. "Community Literacy as Civic Dialogue" *Community Literacy Journal* 1.1 (2006): 96–108.

—. "Counterpublics in Public Housing: Reframing the Politics of Service-Learning." *College English* 67.5 (2005): 461–82.

—. "Public Rhetoric and Public Safety at the Chicago Transit Authority: Three Approaches to Accident Analysis." *Journal of Business and Technical Communication* 16.3 (2002): 277–305.

—. "Service Learning and Social Change: The Case for Materialist Rhetoric." *College Composition and Communication* 57.4 (2006): 667–93.

—. "Sophists for Social Change." *Rhetoric and Social Change: The Public Work of Scholars and Students*. Ed. John Ackerman and David Coogan, in prep.

Cressy, David. "The Environment for Literacy: Accomplishment and Context in Seventeenth Century England and New England." *Literacy in Historical Perspective*, Ed. Daniel P. Resnick. Washington, DC: Superintendent of Documents, U.S. Government Printing Office, 1983. 23–42.

Crow, Graham, and Graham Allan. *Community Life: An Introduction to Local Social Relations*. New York: Harvester / Wheatsheaf, 1994.

Cushman, Ellen. "Response to 'Accepting the Roles Created for Us: The Ethics of Reciprocity.'" *College Composition and Communication* 56.1 (2004): 150–53.

—. "The Rhetorician as an Agent of Social Change." *College Composition and Communication* 47.1 (1996): 7–28.

—. *The Struggle and the Tools: Oral and Literate Strategies in an Inner City Community*. New York: SUNY P, 1998.

—. "Sustainable Service Learning Programs." *College Composition and Communication* 54.1 (2002): 40–65.

—. "Toward a Praxis of New Media: The Allotment Period in Cherokee History. *Reflections: A Journal of Writing, Community Literacy, and Service-Learning* 5 (2006): 111-32.

Cushman, Ellen, Stuart Barbier, Catherine Mazak, and Robert Petrone. "Family and Community Literacies." *Research on Composition: Multiple Perspectives on Two Decades of Change*. Ed. Peter Smagorinsky. New York: Teachers College P, 2000. 187–217.

Cushman, Ellen, Eugene R. Kintgen, Barry M. Kroll, and Mike Rose, eds. *Literacy A Critical Sourcebook*. Boston: Bedford/St. Martin's P, 2001.

Deans, Thomas. *Writing Partnerships: Service-Learning in Composition*. New York: NCTE, 2000.

Dewey, John. *Characters and Events*. New York: Holt, Rinehart, and Winston, 1939. 74–102.

—. "The Need for a Recovery of Philosophy," *On Experience, Nature, and Freedom: Representative Selections*, ed. Richard J. Bernstein, Library of Liberal Arts. New York: Bobbs-Merrill, 1960. 19–69.

—. "Quest for Certainty." *John Dewey: The Later Works: 1925–1953*. Ed. Jo Ann Boydston. 4 vols. Carbondale: Southern Illinois UP, 1988.

Eliasoph, Nina. *Avoiding Politics: How Americans Produce Apathy in Everyday Life*. New York: Cambridge UP, 1998.

Engeström, Yrjö. "Activity Theory and Individual and Social Transformation." *Perspectives on Activity Theory: Learning in Doing: Social, Cognitive and Computational Perspectives*. Ed. Yrjö Engeström, Reijo Miettinen, and Raija-Leena Punamäki. Cambridge, UK: Cambridge UP, 1999. 19–38.

—. *Interactive Expertise: Studies in Distributed Working Intelligence*. Helsinki, Finland: Dept. of Education. University of Helsinki, 1992.

Faber, Brenton. *Community Action and Organizational Change: Image, Narrative, Identity*. Carbondale: Southern Illinois UP, 2002.

Farr, Marcia, "*En Los Dos Idioma:* Literacy Practices among Chicago Mexicanos." *Literacy Across Communities*. Ed. Beverly J. Moss. Cresskill: Hampton P, 1994. 9–47.

—, ed. *Latino Language and Literacy in Ethnolinguistic Chicago*. Mahwah: Lawrence Erlbaum Associates, 2004.

—. *Rancheros in Chicagoac'an: Ways of Speaking and Identity in a Transnational Mexican Community*. Austin: U of Texas P, 2006.

Farr, Marcia, and Eliaz Dominguez Barajas. "Mexicanos in Chicago: Language Identity and Education." *Latino Language and Literacy in Ethnolinguistic Chicago*. Ed. Marcia Farr. Mahwah: Lawrence Erlbaum Associates. 35–66.

Fasold, Ralph W. "Motivations and Attitudes Influencing Vernacular Literacy: Four African Assessments." *Vernacular Literacy: A Re-Evaluation*. Ed. Andrée Tabouret-Keller et al. Oxford, UK: Clarendon P, 1997. 246–71.

Finn, Patrick. *Literacy With an Attitude: Educating Working-Class Children in Their Own Self-Interest*. Albany: SUNY P. 1999.

Fishman, Jenn, Andrea Lunsford, Beth McGregor, and Mark Otuteye. "Performing Writing, Performing Identity." *College Composition and Communication* 52.2 (2005): 224–52.

Fitzgerald, Katheryn. "A Rediscovered Tradition: European Pedagogy and Composition in Nineteenth-century Midwestern Normal Schools. *College Composition and Communication*. 53.2 (2001): 224–50.

Flanagan, John C. "The Critical Incident Technique." *Psychological Bulletin*. 5.4 (1954): 327-358.

Fleming, David. "Subjects of the Inner City: Writing the People of Cabrini-Green." *Towards a Rhetoric of Everyday Life: New Directions in Research on Writing, Text, and Discourse.* Ed. Martin Nystrand and John Duffy. Madison: U Wisconsin P, 2003. 207–44.

—. "The Very Idea of a *Progymnasmata*." *Rhetoric Review* 22.2 (2003): 105–20.

Flower, Linda. "Can You Build a Transformative (Local) Public Sphere? Spaces for Alternative Representations of Identity and Agency in Marginalized Youth." Berkeley: NCTE Assembly for Research. February 19–21, 2004.

—. *Community Literacy and the Rhetoric of Engagement.* Carbondale: Southern Illinois UP, 2008.

—. *The Construction of Negotiated Meaning: A Social Cognitive Theory of Writing.* Carbondale: Southern Illinois UP, 1994.

—. "An Experimental Way of Knowing." *Learning to Rival: A Literate Practice for Intercultural Inquiry.* Mahwah: Lawrence Erlbaum Associates, 2000. 49–80.

—. "Intercultural Knowledge Building: The Literate Action of a Community Think Tank." *Writing Selves, Writing Societies: Research from Activity Perspectives.* Ed. Charles Bazerman and David Russell. 239–70. Fort Collins: WAC Clearinghouse, 2002. http://wac.colostate.edu/books/selves_societies/

—. "Intercultural Inquiry and the Transformation of Service." *College English* 65.2 (2002): 181–201.

—. "Literate Action." *Composition in the Twenty-First Century: Crisis and Change.* Ed. Lynn Z. Bloom, Donald A. Daiker and Edward M. White. Carbondale: Southern Illinois UP, 1996. 249–60.

—. "Negotiating the Meaning of Difference." *Written Communication* 13.1 (1996) 44–92.

—. "Partners in Inquiry: A Logic for Community Outreach." *Writing the Community: Concepts and Models for Service-Learning in Composition.* Ed. Linda Adler-Kassner, Robert Crooks, and Ann Watters. Washington, DC: American Association for Higher Education, 1997. 95–117.

—. *Problem-Solving Strategies for Writing in College and Community.* Fort Worth: Harcourt Brace, 1998.

—. "Talking Across Difference: Intercultural Rhetoric and the Search for Situated Knowledge." *College Composition and Communication* 55.1 (2003): 38–68.

—. "Teachers as Theory Builders." *Making Thinking Visible: Writing, Collaborative Planning, and Classroom Inquiry.* Ed. Linda Flower, David L. Wallace, Linda Norris, and Rebecca E. Burnett. Urbana: NCTE, 1994. 1–22.

—. "Tertulia." *Latino/a Discourses: On Language, Identity and Literacy Education.* Ed. Michelle Hall Kells, Valerie Balester, and Victor Villanueva. Portsmouth: Boynton, 2004. 128–31.

Flower, Linda, and Julia Deems. "Conflict in Community Collaboration." *New Perspectives on Rhetorical Invention*. Ed. Janet M. Atwill and Janice M. Lauer. Knoxville: U Tennessee P, 2002. 96–130.

Flower, Linda, and Shirley Brice Heath. "Drawing on the Local: Collaboration and Community Expertise." *Language and Learning Across the Disciplines* 4.3 (2004): 43–65.

Flower, Linda, Elenore Long, and Lorraine Higgins. *Learning to Rival: A Literate Practice for Intercultural Inquiry*. Mahwah: Lawrence Erlbaum Associates, 2000.

Flower, Linda, David L. Wallace, Linda Norris, and Rebecca E. Burnett. eds. *Making Thinking Visible: Writing, Collaborative Planning, and Classroom Inquiry*. Urbana: NCTE, 1994.

Fraser, Nancy. "Rethinking the Public Sphere: A Contribution to the Critique of Actually Existing Democracy." *Habermas and the Public Sphere*. Ed. Craig Calhoun. Cambridge, MA: MIT P, 1993. 109–42.

Freire, Paulo. *Pedagogy of the Oppressed*. Trans. Myra Bergman Ramos. New York: Continuum Publishing Company, 1970.

Fusion. Mills Theater, Bay Path College, Longmeadow. 4 April 2006.

Gardner-Chloros, Penelope. "Vernacular Literacy in New Minority Settings in Europe." *Vernacular Literacy: A Re-Evaluation*. Ed. Andrée Tabouret-Keller et al. Oxford, UK: Clarendon P, 1997. 189–221.

Gardner, Howard. *Multiple Intelligences: New Horizons*. 1993. New York: Basic Books, 2006.

Gastil John, and Peter Levine, eds. *The Deliberative Democracy Handbook*. San Francisco: Jossey-Bass, 2005.

Gee, James Paul. "Literacy, Discourse, and Linguistics: Introduction." *Journal of Education* 171.1 (1989): 5–17.

Geertz, Clifford. *Local Knowledge: Further Essays in Interpretative Anthropology*. New York: Basic Books, 1983.

Geisler, Cheryl. "How Ought We to Understand the Concept of Rhetorical Agency? Report from the ARS." *Rhetoric Society Quarterly* 34.3 (2004): 9–17.

Gelb, Richard. "The Magic of Verbal Art: Juanita's Santeria Initiation." *Latino Language and Literacy in Ethnolinguistic Chicago*. Ed. Marcia Farr. Mahwah: Lawrence Erlbaum Associates, 2005. 323–49.

Gerbault, Jannine. "Pedagogical Aspects of Vernacular Literacy." *Vernacular Literacy: A Re-Evaluation*. Ed. Andrée Tabouret-Keller et al. Oxford, UK: Clarendon P, 1997. 142–85.

Gere, Ann Ruggles. *Intimate Practices: Literacy and Cultural Work in U.S. Women's Clubs, 1880–1920*. Urbana: U of Illinois P, 1997.

Gilgoff, Dan. "Hot Spot: All the Issues that are Key to this Fall's Elections are on Display in Ohio." *U.S. News & World Report*. 19 Jun. 2006: 30–35.

Gilmore, Perry. "'Gimme Room'": School Resistance, Attitude and Access to Literacy." *Rewriting Literacy: Culture and the Discourse of the Other.* Ed. Candace Mitchell and Kathleen Weiler. New York: Bergin & Garvey, 1991. 57–73.

Gilyard, Keith. "African American Contributions to Composition Studies." *College Composition and Communication* 50.4 (1999): 626–44.

—, ed. *Race, Rhetoric, and Composition.* Portsmouth: Heinemann-Boynton/ Cook, 1999.

—. *Voices of the Self: A Study of Language Competence.* Detroit: Wayne State UP, 1991.

Gold, David. "Nothing Educates Us Like a Shock: The Integrated Rhetoric of Melvin B. Tolson." *College Composition and Communication* 55.2 (2003): 226–253.

Goldblatt, Eli. "Alinsky's Reveille: A Community-Organizing Model for Neighborhood-Based Literacy Projects." *College English* 67.3 (2005): 274–94.

—. "Van Rides in the Dark: Literacy as Involvement." *Journal for Peace and Justice Studies* 6.1 (1994): 77–94.

Goody, Jack. *The Domestication of the Savage Mind.* Cambridge, UK: Cambridge UP, 1971.

Gorzelsky, Gwen. *The Language of Experience: Literate Practices and Social Change.* Pittsburgh: U Pittsburgh P, 2005.

—. "Shifting Figures: Rhetorical Ethnography." *Ethnography Unbound: From Theory Shock to Critical Praxis.* Ed. Gilbert Brown and Sidney I. Dobrin. Albany: SUNY P, 2004. 73–97.

Grabill, Jeffery T. *Community Literacy Programs and the Politics of Change.* Albany: SUNY P, 2001.

—. "The Written City: Urban Planning, Computer Networks, and Civic Literacies." *City Comp: Identities, Spaces, Practices.* Ed. Bruce McComiskey and Cynthia Ryan. Albany: SUNY P, 2003. 128–40.

Grabill, Jeffery T., and Michele Simmons. "Toward a Critical Rhetoric of Risk Communication: Producing Citizens and the Role of Technical Communicators." *Technical Communication Quarterly* 7.2 (1998): 415–41.

Greene, Ronald Walter. "Rhetorical Pedagogy as a Postal System: Circulating Subjects through Michael Warner's 'Publics and Counterpublics.'" *Quarterly Journal of Speech* 88.1 (2002): 434–43.

Guerra, Juan C. "Emerging Representations: Situated Literacies and the Practice of Transcultural Repositioning." *Latino/a Discourses: On Language, Identity and Literacy Education.* Ed. Michelle Hall Kells, Valerie Balester, and Victor Villanueva. Portsmouth: Boynton, 2004. 7–23.

Habermas, Jürgen. *The Structural Transformation of the Public Sphere: An Inquiry into a Category of Bourgeois Society*. Trans. Thomas Burger and Frederick Lawrence. Cambridge: MIT P, 1989.

Halliday, M. A. K. *Learning How to Mean*. London, UK: Arnold P, 1975.

Halloran, S. Michael. "Further Thoughts of the End of Rhetoric." *Defining New Rhetorics*. Ed. Theresa Enos and Stuart C. Brown. Newsbury Park: Sage Publications, 1993. 109–19.

—. "On the End of Rhetoric, Classical and Modern." *College English* 36 (1975): 621–31.

—. "Rhetoric in the American College Curriculum: The Decline of Public Discourse." *Pre/Text* 3 (1982): 245–69.

Harris, Joseph. Rev. of *Writing Partnerships: Service-Learning in Composition*, by Thomas Deans. *Reflections: A Journal of Writing, Community Literacy* 2.1 (2001): 15–17.

Harris, Joyce L., Alan G. Kamhi, and Karen E. Pollock, eds. *Literacy in African American Communities*. Mahway: Lawrence Erlbaum Associates, 2001.

Hauser, Gerard. "Rhetorical Democracy and Civic Engagement." *Rhetorical Democracy: Discursive Practices of Civil Engagement*. Ed. Gerard Hauser and Amy Grim. Mahwah: Lawrence Erlbaum Associates, 2004. 1–14.

—. *Vernacular Voices: The Rhetoric of Public and Public Spheres*. Columbia: U South Carolina P, 1999.

Haskins, Ekaterina V. *Logos and Power in Isocrates and Aristotle*. Columbia: U of South Carolina P, 2004.

Havelock, Eric. *Origins of Western Literacy*. Toronto: Institute for Studies in Education, 1976.

Heath, Shirley Brice. *Ways with Words: Language, Life, and Work in Communities and Classrooms*. New York: Cambridge UP, 1983.

Heath, Shirley Brice, and Laura Smyth. *ArtShow: Youth and Community Development: A Resource Guide*. Washington, DC: Partners for Livable Communities, 1999.

Heller, Caroline E. *Until We are Strong Together: Women Writers in the Tenderloin*. New York: Teachers College P, 1997.

Higgins, Lorraine. Rev. of *Portraits of Literacy Across Families, Communities, and School.*, Ed. Jim Anderson, Maureen Kendrick, Theresa Rogers, and Suzanne Smythe. *Reflections: A Journal of Writing, Community Literacy* 6.1 (2007): 185–89.

Higgins, Lorraine, and Lisa D. Brush. "Personal Experience Narrative and Public Debate: Writing the Wrongs of Welfare." *College Composition and Communication*. 57.4 (2006): 694–729.

Higgins, Lorraine, Elenore Long, and Linda Flower. "A Rhetorical Model of Community Literacy." *Community Literacy Journal* 1.1 (2006): 9–42.

Hobsbawm, Eric. *Age of Extremes: The Short Twentieth Century 1914–1991.* New York: Viking Penguin, 1994.

Holmes, David G. *Revisiting Racialized Voice: African American Ethos in Language and Literature.* Carbondale: Southern Illinois UP, 2004.

hooks, bell. *Yearning: Race, Gender and Cultural Politics.* Boston: South End P, 1990.

hooks, bell, and Cornel West. *Break Bread: Insurgent Black Intellectual Life.* Boston: South End P, 1991.

Horner, Bruce, and John Trimbur. "English Only and U.S. College Composition." *College Composition and Communication* 53.4 (2002): 594–630.

Howard, Ursula. "History of Writing in the Community." *Handbook of Research on Writing: History, Society, School, Individual, Text.* Ed. Charles Bazerman. Mahwah: Lawrence Erlbaum Associates, 2008. 237-54.

Hull, Glynda. "Hearing Other Voices: A Critical Assessment of Popular Views on Literacy and Work." *Harvard Educational Review* 63.1 (1993): 21–49.

—. "Transforming Literacy: Adventures in Digital Multi-Modality." National Writing Project Spring Meeting. Washington, DC. 7 April 2006. <http://www.writingproject.org/cs/nwpp/print/nwpr/2321>.

Hull, Glynda, and Michael Angelo James. "Geographies of Hope: A Study of Urban Landscape and a University-Community Collaborative." *Blurring Boundaries: Developing Writers, Researchers, and Teachers: A Tribute to William L. Smith.* Ed. Peggy O'Neill. Cresskill: Hampton P, 2007. 255-90.

Hull, Glynda, and Mira-Lisa Katz. "Crafting an Agentive Self: Case Studies of Digital Storytelling." *Research in the Teaching of English* 41.1 (2006): 43–81.

Hull, Glynda, and Katherine Schultz, eds. *School's Out: Bridging Out-of-School Literacies with Classroom Practice.* New York: Teachers College P, 2002.

Hull, Glynda, and Jessica Zacher. "What is After-School Worth? Developing Literacy and Identity Out of School." *Adolescent Literacy* 3 (2004): 38 pars. 27 Sept. 2006 <http://www.annenberginstitute.org/VUE/spring04/Hull.html>

Hurtig, Janice. "Resisting Assimilation: Mexican Immigrant Mothers Writing Together." *Latino Language and Literacy in Ethnolinguistic Chicago.* Ed. Marcia Farr. Mahwah: Lawrence Erlbaum Associates, 2005. 247–75.

Isocrates. *Against the Sophists and Antidosis.* Trans. George Norlin. London, UK: William Heinemann, 1962.

Jarratt, Susan C. "Feminism and Composition: The Case for Conflict." *Contending with Words: Composition and Rhetoric in a Postmodern Age.* Ed.

Patricia Harkin and John Schilb. New York: Modern Language Association P, 1991. 105–23.

Jordan, Heather L. H. Rev. of *ArtShow 2 Grow* by Shirley Brice Heath. *Community Literacy Journal* 1.1 (2006): 117–21.

Kells, Michelle Hall. "Writing Across Communities: Deliberation and the Discursive Possibilities of WAC." *Reflections: A Journal of Writing, Community Literacy, and Service-Learning.* 6 (2007): 87-108.

Kells, Michelle Hall, Valerie Balester, and Victor Villanueva, eds. *Latino/a Discourses: On Language, Identity and Literacy Education.* Portsmouth: Boynton, 2004.

Killingsworth, Jimmie. "Discourse Communities—Local and Global." *Rhetoric Review* 11.1 (1992): 110–22.

Kinloch, Valerie Felita. "Revisiting the Promise of Students' Right to Their Own Language: Pedagogical Strategies." *College Composition and Communication* 57.1 (2005): 83–113.

Kissling, Frances, and Serra Sippel. "Women under Oppressive Regimes: Women and Religious Fundamentalism." *Conscience.* 31 Jan. 2002: 10.

Knobel, Michele. *Everyday Literacies: Students, Discourse, and Social Practice.* New York: Peter Lang Publishing, 2002.

Kochman, Thomas. *Black and White Styles in Conflict.* Chicago: U of Illinois P, 1981.

Kulick, Don, and Christopher Stroud. "Conceptions and Uses of Literacy in a Papua New Guinean Village." *Cross-cultural Approaches to Literacy.* Ed. Brian Street. Cambridge, UK: Cambridge UP, 1993. 30–61.

Labov, William. *Language in the Inner City: Studies in the Black English Vernacular.* Philadelphia: U of Pennsylvania P, 1972.

Lakoff, George, and Mark Johnson. *Metaphors We Live By.* Chicago: U Chicago P, 2003.

Lauer, Janice M. *Invention in Rhetoric and Composition.* West Lafayette: Parlor P, 2004.

Lavadenz, Magaly. "*Como Hablar En Silencio* (Like Speaking in Silence): Issues of Language, Culture and Identity of Central Americans in Los Angeles." *Building on Strength: Language and Literacy in Latino Families and Communities.* Ed. Ana Celia Zentella. New York: Teachers College P, 2005. 93–110.

Lawrence, Susan. *Reading Other's Realities: Double-Sided Discourse Moves.* Ms. Pittsburgh: Carnegie Mellon, 1996.

Le Page, R. B. "Social Contexts Conducive to the Vernacularization of Literacy." *Vernacular Literacy: A Re-Evaluation.* Ed. Andrée Tabouret-Keller et al. Oxford, UK: Clarendon P, 1997. 23–81.

Logan, Shirley Wilson. *We are Coming: The Persuasive Discourse of Nineteenth-Century Black Women.* Carbondale: Southern Illinois UP, 1999.

Long, Elenore. "Community Literacy: Negotiating Difference in Contemporary Public Spheres." *Proceedings of the Fifth Conference of the International Society for the Study of Argumentation*. Amsterdam, 25–28 June 2002. Ed. Frans H. van Eemeren, J. Anthony Blair, Charles A. Willard, and A. Francisca Snoeck Henkemans. Rozenberg: Amsterdam, Neth, 2002. 691–96.

—. "The Rhetoric of Literate Social Action: Mentors Negotiating Intercultural Images of Literacy." Diss. Carnegie Mellon U, 1994.

—. "The Rhetoric of Social Action: College Mentors Inventing the Discipline." *Inventing a Discipline: Rhetoric Scholarship in Honor of Richard E. Young*. Ed. Maureen Daly Goggin. Urbana: NCTE, 2000. 289–318.

—. "The Rhetorical Education of Gatekeepers in Training." *Reflections: A Journal of Writing, Community Literacy*, forthcoming.

Long, Elenore, Wayne C. Peck, and Joyce A. Baskins. "STRUGGLE: A Literate Practice Supporting Life-Project Planning." *School's Out: Bridging Out-of-School Literacies with Classroom Practice*. Ed. Glynda Hull and Katherine Schultz. New York: Teachers College P, 2002. 131–61.

Lyons, Scott Richards. "Rhetorical Sovereignty: What do American Indians Want from Writing?" *College Composition and Communication* 51 (2004): 447–68.

Marzluf, Phillip P. "Diversity Writing: Natural Languages, Authentic Voices." *College Composition and Communication* 57.3 (2006): 503–22.

Mathieu, Paula. "Not Your Mama's Bus Tour: A Case for Radically Insufficient Writing." *City Comp: Identities, Spaces, Practices*. Ed. Bruce McComisky and Cynthia Ryan. Albany: SUNY P, 2003. 71–83.

—. *Tactics of Hope: The Public Turn in English Composition*. Portsmouth, NH: Boynton/Cook, 2005.

McComiskey, Bruce, and Cynthia Ryan, eds. *City Comp: Identity, Spaces, Practices*. Albany: SUNY P, 2003.

McGee, Michael. "The 'Ideograph': A Link between Rhetoric and Ideology." *Quarterly Journal of Speech* 6 (1980): 1–16.

—. "Text, Context, and the Fragmentation of Contemporary Culture." *Western Journal of Speech Communication* 54 (1992): 97–119.

McKenzie, John. *Perform or Else: From Discipline to Performance*. London, UK: Routledge, 2001.

McKnight, John. *The Careless Society: Community and its Counterfeits*. New York: Basic Books, 1996.

McLaughlin, Milbrey W., Merita A. Irby, and Juliet Langman. *Urban Sanctuaries: Neighborhood Organizations in the Lives and Futures of Inner-City Youth*. San Francisco: Jossey-Bass, 2001.

Miller, Keith D. *Voices of Deliverance: The Language of Martin Luther King, Jr. and Its Sources*. New York: Free P, 1992.

Moll, Luis C., and Norma González. "Lessons from Research with Language-Minority Children." *Journal of Reading Behavior* 26.4 (1994): 439–56.

Moss, Beverly J. *A Community Text Arises: A Literate Text and a Literacy Tradition in African-American Churches.* Cresskill: Hampton P, 2002.

—, ed. *Literacy Across Communities.* Cresskill: Hampton P, 1994.

—. "From the Pews to the Classrooms: Influences of the African American Church on Academic Literacy." *Literacy in African American Communities.* Ed. Joyce L. Harris, Alan G. Kamhi, and Karen E. Pollock. Mahway: Lawrence Erlbaum Associates, 2001. 195–212.

Murphy, John M. "Presence, Analogy, and Earth in the Balance." *Argumentation and Advocacy* 31 (1994): 1–16.

Murphy, Patricia, and James Cunningham. *Organizing for Community Controlled Development: Renewing Civil Society.* Thousand Oaks: Sage Publications, 2003.

Norgaard, Rolf. "The Rhetoric of Writing Requirements." *Rhetoric, Cultural Studies, and Literacy.* Ed. Fred Reynolds. Hillsdale: Lawrence Erlbaum, 1995. 153-60.

Nystrand, Martin, and John Duffy, eds. *Towards a Rhetoric of Everyday Life: New Directions in Research on Writing, Text, and Discourse.* Madison: U of Wisconsin P, 2003.

Ong, Walter. *Orality and Literacy.* New York: Routledge, 2002.

Parks, Stephen. *Class Politics: The Movement for the Students' Right to their Own Language.* Urbana: NCTE, 1999.

Parks, Steve, and Eli Goldblatt. "Writing beyond the Curriculum: Fostering New Collaborations in Literacy." *College English* 62.5 (2000): 584–606.

Peck, Wayne. "Community Advocacy: Composing for Action." Diss. Carnegie Mellon U, 1991.

Peck, Wayne, Linda Flower, and Lorraine Higgins. "Community Literacy." *College Composition and Communication* 46.2 (1995): 199–222.

Peck, Wayne, and Jan Leo. *Telling Our Stories: Voices from the GLBT Community.* The Community House Church and Learning Center. Pittsburgh, 2006.

Perelman, Chaïm, and L. Olbrechts-Tyteca. *The New Rhetoric: A Treatise on Argumentation.* Trans. John Wilkinson and Purcell Weaver. Notre Dame: U of Notre Dame P, 1969.

Pezzullo, Phaedra C. "Resisting 'National Breast Cancer Awareness Month': The Rhetoric of Counterpublics and their Cultural Performances." *Quarterly Journal of Speech* 89.4 (2003): 345–65.

Pineau, Elyse Lamm. "Critical Performative Pedagogy: Fleshing Out the Politics of Liberatory Education." *Teaching Performance Studies.* Ed. Nathan Stucky and Cynthia Wimmer. Carbondale: Southern Illinois UP, 2002. 41–54.

Pough, Gwendolyn D. "Empowering Rhetoric: Black Students Writing Black Panthers." *College Composition and Communication* 53.3 (2002): 466-86.

Powell, Malea. "Rhetorics of Survivance: How American Indians use Writing." *College Composition and Communication* 53.3 (2002): 396–434.

Prendergast, Catherine. *Literacy and Racial Justice: The Politics of Learning after Brown v. Board of Education.* Carbondale: Southern Illinois UP, 2003.

—. "Race: The Absent Presence in Composition Studies." *College Composition and Communication* 50.1 (1998): 36–53.

Qualls, Constance Dean. "Public and Personal Meanings of Literacy." *Literacy in African American Communities.* Ed. Joyce L. Harris, Alan G. Kamhi and Karen E. Pollock. Mahwah: Lawrence Erlbaum Associates, 2001. 1–19.

Reder, Stephen, and Karen Reed Wikelund. "Literacy Development and Ethnicity: An Alaskan Example." *Cross-cultural Approaches to Literacy.* Ed. Brian Street. Cambridge, UK: Cambridge UP, 1993. 176–97.

Richardson, Elaine. *African American Literacies.* New York: Routledge, 2002.

Roberts-Miller, Patricia. "Discursive Conflict in Communities and Classrooms." *College Composition and Communication* 54.4 (2003): 536–57.

Royster, Jacqueline Jones. *Traces in the Stream: Literacy and Social Change among African American Women.* Pittsburgh: U of Pittsburgh P, 2000.

Royster, Jacqueline Jones, and Jean C. Williams. "History in the Spaces Left: African American Presence and Narratives of Composition Studies." *College Composition and Communication* 50.4 (1999): 563–84.

—. "Reading Past Resistance: Response to Valerie Balester." *College Composition and Communication* 52.1 (2000): 133–42.

Rude, Carolyn. "Toward and Expanded Concept of Rhetorical Delivery: The Uses of Reports in Public Policy Debates." *Technical Communication Quarterly* 13.3 (2004): 271–88.

Schriver, Karen. *Dynamics in Document Design.* New York: John Wiley & Sons, 1997.

Schultz, Katherine, and Glynda Hull. "Locating Literacy Theory in Out-of-School Contexts." *School's Out: Bridging Out-of-School Literacies with Classroom Practice.* Ed. Glynda Hull and Katherine Schultz. New York: Teachers College P, 2002. 11–31.

Scribner, Sylvia, and Michael Cole. *Psychology of Literacy.* Cambridge, MA: Harvard UP, 1981.

Shaull, Richard. Foreword. *Pedagogy of the Oppressed.* By Paulo Freire. Trans. Myra Bergman Ramos. New York: Continuum Publishing Company, 1970. 11–16.

Shor, Ira, and Caroline Pari. *Critical Literacy in Action: Writing Words, Changing Worlds/A Tribute to the Teachings of Paulo Freire.* Portsmouth: Boynton/Cook, 1999.

Simmons, W. Michele, and Jeffery T. Grabill. "Toward a Civic Rhetoric for Technologically and Scientifically Complex Places: Invention, Performance, and Participation." *College Composition and Communication* 58.3 (2007): 419–48.

Sleeter, Christine, and Dolores Delgado Bernal. "Critical Pedagogy, Critical Race Theory and Antiracist Education." *Handbook of Research on Multicultural Education.* Ed. James A. Banks and Cherry A. McGee Banks. 2nd ed. San Francisco: Jossey-Bass, 2003. 240–58.

Smith, Sean. "The Celebrity: Brad Pitt." *Newsweek.* 10 July 2006: 59–61.

Smitherman, Geneva. "CCCC's Role in the Struggle for Language Rights." *College Composition and Communication* 50 (1999): 349–76.

—. *Talkin and Testifyin: The Language of Black America.* Detroit: Wayne State UP, 1986.

Springsteen, Karen. *Rev. of ArtShow: Youth and Community Development. Community Literacy Journal* 1.1 (2006): 115–16.

Squires, Catherine. "Rethinking the Black Public Sphere: An Alternative Vocabulary for Multiple Public Spheres." *Communication Theory* 12.4 (2002): 446–68.

Stock, Patricia Lambert, and Janet Swenson. "The Write for Your Life Project: Learning to Serve by Serving to Learn." *Writing the Community: Concepts and Models for Service-Learning in Composition.* Ed. Linda Adler-Kassner, Robert Crooks, and Ann Watters. Washington, DC: American Association for Higher Education, 1997. 153–66.

Stone, Diane. "Introduction: Think Tanks, Policy Advice and Governance." *Think Tank Traditions: Policy Research and the Politics of Ideas.* Ed. Diane Stone and Andrew Denham. New York: Manchester UP, 2004. 1–16.

Street, Brian. *Cross-cultural Approaches to Literacy.* Cambridge, UK: Cambridge UP, 1993.

—. *Literacy in Theory and Practice.* Cambridge, UK: Cambridge UP, 1984.

"Students' Right to Their Own Language." *Spec. issue of College Composition and Communication* 25 (1974): 1–32.

Swan, Susan. "Rhetoric, Service, and Social Justice." *Written Communication* 19.1 (2002): 76–108.

Tabouret-Keller, Andrée. "Conclusion." *Vernacular Literacy: A Re-Evaluation.* Ed. Andrée Tabouret-Keller et al. Oxford, UK: Clarendon P, 1997. 316–27.

Tabouret-Keller, Andrée, Robert B. Le Page, Penelope Gardner-Chloros, and Gabrielle Varros, eds. *Vernacular Literacy: A Re-Evaluation.* Oxford, UK: Clarendon P, 1997.

Tannen, Deborah. *You Just Don't Understand: Women and Men in Conversation.* New York: Harper Paperbacks, 2001.

Terkel, Studs. *Hope Dies Last: Keeping the Faith in Difficult Times.* New York: New P, 2003.

Trimbur, John. "Articulation Theory and the Problem of Determinism: A Reading of *Lives on the Boundary.*" *Journal of Advanced Composition* 13.1 (1993): 33–50.

—. "Composition and the Circulation of Writing." *College Composition and Communication* 51.2 (2000): 188–219.

Tusting, Karin. "The New Literacy Studies and Time: An Exploration." *Situated Literacies: Reading and Writing in Context.* Ed. David Barton, Mary Hamilton, and Roz Ivanič. New York: Routledge, 2000. 35–53.

United Nations' Educational, Scientific and Cultural Organization. *The Use of Vernacular Languages in Education.* Paris, Fr, 1953.

Villanueva, Victor. "On the Rhetoric and Precedents of Racism. *College Composition and Communication* 50.4 (1999): 645–61.

Waller, James. *Becoming Evil: How Ordinary People Commit Genocide and Mass Killing.* New York: Oxford UP, 2002.

Warner, Michael. *Publics and Counterpublics.* New York: Zone Books, 2005.

Weinstein-Shr, Gail. "Literacy and Social Process: A Community in Transition." *Cross-cultural Approaches to Literacy.* Ed. Brian Street. Cambridge, UK: Cambridge UP, 1997. 272–93.

Weis, Lois. Foreword. *The Cultural Production of the Educated Person: Critical Ethnographies of Schooling and Local Practice.* Ed. Bradley A. Levinson, Douglas E. Foley and Dorothy C. Holland. Albany: SUNY P, 1996. i-ix.

Weisser, Christian. *Moving Beyond Academic Discourse: Composition Studies and the Public Sphere.* Carbondale: Southern Illinois UP, 2002.

Welch, Nancy. "Living Room: Teaching Public Writing in a Post-Publicity Era." *College Composition and Communication* 56.3 (2005): 470–92.

Wells, Susan. "Rogue Cops and Health Care: What Do We Want from Public Writing." *College Composition and Communication* 47.3 (1996): 325–41.

West, Cornel. *The American Evasion of Philosophy: A Genealogy of Pragmatism.* Madison, WI: U of Wisconsin P, 1989.

—. *Democracy Matters: Winning the Fight Against Imperialism.* New York: Penguin, 2005.

—. *Keeping Faith: Philosophy and Race in America.* New York: Routledge, 1993.

—. *Race Matters.* New York: St. Martin's P, 1992.

Wible, Scott. "Pedagogies of the 'Students' Right' Era: The Language Curriculum Research Group's Project for Linguistic Diversity." *College Composition and Communication* 57.3 (2006): 442–78.

Willinsky, John. *The New Literacy: Redefining Reading and Writing in the Schools.* New York: Routledge, 1990.

Wilson, William Julius. *When Work Disappears: The World of the New Urban Poor.* New York: Alfred A. Knopf, 1996.

Woolf, Virginia. "Professions for Women." *The McGraw-Hill Reader: Issues Across the Disciplines.* Ed. Gilbert H. Miller. New York: McGraw-Hill, 2000. 325–29.

Yeager, Patricia. *Dirt and Desire: Reconstructing Southern Women's Writing, 1930–1990.* Chicago: U of Chicago P. 2000.

Young, Amanda. "Patients as Problem Solvers: Toward a Rhetoric of Agency in Healthcare." Diss. Carnegie Mellon U, 2000.

Young, Amanda, and Linda Flower. "Patients as Partners: Patients as Problem-Solvers." *Health Communication* 14.1 (2001): 68–97.

Young, Iris Marion. *On Female Body Experience: "Throwing Like a Girl" and Other Essays.* New York: Oxford UP, 2005.

—. *Inclusion and Democracy.* New York: Oxford UP, 2002.

—. *Intersecting Voices: Dilemmas of Gender, Political Philosophy, and Policy.* Princeton, NJ: Princeton UP, 1997.

Young, Richard E., Alton L. Becker, and Kenneth L. Pike. *Rhetoric: Discovery and Change.* Orlando, FL: Harcourt, 1970.

Zentella, Ana Celia, ed. *Building on Strengths: Language and Literacy in Latino Families and Communities.* New York: Teachers College P, 2005.

About the Author

After completing a postdoctoral fellowship through Pittsburgh's Community Literacy Center and Carnegie Mellon University, Elenore Long continued to direct community-literacy initiatives with Wayne Peck and Joyce Baskins. With Linda Flower and Lorraine Higgins, she published *Learning to Rival: A Literate Practice for Intercultural Inquiry*. They recently published a fifteen-year retrospective for the *Community Literacy Journal*. She currently directs the composition program and Writers' Center at Eastern Washington University.

Index

Abelson, Donald, 122
Ackerman, John, 244–245
activism: knowledge, 52, 125, 129–130, 178, 205; political, 41, 200; progressive, 195; secular, 73; social, 64–65; through educational initiatives, 44
activist rhetoric, 15, 49, 51, 118, 131–132, 134–135, 153, 234
African American communities, literacy in, 47, 55, 58–59, 64, 69, 258n, 259n
African American freedom struggle, 27, 124, 195
African Methodist Episcopal Church (AME), 9, 64–70, 73, 76, 81, 84, 259n
agencies, social and human service, 4, 28, 94, 96, 98, 104, 134, 164, 187, 201, 205, 223
agency: cultural, 20, 23, 68, 71; linguistic, 20, 23, 98–99, 102, 104, 202, 206, 221; rhetorical, 191, 193–194, 202, 210, 225
Alinsky, Saul, 4, 6, 10, 26, 40, 46, 51, 106–116, 118, 129–130, 134–135, 178, 182, 201, 205, 229, 261n
Allen, Graham, 28, 35
Almighty Latin Kings Nation, 137–142, 149–150, 231, 257n
alternative discourse, 12, 41, 54, 119–120, 126, 169, 200, 215, 235, 245, 249

Anderson, Jim, 31, 215
Anzaldua, Gloria, 9, 208
appropriation: cultural, 23, 14, 144, 147-148, 202, 211
argumentation, 52, 91, 123, 171, 210
Aristotle, 3, 195, 258n, 263n
Arola, Jill, 252n
articulation theory, 66
ArtShow (youth project), 44, 133, 190, 196–197, 257n, 262n
assessment, writing, 116–117
Atwill, Janet, 3, 19, 212, 227, 258n, 263n
audience: and its reach, 33; and its stakeholders, 181; immediate, 188, 197; resistant, 83, 186; responsive, 56, 153, 197; sympathetic, 149
autonomous model of literacy, 20, 29–30, 41, 200

Bacon, Nora, 167, 215
Balester, Valerie, 31, 237
Ball, Arnetha, 35
Barajas, Eliaz Domingues, 39, 251
Barbier, Stuart, 5, 15
Barton, David, 5, 7, 9, 15–19, 22–24, 31–32, 35, 37, 41, 85–90, 92–95, 104, 162, 216–217, 254n
Baskins, Joyce, 12, 44, 135, 252n
Bazerman, Charles, 116–117, 236
Bean, Janet, 35
Becker, Alton, 27

Belenky, Mary Field, 258n
belletristic literacies, 23, 78
Bennett, Susan, 56
Benson, Chris, 46
Bernal, Dolores Delgado, 40
Besnier, Niko, 21
Biber, Douglas, 21
Bible, 65, 69, 236, 259n
binary opposites (dichotomies), 24,
    38, 85, 100, 149, 212
Bitzer, Lloyd, 253n
Black Action Movement (BAM),
    174–175
Black English Vernacular (BEV),
    34– 35, 257n
Black Panther Party (BPP),
    172–173
Bond, Lynne, 258n
border crossing: cultural, 3; discur-
    sive, 3, 9, 147, 251; institutional,
    162; political, 24, 164; strategic,
    41
boundaries: institutional, 113, 118,
    162, 221
Bourdieu, Pierre, 129
Branch, Kirk, 19, 53–54, 163,
    217, 252n, 253n, 258n
Brandt, Deborah, 6–7, 9, 18–20,
    23, 36, 40, 64–74, 76, 81, 84,
    158, 199, 203, 211, 218–219,
    222, 259n
Britton, James, 79
Bruch, Patrick, 34–35, 255n
Brush, Lisa, 9, 19, 38, 81–84, 131,
    148, 233–234
Burke, Kenneth, 18, 244
Burnett, Rebecca, 179
Burton, Vicki Tolar, 256n
Busch, Amy, 35
Bush, George, 19

Calhoun, Craig, 257n
Camitta, Miriam, 31

Canagarajah, Suresh, 35, 48, 154,
    156, 158, 162, 254n
cancer, 145, 149–150
Cárdenas, Diana, 164–165, 238
Carnegie Mellon University
    (CMU), 6, 44, 131, 135, 164,
    168, 176–177, 239–240
Carrington, Lawrence, 30
Chaiklin, Seth, 20
challenges: boys' public-stage, 61,
    258n
change: agent, 50; discovery and,
    27, 115–116, 225; manage-
    ment consultant, 51; of everyday
    practices, 123, 150; social, 4,
    25, 27, 40, 48, 50, 66, 93, 104,
    155, 159, 164, 170–174, 181,
    185, 192, 198, 202, 218, 222,
    224, 235–236, 245, 250; within
    organizations, 50, 131
Charney, Davida, 4, 48
Charpentier, Jean-Michel, 33,
    255n, 256n
Christian, Scott, 26, 46, 249
Cintron, Ralph, 7, 10, 17, 19,
    20–21, 23, 38–39, 41, 137–144,
    146, 148, 150–153, 170–171,
    175, 198–199, 211–212,
    219–220, 238, 244, 252n, 262n
circulation, 117, 167, 187, 189,
    203, 231, 248
citizens, 11, 14, 41–42, 74, 103,
    113, 122, 131, 171, 176, 191,
    195, 198, 231, 244, 246, 249,
    252n, 256n
civic education, 40, 176
civil rights, 67, 73, 226, 240,
    256n, 259n
class struggle, 14, 24, 37, 40, 102,
    172–173, 175, 204, 222, 252n
Clinton, William (Bill), 19, 173
cognitive rhetoric, 26–27, 49
Cole, Michael, 21, 29, 204, 207

collaboration: among kith and kin, 97; and knowledge building, 27, 245; between/among commu- nity-university partners, 26, 51, 97, 106, 189; commitment to, 39, 221; conflict within, 10, 50, 51, 112, 185–187, 227; strategies for, 27, 245
collaborative planning, 51, 179, 186, 200
Collins, Paul, 4
communication: intercultural, 9, 42
communications: technical, 164, 166
communicative democracy, 42, 82, 84, 122, 201
community conversations, 226, 233
Community Literacy Center (CLC), 6, 12, 19, 25–27, 35, 44, 47, 49, 50, 72, 118, 121, 135, 143, 166, 168, 176–179, 183, 188–189, 193–194, 201, 209, 223, 226–227, 234, 239, 245, 247, 261n
community organizers, 4, 109, 180, 220
community organizing: its legacy, 109; Open Doors as an example of, 10, 52, 106–110, 112–117, 129–130, 133, 229; techniques for, 106–107, 109, 112
community think tank: as techne, 120, 125; definition, 45; diversity within, 119; goals of, 10; history of its methods, 121, 123; on worklife issues, 121–122, 164, 183, 187, 198; securing funding for, 135
community-literacy studies, 3–7, 11–12, 19, 22, 24–25, 27, 35, 52, 54, 84, 134, 142, 199, 214, 253n, 256n, 260n

compositionists, 109, 112, 132, 192, 231, 237, 249
computer-based interventions, 12–13, 45–46, 99, 111, 168, 183, 237, 244, 246
Comstock, Michelle, 12, 40, 134, 260n, 263n
Conference on College Com- position and Communication (CCCC), 6, 34–35, 193
conflict: and ideographic analysis, 52; built into community think tank's design, 119; in community organizing, 112; in rhetorical invention, 115, 134, 211; in Tenderloin Women's Writing Workshop, 77, 103, 115; inter- personal, 77, 103; prevalence in local public life, 10, 51, 227
consensus: rhetoric of, 4, 10, 51–53, 109, 112, 115, 176
consensus-building literacies, 23, 110, 112
context: and New Literacy Studies, 18; as defined by the local public framework, 18; inspired, 64, 72
Coogan, David, 14, 25, 40, 48, 51–53, 142, 156, 158–160, 162, 176, 178, 180, 182, 185–186, 188–190, 195, 199, 220, 258n, 261n, 263n
corporations, 11, 114, 145, 148, 150, 171
counterpublic, 42–43, 54, 142–143, 149, 156, 160, 162, 171, 173, 184, 202, 225, 235, 247, 249
Cressy, David, 30
critical consciousness, 54, 63, 65, 72–73, 78, 98, 208, 215, 221- 222
critical race theory, 62

critical-rational discourse, 43,
201–202, 210, 249
Crow, Graham, 5, 28, 35, 53
cultural agency, 20, 23, 66, 68, 71,
202
cultural appropriation, 23, 144,
202
cultural imaginary, 20, 23, 138,
202
cultural theory, 166
Cunningham, James, 109
Cushman, Ellen, 4–5, 7, 10, 12,
15, 17, 20, 23–25, 28, 35, 38,
41, 85, 95–98, 100–104, 114,
116, 134, 163–165, 211, 221–
222, 251, 254n, 260n, 263n

de Beauvoir, Simone, 259n
de Certeau, Michel, 38, 53, 140,
242
Deans, Thomas, 48, 156, 198, 215,
222–223, 261n
Deem, Melissa, 152, 262n
Deems, Julia, 10, 50, 51, 227
deliberation: alternative models
for, 44, 47, 50, 176, 180, 201; as
a feature of community literacy,
37; computer-supported, 13,
196; that brackets difference, 42,
82, 131; that uses diversity as a
resource for inquiry and action,
42, 132
Deluca, Kevin Michael, 153
democracy: communicative, 84,
201; deliberative, 234; participatory, 41–42, 143
design literacies, 23, 124–126,
130, 148, 196, 202, 210
Dewey, John, 40, 49, 121, 223,
261n
dialects, 41, 77, 238
dialogue: and difference, 19,
49, 127, 166, 185, 188, 235;

community problem-solving,
27, 45, 49, 106, 121, 143, 169,
179–180, 183, 215, 226, 247;
computer-supported, 183; generative, 118, 130; inquiry-driven,
251; narrative in, 233; public, 40
dichotomies. See binary opposites.
digital technologies, 12, 45–46,
184, 237, 263n
Digital Underground Storytelling
for Youth (DUSTY), 12, 46–47,
184, 237
discourse: alternative, 12, 41, 54,
119–120, 126, 169, 200, 215,
235, 245, 249; definition, 202;
dominant, 83, 171, 203, 216,
234; formal, 35, 47; hybrid, 41,
89, 182, 200; professional, 10,
34, 46–48, 82, 96, 108, 155,
163–165, 167, 170, 176, 181,
201, 224, 248; tenor of, 8, 18,
20–21, 59, 78, 145, 149, 208
diversity: and conflict, 77, 103,
119; and deliberative democracy, 54; as resource for building
knowledge, 119; cultural, 26; linguistic and rhetorical, 34; within
the community think tank, 119
domain: definition, 32, 86, 203;
hybrid, 5, 32, 89; private, 32, 86,
203; public, 8, 28, 31, 35, 86,
89, 162
Duffy, John, 16, 243–244, 253n
economy: of efficiency, 9, 67, 69,
76, 203; of excess, 67, 203
edgeworker, 175

Eliasoph, Nina, 42
engagement: democratic, 43;
emancipatory, 30; public/civic,
4, 35, 43, 54, 121, 167, 174;
rhetoric of, 8, 25–26, 136, 210;
rhetorical, 134–135, 160, 225;
social, 84, 124, 207, 238

Engeström, Yrjö, 115, 123, 261n
ethics, 3, 25, 73, 101, 108,
  164–165, 169
expertise: community-based, 48,
  170, 176, 245, 248, 262n

Faber, Brenton, 40, 50–51, 116,
  134, 174, 181, 198, 214,
  223–224
facilitators, 30, 39, 79–82, 224,
  233, 259n
Farr, Marcia, 31, 39, 40, 251
Fasold, Ralph, 253n, 254n, 256n
Finn, Patrick, 40
Fishman, Jenn, 156, 191–192,
  263n
fissures, 138–139, 146, 171
Fitzgerald, Katheryn, 256n
Fleming, David, 131, 195, 244,
  256n
Flower, Linda, 4, 6–10, 12, 17,
  19, 22–23, 25–27, 35, 40–41,
  44, 47–51, 54, 106, 118–120,
  122–125, 127–130, 132–135,
  142–143, 152, 156, 163, 166,
  168–169, 176, 178–190, 194–
  199, 201, 206–208, 210–215,
  223–228, 234, 238, 240, 245,
  250, 252n, 253n, 257n, 259n,
  261n, 262n, 263n
Fraser, Nancy, 5, 9, 28, 41–42, 62,
  220, 249, 257n
freedom struggle, 24, 102, 204,
  222
Freire, Paulo, 26–27, 29, 40, 76,
  223, 233, 249, 261n
funding, 76, 84, 98, 109, 115–
  117, 130, 133, 135, 161, 212
Fusion, 148
fussing, 58, 59

gangs, 10, 72, 137–143, 146–148,
  150, 171, 211, 219, 241, 244

Gardner, Howard, 38, 115, 253n,
  255n
Gardner-Chloros, Penelope, 38,
  253n, 255n
Gastil, John, 13
gatekeepers, 10, 96– 97, 100–104,
  114, 165, 210, 260n
gatekeeping encounter, 10, 17, 24,
  38, 96–99, 100–101, 103–104,
  114, 124, 203, 206, 211,
  221–222, 251, 261n
Gee, James Paul, 119, 202
Geertz, Clifford, 19, 233
Geisler, Cheryl, 67
Gelb, Richard, 39
gender, 31, 57, 102, 159, 209,
  222, 256n
genres, 47, 78–79, 82, 173, 228
geography, 12, 15, 46–47, 57, 61
Gerbault, Jannine, 30, 38, 40,
  254n
Gere, Ann Ruggles, 171, 257n
Gilgoff, Dan, 19
Gilmore, Perry, 11, 20, 39,
  144–148, 152
Gilyard, Keith, 35, 257n
girl talk, 58, 59
Gold, David, 257n
Goldblatt, Eli, 4, 6, 7, 10, 21, 23,
  26, 40, 46, 48, 51, 53, 106–118,
  129–130, 134–136, 154, 156,
  158–159, 161, 178, 182, 229,
  261n
González, Norman, 40
Goody, Jack, 29
Gorzelsky, Gwen, 259n, 263n
government, 19, 65, 88, 98, 109,
  114, 131–132, 138–139, 187,
  201, 254n
Grabill, Jeffery, 6, 12, 40, 48–51,
  72, 76, 94, 113, 134, 163, 164–
  165, 167–168, 191, 195–196,

230, 240, 246–247, 252n, 257n, 259n, 261n, 262n, 263n
graffiti, 109, 141, 144, 171, 220
graphic organizers, 169, 233, 248
great divide, 29, 33, 204
Greenblatt, Stephen, 191, 193–194
Greene, Ronald Walter, 165, 169, 230
Guerra, Juan, 41, 238, 263n

Habermas, Jürgen, 41, 43, 50, 113, 122, 143, 226, 249, 257n
Halliday, M. A. K., 60
Halloran, S. Michael, 26, 256n
Hamilton, Mary, 5, 7, 9, 15–19, 22–24, 31–32, 35, 38, 41, 85– 90, 92–95, 104, 162, 216–217, 254n
Harris, Alan, 258n
Harris, Joyce, 231
Haskins, Ekaterina, 263n
Hauser, Gerard, 20, 42, 122, 131
Havelock, Eric, 29
health, 28, 30, 45, 126, 129, 149, 169, 173, 231, 233, 235, 250, 256n
healthcare, 187, 198
Heath, Shirley Brice, 7–8, 17–18, 21, 23, 36, 38–39, 44, 48, 54–63, 133–134, 156, 176, 189, 190–191, 197–199, 206, 214, 222, 232, 258n, 261n
Heller, Caroline, 7, 9, 21, 23, 36, 39, 74–81, 84, 115, 199, 232, 259n, 260n
heuristic: cultural-circuit, 166– 167; for collaborative inquiry, 250; for comparing local publics, 207; for listening, 165
hidden logic, 83, 127, 188, 204, 225
hidden transcript, 38, 41, 100, 103–104, 124, 204

Higgins, Lorraine, 6, 9, 19, 27, 35–36, 38, 40–41, 44, 49, 51, 54, 81–84, 120, 131–132, 135, 142– 143, 148, 178, 180–181, 185–186, 216, 227–228, 233–234, 245, 253n, 257n, 261n, 262n
Highlander Folk School, 218, 252n; and its method, 53
Hmong: Chou Chang as literacy broker, 24
Hobsbawm, Eric, 253n
Holmes, David, 257n
homelessness, 74, 79, 103, 172, 240, 245
homeplace, 41, 65, 156, 159, 200, 258n
hooks, bell, 65, 115, 233, 258n, 259n
hope: geographies of, 66; public, 262n; tactics of, 25, 53–54, 240, 242, 259n, 262n; tenacity of, 261n; tragicomic commitment to, 43
Horner, Bruce, 254n
housing, 57, 73, 88, 96, 98–99, 103, 109, 116, 131, 158, 162, 166, 205, 221, 233, 244, 260n
Howard, Ursula, 235, 253n
Hull, Glynda, 12, 31, 40, 44, 46–47, 66–67, 184, 196, 237, 240
Hurtig, Janice, 39

identities: oppositional, 54, 142, 202, 249; personal, 31, 209; pro- fessional, 10; provisional/negoti- ated, 241; public, 182; shared, 42; social, 58, 129
ideographic analysis, 185–187
ideographs, 52, 186, 208
ideological model of literacy, 18, 30, 31, 50, 204, 207, 209

Illinois Institute of Technology
  (IIT), 158–159, 162, 176–177,
  220
illiteracy, 29, 49, 253n
immigrant parents, 39, 216
immigration, 14, 251
inquiry-driven literacies, 23, 124,
  126
inspired context, 9, 64, 81, 196,
  204
institutional design: participatory,
  40, 50, 72, 113, 230
institutional worker, 96, 101–102,
  203–205, 210, 221
institutions: and bureaucracy, 41;
  as threat to sovereignty, 62; definition, 252n; examples, 32, 37;
  in relation to local publics, 7, 57
intercultural inquiry, 9, 12, 15,
  27, 49, 119, 121, 123–125,
  130, 132–133, 136, 176–178,
  180–182, 186–190, 201, 205,
  209, 214, 220, 223, 225–226,
  228, 234, 245, 247
International Group for the Study
  of Language Standardization and
  the Vernacularization of Literacy
  (IGLSVL), 32–33, 38, 254n,
  255n
Interprofessional Research Project
  (IPRP), 158–159, 162, 176, 178,
  189
intervention, 10, 50, 51, 222
invention: rhetorical, 22, 26, 61,
  79–80, 92, 101, 190, 208, 244
Irby, Merita, 44, 72, 190, 241
Isocrates, 3, 195, 263n
Ivanič, Roz, 5, 31

James, Michael Angelo, 47, 66
Jarratt, Susan, 82–83
Johnson, Mark, 17

Jordan, Heather, 70– 71, 257n,
  262n

Kamhi, Alan, 31, 35, 231, 258n
Katz, Mira-Lisa, 12, 47, 67, 184,
  196, 237
Kells, Michelle Hall, 31, 35, 237
Kendrick, Maureen, 31, 215
Killingsworth, Jimmie, 19
Kinloch, Valerie Felita, 35
Kintgen, Eugene, 222, 254n
Kissling, Frances, 19
Knobel, Michele, 15, 253n
knowledge activism, 52, 125,
  129–130, 178, 205
Kochman, Thomas, 258n
Kroll, Barry, 222, 254n
Kulick, Don, 31

Labov, William, 47, 231, 257n
Lakoff, George, 17
landlords, 45, 51, 77, 96, 99, 102,
  227
landlord-tenant relations, 45, 227
Langman, Juliet, 44, 72, 190, 241
language learning: participatory,
  60–61, 251
language rights, 8, 24, 26, 28, 34,
  38
Latino/a communities, literacy in,
  31, 108, 134, 144, 219–220,
  237–239, 251
Lauer, Janice, 22, 227
Lavadenz, Magaly, 24, 41, 251
Lave, Jean, 20
Lawrence, Susan, 12, 166
Leo, Jan, 183
Levine, Peter, 13
Lindquist, Evert, 122
linguistic agency, 20, 23, 98–99,
  102, 104, 202, 205, 221
literacies: belletristic, 23, 36;
  consensus-building, 10, 176;

design, 23, 124–126, 130, 148, 196, 202, 210; inquiry-driven, 126, 251; institutional, 23–24, 71, 100–101, 211; interpretative, 69–70, 154, 158–159; mobilizing, 23, 90–91; performative, 54, 59, 154, 196; situated-public, 15–16, 20, 37, 39–41, 47, 62, 153, 156–157, 208; tactical, 23, 140, 144, 154, 171, 173–175; vernacular, 8, 26, 34–35, 54, 95, 147, 212

literacy event, 56, 97–98, 206, 232, 242–243; definition, 206

literacy sponsors. *See also* sponsorship, 6, 81, 216

literate (rhetorical) performance, 195–196, 207

literate act, 22; definition, 206

literate action, 27, 120–121, 128–129, 196, 208, 225

literate practice: and tenuous connection to democratic values, 95; and the enactment of social values, 65, 73; and the vitality of local publics, 7; as defined by Scribner and Cole, 21, 29, 207; as defined by Street, 21, 207; capping, 258n; characteristic of community literacy, 37; circulation of, 73; protest writing, 73; rhetorical power of urban teens, 47; rivaling, 149, 168, 227, 228; signifying, 47; stepping, 20, 146–148, 262n; transformation of, 19, 69

local public: as community-organizing effort, 107; as cultural womb, 64; as garden, 74; as gate, 96; as link, 85; as shadow system, 137; as theater, 55; definition, 5

local public framework, 7, 8, 16, 19, 20, 22, 24, 207, 252n

Logan, Shirley Wilson, 147, 257n

Long, Elenore, 6, 10, 12, 27, 35, 44, 48, 54, 132, 142, 176, 178, 180–181, 185–187, 194, 227–228, 234, 239, 252n, 253n, 257n, 261n

Lunsford, Andrea, 263n

Lyons, Scott, 9, 48, 61, 62, 190, 196, 209

Marback, Richard, 34, 35, 240, 255n

Marzluf, Phillip, 35

materialist rhetoric, 52, 176–178, 180, 182, 186, 188, 208

Mathieu, Paula, 25, 48, 53–54, 94, 134, 170, 172, 240, 242, 259n, 262n

Mazak, Catherine, 5, 15

McComiskey, Bruce, 262n

McGee, Michael, 52, 263n

McGregor, Beth, 192

McKenzie, John, 192

McKnight, John, 97, 165

McLaughlin, Milbrey, 44, 72, 190, 241

mentors, 6, 35, 44–45, 81, 166, 177–179, 181, 187–188, 193–194, 225–226, 237, 240

mestiza public, 9, 208

metaphor, 7–8, 11, 16–17, 23, 74, 144, 183, 189, 199, 208, 218

métis, 53, 258n. *See also* techne.

Miller, Keith, 244, 257n

minority culture, 41, 211, 238

minority-group practices, 16, 31, 36, 209

Moll, Luis, 40

Moss, Beverly, 31, 35–36, 40, 238, 242–243, 259n

mother tongue, 29, 34, 254n, 255n, 256n

mother wit, 258n

movements: Black Action, 174;
Black Power, 172; civil rights, 67,
73, 240, 256n, 259n; labor, 172;
social, 66, 72, 172–173, 216,
222, 236
multimedia, 45, 183
multimodality, 12
Murphy, John, 17
Murphy, Patricia, 109
mutuality, 97, 106
narratives: default, 233; multimodal, 237; of identity, 191; problem, 161; publicly persuasive, 38,
83, 233–234, 237; ritualized, 59;
subaltern, 141; organizational, 50

National Breast Cancer Awareness
Month (NBCAM), 149
National Writing Project (NWP),
46, 257n
negotiation theory, 128–129, 208,
211
neighborhoods, 5, 44, 74, 108–
109, 112–115, 158, 201, 232
neighbors, 51, 57, 75, 110
network: definition, 86; informal,
89; mental, 123–124, 212;
social, 40, 86–87, 102
Neuwirth, Christine, 4, 48
New Ghost Dance, 9, 61– 62, 190,
196, 209
New Literacy Group (NLG), 20,
30–32, 39, 209, 254n
New Literacy Studies (NLS), 30,
204, 207, 209, 215
new media, 12
nonprofit organizations, 111, 133
Norris, Linda, 179
Nystrand, Martin, 15, 243–244,
253n

Olbrechts-Tyteca, L., 17
Ong, Walter, 29

organizations: and democratic
practice, 95, 126; commu-
nity, 44, 46, 81, 88, 90, 113,
117, 133, 148, 167, 212, 223,
241–242; doing science, 246;
hybridity of, 88; identities, 223;
institutional, 196; partnering, 50,
52; resources for, 89; sponsoring,
51, 74; transformational, 261n
Otuteye, Mark, 191
outcomes: as measures of effectiveness, 112, 117, 136, 222; as unit
of meaning, 4, 27, 128; intercultural, 134; of New Ghost Dance,
62; options-and-outcomes strategy, 126–127, 168; place within
rhetorics of sustainability, 134;
practical, 176, 185

paideutic rhetorical education,
191, 195, 196
Pari, Caroline, 40
Parks, Stephen, 35, 46, 107–108,
170, 256n
partners: community, 3, 48–49,
51, 53, 114, 129–130, 155,
159–161, 169, 179–182, 185,
187, 198–199, 205, 208, 211,
229; institutional, 15, 135; university, 8, 27, 49, 52, 106, 117,
129, 130, 134, 156, 182, 215,
222, 229, 237, 246
patients, 52, 169, 250
Peck, Wayne, 6, 9, 12, 27, 37, 38,
40–41, 44, 49, 51, 120, 135,
143, 178, 183, 245, 252n, 261n,
262n
pedagogies: Freirian, 29, 40;
inquiry-driven, 48, 175, 181,
185, 189; institutional, 11,
48, 163–167, 170, 175, 262n;
interpretative, 11, 48, 158–161,
163, 262n; performative, 11, 48,

161, 189–190, 262n; tactical, 48,
    170–171, 175, 190
Perelman, Chaïm, 17
performance: and inquiry, 196–
    197; and the New Ghost Dance,
    196; public, 9, 20, 39, 55–58,
    61–62, 156, 189, 191–192, 196,
    210, 262n; RavenLight's, 151,
    153, 262n; rhetorical, 120, 189–
    191, 195–196, 207, 246; ritual-
    ized, 55; theatrical, 39, 55, 63,
    191, 197, 263n; within ArtShow,
    197; world-making power of, 9,
    21, 39, 63, 191, 197–198
Pezzullo, Phaedra, 11, 144–145,
    148–153, 262n
phronesis, 27
Pike, Kenneth, 27
Pineau, Elyse Lamm, 192
playsongs, 56, 59, 145, 147
poetic world-making, 9
police, 14–15, 99, 139, 143, 150,
    152, 154, 171, 213, 226
Pollock, Karen, 31, 35, 231, 258n
Pough, Gwendolyn, 48, 170,
    172–175
poverty, 14, 38, 49, 65, 76, 81,
    184, 204, 237, 253n
Powell, Malea, 257n
pragmatism: prophetic, 4, 49, 104,
    124, 195, 209
praxis, 12, 40, 223
Prendergast, Catherine, 62, 258n
prison, 142, 159; correctional
    discourse of, 218
private-public intersections, 9,
    24, 38, 85, 87, 159, 217, 259n,
    262n
problem-solving dialogues, 183
problem-solving strategies, 45, 49,
    84, 120, 168–169, 177, 179,
    185–186, 226, 250

prophetic pragmatism, 4, 49, 104,
    124, 195, 209
publications, 6, 29, 46, 49, 53, 79,
    122, 187–188, 199, 221, 229,
    246
publics: alternative, 5, 42, 247;
    counter-, 42–43, 54, 142–143,
    149, 247, 249; local, 5, 7, 16,
    35, 48, 55, 61, 64, 72, 74, 85,
    96, 103, 106–107, 115, 117–
    118, 132, 137, 207; mestiza, 9;
    virtual, 12
public-spheres studies, 8, 26, 28,
    43, 54, 62, 88, 152, 261n

Qualls, Constance Dean, 15

racism, 25, 63, 76, 100, 147, 204,
    221, 231, 238, 252n, 258n,
    261n
rational-critical discourse, 43,
    201–202, 210, 249
rationality, 43, 138–139, 152, 210,
    212
RavenLight, 150–153, 171
Reder, Stephen, 31
reflection, 27, 126, 161, 177–178,
    194, 223, 245–246, 261n
respect, 15, 27, 33, 45, 97, 99,
    110, 113–114, 137–139,
    143–144, 171, 187, 207, 212,
    219, 222, 239
rhetor, 117, 128, 196
rhetoric: embodied, 153, 262n;
    local public, 17–18, 156, 199;
    materialist, 52, 176–178, 180,
    182, 186, 188; of consensus, 10,
    176; of engagement, 8, 25–26,
    136, 210; performative, 132,
    191, 195; public, 82, 199, 209,
    244; social-cognitive, 26–27,
    40, 49, 121, 123, 212; sophistic,
    123; transformative, 9, 64

rhetoric and composition, 5, 7, 24, 27, 30, 34–35, 37–38, 129, 154, 239–240, 244–245, 249

rhetorical agency, 191, 193–194, 202, 210, 225

rhetorical intervention, 8, 25, 35, 43, 49, 50–51, 54, 134, 157, 202, 210– 211, 223, 251

rhetorical invention, 8, 10, 16, 18, 22–23, 60, 70, 79, 92, 101–102, 112, 128–129, 141, 144, 148, 200, 208, 211, 227, 246–247

rhetorical sovereignty, 62, 190, 211

rhetorical theory, 3, 11, 190, 207

rhetorician, 38, 104, 130, 234, 255n; activist, 15, 49, 51, 118, 131–132, 134–135, 153, 234

rhetorics of sustainability, 134, 211

rights: civil, 67, 73, 226, 240, 256n, 259n; human, 14, 32, 142, 253n, 255n; land, 85, 88, 92; language, 8, 24, 26, 28, 34, 38; legal, 92

rival-hypothesis thinking, 125–127, 149, 168, 182, 186, 188, 227–228, 235; strong stance, 124, 126, 152, 209, 228

rival-reading technique, 125, 166–167, 176, 182, 263n

Roberts-Miller, Patricia, 5, 132

Rogers, Theresa, 31, 215

Rose, Mike, 66, 222, 254n

Royster, Jacqueline Jones, 22, 257n

Rude, Carolyn, 174

Ryan, Cynthia, 240, 262n

sanctuary: urban, 72, 242

schooling, 47, 55, 223, 254n

Schriver, Karen, 188

Schultz, Katherine, 31

Scribner, Sylvia, 29, 204, 207

sermons, 36, 71, 243

service-learning, 5, 48–49, 154, 164, 166–167, 214–215, 222–223

shadow system, 7, 10, 15, 17, 21, 23, 48, 137–146, 148, 150, 170–171, 189, 212

Shaull, Richard, 30

Shor, Ira, 40

Simmons, Michele, 48, 163–168, 191, 195–196, 246–247, 252n, 263n

Sippel, Serra, 19

Sleeter, Christine, 40

Smith, Sean, 14

Smitherman, Geneva, 34–35, 147, 231, 258n

Smyth, Laura, 44, 190

Smythe, Suzanne, 31, 215

sophists, 48, 123, 190, 195

sovereignty: rhetorical, 211

Soyinka, Wole, 255n

space: discursive, 7, 11, 14, 16–17, 20, 22, 24, 28, 34, 39, 41, 75, 85, 88, 100, 150, 175, 199, 208, 211; local public, 97; material, 15, 39; physical, 10, 12, 61, 66, 75; public, 35, 54, 63, 88, 114, 145, 162, 257n; rhetorical, 34, 97, 99, 163, 165, 172, 246; urban, 240

sponsorship, 6, 7, 22, 40, 67, 68, 84, 131

Springsteen, Karen, 257n, 262n

Squires, Catherine, 94, 142, 247

stakeholders, 15, 52, 117, 122, 125, 127, 178–181, 186–188, 192, 207, 209, 224, 235

stepping, 20, 146, 147–148, 262n

Stock, Patricia Lambert, 44, 46, 47

Stone, Diane, 119, 261n

Street, Brian, 5, 18, 20–21, 30–31, 108, 207, 229

STRUGGLE (literacy project), 252n

subaltern. *See also* counterpublic,
142–143, 148, 202, 250
sustainability: as one among other
measures of a local public's merit,
84, 134; definition, 212; institutional, 9, 134, 242; of literacy
programs, 22
Swan, Susan, 48, 82, 163–164,
168–170, 240, 247, 248
Swenson, Janet, 44, 46– 47
system world, 18, 137–142, 146,
148, 150, 153, 171

Tabouret-Keller, Andrée, 31–32,
34, 38–39, 254n
tactics, 23, 53–54, 61, 101, 109,
140–141, 143–144, 148, 154,
155, 157, 170–175, 201, 218,
219, 242, 261n
Takayoshi, Pamela, 263n
Tannen, Deborah, 165
techne, 43, 48–49, 52–53,
166–167, 172, 185, 212, 228,
242, 245, 247, 258n
TeenTalk (youth project), 44, 190,
241, 262n
tenants, 51
Tenderloin Reflection and Education Center (TREC), 74–76, 79,
84, 233
Tenderloin Women's Writing
Workshop (TWWW), 9, 73–79,
81–84
Terkel, Studs, 261n
theory: activity, 116; and traditions
of praxis, 27; building, 17, 27,
43, 50, 128, 134–135, 196, 244,
253n; critical race, 62; democratic, 41; drama, 192; -driven
action, 3, 108; negotiation, 128–
129, 208, 211; of articulation,
66; of excess, 67; of negotiated
meaning making, 128–129, 194,

208; of public deliberation, 50;
of rhetorical performance, 195;
public spheres, 249; rhetorical,
3, 11, 190, 207; social cognitive,
120, 225; sociolinguistic, 38;
working, 17, 24, 27, 62, 100,
123, 127, 135, 192, 199, 208,
211–212, 253n
topoi, 131, 138–139, 141, 144,
146, 152, 171, 212
Toxic Link Coalition (TLC), 11,
145, 149, 150, 152–153
transcript: hidden, 38, 41, 100,
103–104, 124, 204; public, 38,
100, 204, 210, 247
transformation: material, 12;
personal and public, 186, 261n;
rhetoric of, 9, 64
transformed understanding, 10,
106, 205, 212, 225–226
Trimbur, John, 66–67, 162, 231,
254n
trust, 11, 80, 113, 151–152, 262n
Tusting, Karin, 31

UNESCO, 29, 32, 34, 38, 253n,
254n, 255n, 256n
urban sanctuary, 72, 242

vernacular literacies, 8, 26–28, 30,
32–35, 38–39, 42–43, 47, 54,
89, 94–95, 120, 122, 146–147,
201, 203, 212, 253n, 254n,
255n, 256n
vernacularization, 29, 32, 254n,
255n, 256n
violence, 11, 139, 147, 150–153,
247
voice, 74, 79, 171, 225, 233

Wallace, David, 179
Waller, James, 253n

Warner, Michael, 5, 9, 17, 43, 54, 63, 66, 72, 141–142, 165, 169, 191, 199, 203, 230, 248–249, 253n
Weinstein-Shr, Gail, 24
Weinstock, Jacqueline, 258n
Weis, Lois, 259n
Weisser, Christian, 5, 26– 27, 30, 157, 162, 249, 261n
Welch, Nancy, 12, 14, 48, 154, 156, 170–175, 198, 252n
welfare, 4, 38, 82–83, 99, 102–103, 113, 115, 121–122, 130–131, 175, 183, 233–234
Wells, Susan, 14– 15, 156, 173, 191, 229
West, Cornel, 4, 25, 43, 46, 53, 104, 115, 124, 152, 184, 209– 210, 237, 253n, 255n, 261n
Wible, Scott, 35
Wikelund, Karen Reed, 31
Williams, Jean, 22
Willinsky, John, 9, 64
Wilson, William Julius, 81
Woolf, Virginia, 259n

workers, 96, 101–102, 205, 221; institutional, 96, 101–102, 114, 203–205, 210, 221
working theory, 17, 24, 27, 62, 100, 123, 127, 135, 192, 199, 208, 211–212, 253n; definition, 249; student's, 132
workplace, 5, 32, 45, 86, 216–217, 236
Write For Your Life (WFYL) (educational initiative), 45

Young, Amanda, 12, 168–169, 176, 183, 250
Young, Iris Marion, 14, 43, 50, 65, 82, 83, 117, 131, 166, 201, 252n, 257n, 259n
Young, Richard, 27
youth, 44–47, 119, 131, 133, 146, 170, 197, 216, 226, 237, 241, 244–245, 248, 262n

Zacher, Jessica, 44, 47
Zentella, Ana Celia, 251, 254n